Reader's Digest® Paperbacks

Informative.....Entertaining.....Essential.....

Berkley, one of America's leading paperback publishers, is proud to present this special series of the best-loved articles, stories and features from America's most trusted magazine. Each is a one-volume library on a popular and important subject. And each is selected, edited and endorsed by the Editors of Reader's Digest themselves!

THEY BEAT THE ODDS

THE EDITORS OF *READER'S DIGEST*

A BERKLEY/READER'S DIGEST BOOK
published by
BERKLEY BOOKS, NEW YORK

THEY BEAT THE ODDS

A Berkley/Reader's Digest Book, published by arrangement with
Reader's Digest Press

PRINTING HISTORY
Berkley/Reader's Digest edition/February 1983
Second printing / January 1985

A BERKLEY BOOK ® TM 757,375
The name "BERKLEY" and the stylized "B" with design are trademarks
belonging to Berkley Publishing Corporation.
PRINTED IN THE UNITED STATES OF AMERICA

contents

THEY BEAT
THE ODDS

On Gossamer Wings

by Wilbur Cross and James A. Maxtone Graham

THE DAY DAWNED with no wind and a haze over the English Channel. Soon after 8 a.m. on June 12, 1979, nearly a hundred people stood on the French shore at Wissant Beach, Cap Gris-Nez, peering intently toward the British coast at Folkestone, 22 miles away.

"Here it comes!" cried a boy, pointing excitedly to a luminous speck over the glassy swells. Within minutes, the glittering object was recognizable as some sort of aircraft, so low that it seemed almost on a level with a fleet of small boats that accompanied it. The diaphanous shape slowly sharpened in the eyes of the onlookers, like something in a dream becoming reality.

With the motion of a falling feather, the singular craft touched down on the hard sand. *Gossamer Albatross* had just made aviation history: the only Channel crossing ever under the power of the pilot alone. It was a giant advance toward fulfilling one of man's earliest dreams: to fly through the air at will, using only the energy supplied by his own muscles.

The dream has fascinated inventors since the ancient Greeks and Chinese, though most of those who attempted to create wings for themselves were considered oddballs. The fad revived in the late 1950s when a host of aeronauts—some amateur flying enthusiasts, some highly skilled aeronautical engineers—again began working their way backward in time and forward in technology.

One group allied itself with the birds, determined to simulate wings that could flap effectively. A second group tried to harness the principle of the helicopter, transferring energy from arms and legs to overhead rotors. But the only school that made progress utilized fixed wing and propeller to pull or push an aircraft powered by the pilot pedaling a bicycle-like mechanism.

In 1959 Henry Kremer, a British industrialist, tried to get things moving by offering a prize of $14,000 (later $100,000) to the person who could complete a 1.35-mile figure-eight course. The sport that had once attracted more than its share of crackpots now became a scientific endeavor, sanctioned by many noted aviation groups, including the prestigious Royal Aeronautical Society and the American Institute of Aeronautics and Astronautics.

But for 18 years the Kremer prize went unclaimed, despite hundreds of attempts by dozens of contenders. Then Californian Paul B. MacCready, Jr., rose to the challenge. MacCready was a trophy-winning sailplane pilot, hang-gliding enthusiast and aerodynamicist. As head of a firm specializing in the application of aeronautic principles to solve industrial problems, he had been researching factors vital to manpowered flight: reduced drag, lightweight construction, power transfer and wind-resistant fabrics.

Working with him, among others, were Peter Lissaman, a professional aerodynamicist specializing in lowspeed flight, and Bryan Allen, a biochemist in his mid-20s who had won cycling trophies, was a glider expert and possessed all the attributes of an ideal pilot.

The result of a year's work was *Gossamer Condor,* fabricated from aluminum tubing, piano wire, plastic film, cardboard and cellophane tape. It had a tapering 96-foot wing and a squarish pod body with a 13-foot propeller directly behind. The most unusual feature was the "canard," or small wing, projecting some 15 feet in front, at the end of a long pole. This harked back to the Wright brothers, who had used the principle to help stabilize their craft in flight. But on *Condor* it could be moved by a control lever to aid in changing altitude or turning, minimizing the risks in banking.

On August 23, 1977, after more than 400 test flights, *Gossamer Condor* made history by successfully navigating an official figure-eight course at Shafter Field, near Bakersfield, Calif. The flight lasted just under 7½ minutes at an altitude never more than 12 feet. MacCready and his group thus became winners of the richest prize in aviation history.

Now Henry Kremer announced a new prize: some $205,000 to the first man-powered airplane to cross the English Channel. MacCready and his associates could not ignore the challenge. "The *Condor* was such fun to fly," he explained, "that once we knew it was going to the Smithsonian Institution we sketched out a new, improved version so we would be able to keep flying. Calculations showed this new model could cover the distance and so we decided to go for the prize."

The second-generation machine, *Gossamer Albatross,* was constructed under the sponsorship of the Du Pont Co. It was designed in the configuration of the earlier bird but using new products and techniques to increase strength and improve performance. With carbon-filament tubing (extremely light and strong and developed to replace metal parts in high-performance jets), epoxy resins for adhesives, and Mylar, a transparent plastic film .0005 inch thick, the group reduced the basic weight of the new craft from the *Condor*'s 70 pounds to 55. By running all of the design alternatives through a computer programmed for aerodynamic output, MacCready and Lissaman also were able to effect structural refinements that otherwise would have been possible only after months of experimentation.

MacCready's group arrived at Folkestone, on the English Channel, in mid-May 1979. As they looked out at the ever-present whitecaps dancing across the Strait of Dover, they grew increasingly worried that they had never once flown over water, not so much as a pond. Weather was another concern. Wind conditions for a Channel crossing usually are favorable only a half-dozen days in May and June. But they were well into June without any sign of a weather break.

Other problems also had to be faced. A moderate-sized

freighter causes air turbulence in its wake that would rock one of these flying machines up to a mile away; even small boats could cause problems if they approached too close. A helicopter closer than 2000 feet on any side, or overhead at almost any height, would be disastrous. Gusts of more than six miles an hour could endanger the pilot's control, while a modest headwind could slow the forward speed so that the cyclist could not sustain his exertions long enough to reach the opposite shore.

After a month of standing by, weather reports indicated a one-to-five chance that there would be a spell of unusual calm over the Channel. At 2:30 a.m. on June 12, the fuselage and wings of *Gossamer Albatross* were gently taken out of her makeshift hangar on the shore and assembled. The wind was near zero but the air was much warmer than hoped for—a discouraging factor for a pilot who would be exerting himself to the limit while sheathed in a cocoon of plastic, with only a small tube in front to provide him with ventilation.

With infinite care, team members pointed the plane southeast, toward the French coast. Pilot Bryan Allen ducked his head under the top of the entrance flap and leaned against the high seat almost in a standing position that allowed him to use his muscle power most efficiently.

Outside, two ground-crew members gripped the cords on either side of the 96-foot wing to steady the plane. Allen started to pedal swiftly and powerfully, and, as he felt the gentle lunge forward, both groundcrew members began running, their hands still steadying the wing on either side.

At 5:51 a.m., the plane took off and gradually assumed its cruising altitude, about 15 feet, and headed out over the water at 11 miles per hour. The two launchers now raced to one of the four inflatable outboard motor boats that would accompany the *Albatross* in her fragile flight.

Inside his plastic pod, Bryan Allen fell into a rhythmic stride. The propeller, as it cut through the air at 100 r.p.m., sounded just right to him. The plane hung in perfect balance.

By mid-Channel, at about 7:15, Allen was experiencing fatigue and control problems created by air turbulence. Suddenly, he heard MacCready's warning shout over his radio transmitter. A supertanker was looming ominously two or three miles off. Following explicit instructions, he gently warped the wing and shifted his own direction slightly to the west to allow the tanker to pass far enough ahead to avoid more heavy turbulence.

But he was now losing altitude. One gust forced the fuselage of the craft to within six inches of the water, but luckily it lasted only a few seconds. And soon Allen could see the thin edge of beach at Cap Gris-Nez. He was perspiring heavily, barely hanging on. As he approached the 2½-hour mark, he still seemed to be far away from the beach. "Leg pains were troubling me badly," he recalls. "Also I was becoming dehydrated. The flight was taking much longer than we had expected, and all the water was gone."

He fought for air in the narrow enclosure. "I wanted to poke my fist through the plastic," he says, "and fill my lungs with fresh air. But I knew that if I did I might cause a drag I could never overcome."

Then he saw the beach drawing closer, now within a few hundred yards. "Wow!" he shouted. "We're going to make it!"

At 8:40, two hours and 49 minutes after taking off, *Gossamer Albatross* settled on the shore, barely beyond the reach of the lapping waters of the Channel. The historic flight was over.

The Incredible Career of Grandma Moses

by Don Wharton

SHE WAS 78 years old when she began painting. She had never received a painting lesson or been inside an art gallery or had more than a few months' schooling of any sort. Her entire life had been spent on farms, 15 years of it as a hired girl. Her hands were now arthritic, and she actually didn't know the difference in artistic value between an original painting and a copy of a pretty postcard. Yet a decade later Anna Mary Robertson Moses was one of the best-known artists in the world.

Her career has no parallel. When she was 90, pictures she had just completed were in galleries and exhibitions in the United States, Austria, Germany, Switzerland, Holland and France. When she reached 100, birthday greetings flooded in from all over the world, including messages from all four living Presidents. When she died in 1961 at 101, it was front-page news across Europe and America. It is only today, with the perspective of a few added years, that we can fathom the full wonder of this fabulous story.

7

Anna Mary Robertson was born in 1860, one of ten children in a frugal farm family in upstate New York, near the Vermont border. At 12, she left home to earn her living as a hired girl. When only 15, she was cooking three meals a day, weeding, washing, cleaning, ironing and churning. She worked like this, for a succession of families, until at 27 she married Thomas Moses, a hired man whom she found "of a good family, very temperate and thrifty."

Moving to Virginia, she not only did the usual work of a farm wife but put in long extra hours to supplement the family income. At one time, she was making and selling 160 pounds of butter a week. When her husband began peddling milk, she had the task of washing, filling and sealing 100 bottles a day. Later, she thought up the idea of making hand-sliced potato chips, at 30 cents a pound, to swap for groceries, and soon she was making them by the barrel for shipment to White Sulphur Springs and Charlottesville. Meanwhile, she was bearing children—ten between 1888 and 1903, of whom only five survived. "Five little graves I left in that beautiful Shenandoah Valley."

This seeming drudgery, accepted, uncomplained at, apparently enjoyed, continued after she moved back to the hills of home in 1905 and settled on a dairy farm in the Hoosick Valley. Year after year, her routine made Monday a washday, Tuesday ironing and mending, Wednesday baking and cleaning, Thursday sewing, Friday sewing and odd jobs such as working in flower and vegetable gardens, Saturday more cleaning—all this in addition to cooking for the whole family, making soap, gathering fruit, canning, rendering lard, trimming and cleaning kerosene lamps. (Not until she was 76 did she have electricity in her home.)

So it is not strange that when she took up painting, it was for practical rather than poetic reasons. "If I didn't start painting," she explained, "I would have raised chickens. I would never sit back in a rocking chair, waiting for someone to help me."

When she was past 70, her husband dead, and housework getting too much for her, she began making bright little pictures of yarn drawn through netting—worsted pictures, they were called. Then her arthritic hands worsened, and in 1938 a sister suggested that painting would be "better and faster." For her first picture she used house paint and a piece of canvas left over from mending a threshing-machine cover.

She thought no more of her painting "than of doing fancywork." She first exhibited her pictures at a local fair, entering them along with some of her canned fruit and raspberry jam. The fruit and jam won a prize, but the paintings were ignored. She next put them on display in a drugstore at nearby Hoosick Falls, in the hope of picking up a few dollars. There they happened to catch the eye of Louis J. Caldor, a middle-aged businessman who was forever buying antiques and Americana. He bought all four, $3 apiece for the small ones and $5 each for two larger ones.

That evening she found he had been told she had ten more pictures and was coming out to the farm the next day to buy the lot. Lying in bed, she got to worrying, because she didn't have that many. But then she recalled a large picture she had painted of the Shenandoah Valley, and she "thought if I could find frames in the morning, I could cut that right in two and make two pictures, which I did, and by so doing I had the ten pictures for him when he came."

These pictures do not rank among her important works, and dealers were not interested in them. But within less than a year, by sheerest chance, Caldor encountered a woman in a New York cafeteria who told him she knew a dealer from Vienna, newly settled in New York because of the war, who was genuinely interested in folk art. This was Otto Kallir, who, when he saw two paintings by this farm woman, wanted to see more. And when he saw more, he wanted to see still more. Within the year, Kallir was giving this unknown painter a "one-man" exhibit, which he cannily entitled "What a Farmwife Painted."

On October 8, 1940, the day before the exhibit opened, there came the turning point in Anna Mary Robertson Moses' professional life: in an unsigned news story in the New York *Herald Tribune*, a reporter referred to the new artist as "Grandma Moses." A desk man stuck this in the headline; it was picked up later by magazines and other newspapers. The name caught on so well that millions of persons never knew her by any other, or had the slightest idea what her full name was. She let strangers call her that to her face, and she came to use the name herself, at 93 slowly penning "Grandma Moses" on nearly 400 Christmas cards. One leading art dealer today contends that, next to the fact that she was a true artist, the most important ingredient in her popularity was this homey name.

In those first years, Grandma Moses wouldn't paint a picture until she had a frame ready and had sawed a piece of masonite to fit it. She rarely painted on canvas. She got friends and relatives to comb their attics for discarded mirror and picture frames, then used hammer, nails and plastic wood to put the dilapidated ones in shape. When the demand for pictures outran her supply of frames, she sold them unframed. But this displeased her—"It's like sending my children out with ragged dresses on them."

She never had a studio, but painted in her farmhouse bedroom, sometimes in the summer used the porch. She did her pictures in batches, like cookies, to save paint, using the same blue for five or six skies, the same greens for all the trees— "this way your paints don't dry up on you." When she was 88, she said, "I can start a batch of five on a Monday, and have them finished off on a Saturday." She painted more than 1500 in her last two decades.

In the early years, when she was asked the prices of her paintings, she replied, "What size do you want?" Pictures ordered by mail were $3 and up. In 1946, she got $250 for a painting—the first time, according to a little notebook in which she recorded all sales, that any picture of hers brought such a price. In the period from 1964 to mid-1967, 68 sold at one gallery at prices ranging from $1250 to $20,000. The most that Grandma Moses herself ever got for one picture was $1000: to paint Eisenhower's Gettysburg home, from photographs he sent to her. This was a gift to him from his cabinet.

It has been said that "Grandma Moses was an industry." In a sense this was true. Under Kallir's astute direction, a firm was set up called Grandma Moses Properties, Inc., which trademarked her name and copyrighted her pictures and sold reproduction rights, with a percentage of every dollar going to the painter. The greeting-card giant, Hallmark, in ten years sold more than 35 million Grandma Moses cards. Still other contracts were made with fabric houses. Altogether, far in excess of a quarter of a million dollars in royalties was passed on to this gentle, spry, birdlike woman. She was exhibited, feted, honored, televised; she was entertained at the White House, adored by millions.

But Grandma Moses never changed her frugal, make-do way of life. She used discarded coffee cans to keep paint in, old cold-cream jars to soak brushes in. Sometimes she worked with a brush long after it was worn down to a nub. Before starting a picture, she gave the masonite board three coats of flat paint—"so I don't have to put on so much of the expensive color paint."

She was keen about being paid a little something for each picture, as if it were a jar of jam, but she was indifferent to *large* sums. When Otto Kallir sent her a $12,000 royalty check in 1947, she didn't cash it. After two letters from him, it still remained uncashed. He visited her at Eagle Bridge, insisted that it be cashed, got her promise, came back the next day and found her sitting at a table loaded with huge stacks of $5 and $10 bills—$12,000 worth. Kallir then insisted that she engage a lawyer to handle her finances.

While everyone thinks of a Grandma Moses picture as a rural landscape with a lovely Green Mountains background, she seldom "painted from nature." She said that sitting out in the open with an easel was "very impracticable." She worked at a table indoors, with "it all up here in my head." She would paint a landscape, and afterward she'd "put in the boys and the cows."

Critics observed that her figures did not cast shadows. She never mastered perspective or proportion—a man in the background might actually be larger than a horse in the foreground. And yet, when her pictures are viewed as a whole, there is a perfection about them that casts a spell and makes people ignore technical oddities and shortcomings.

Grandma Moses soon stopped her early practice of copying postcards and photographs of the Taj Mahal and Lake Geneva's Castle of Chillon. More and more, she "painted her memory." She kept on learning and improving, and hit her stride around 85. Kallir bought whatever she sent him for sale, held back the markedly inferior and exhibited those paintings which in his opinion were most representative of her talent and style.

Anna Mary Robertson Moses was a link between two ages. When she was born, James Buchanan was President, a man whose birth took place in the 18th century. This child, whose first photograph was taken in 1864, her head in a clamp to keep it still and avoid a blur, lived to sleep under an electric blanket and to watch television ("Monotonous"). But there is much more to her appeal than her age or the fact that, like Utrillo, she never went to art school. Many critics say that this appeal is partly nostalgia, for a childhood that was simple and peaceful and happy—the kind of childhood that some had and others wish they had had.

Whatever the nature and origins of Grandma Moses' appeal, it proved to be universal. When her work reached Europe, the critical acclaim was even greater than at home. In Moscow, 100,000 persons went to her exhibit. In Munich, a visitor wrote in the guest book, "One can almost feel the fresh air coming over the hills." And in Salzburg the cashier of the art gallery, who had watched crowds for years, reported, "Ninety-five percent of the visitors left the show in a happy, satisfied mood, with the words, 'It was beautiful.'"

Grandma Moses once said, "I like to paint old-timey things—something real pretty." She did far, far more than that—and lived to see one of her paintings hanging in the White House, another in the Musée National d'Art Moderne at the Louvre (the only American painting there at that time). Jean Cassou, former director of the museum, observed that Grandma Moses "would have us know that there is still a bit of paradise left on this earth."

More important than having her work in the White House or any museum, however, was the fact, recorded by another European, that Grandma Moses made this land "lovable even to those who do not yet know it from personal experience." Anyone can love the earth, but it is incredible that anyone could start out at 78 and learn how to communicate that feeling to multitudes at home and abroad.

The Long Sleep of Gene Tipps

by Joseph P. Blank

THERE WAS never much cause for hope. Yet there was no way for Jack and Gladys Tipps to deny hope. Month after month, year after year, they waited and searched for a sign that their son Gene was breaking out of his mysterious trance.

On May 21, 1967, 20-year-old Gene, an honor student at Cisco Junior College, had been returning from a rodeo to his home in Seymour, Texas, in a car driven by a friend. The car suddenly hit a slick patch on the blacktop, swerved out of control and struck an embankment. Although the driver's injuries were minor, Gene suffered a broken hip and broken pelvis, and was knocked unconscious. He remained in an impenetrable coma for 30 days, then drifted into a semiconscious state, from which he made no advance.

It was a deep, trance-like stupor. Gene didn't recognize his parents, and exhibited nothing of his pre-accident personality. His quick intelligence and easy sense of humor were gone. He

13

was utterly unresponsive. He breathed, but he didn't function as a human being.

The hospital staff concluded, after nearly three more weeks, that it could do nothing more for him. Jack and Gladys Tipps were told to take their son home.

Six months after the accident, Gene was able to shuffle about with the aid of a walker. The neurosurgeon examined him and found no improvement in brain function, however. "He sits in a chair, stares, and does not carry out spontaneous speech," he noted in the records. He told the Tippses that if Gene displayed no flashes of intelligence in a year his brain damage might have to be accepted as permanent.

Gene didn't want to do anything voluntarily. Left to himself, he would sleep 20 hours a day. His parents had to cajole or order him to leave his bed. He had to be forced to wash, shave, comb his hair, brush his teeth. (Even so, his teeth gradually turned brown.) Although he never smiled or laughed, he would answer a direct question with a yes or no. He didn't recognize friends and relatives.

After a year, the Tippses took away Gene's crutches and made him walk on his own. They tried to stimulate him in various other ways. When Jack returned in the evening from his job as a carpenter, he would take Gene for walks and drives. But Gene didn't want to walk, and on drives he fell asleep. Gladys left the television set on all the time, hoping that perhaps a scene or an impression might crack the barriers separating Gene from the world. He sat for so many thousands of hours before the TV set that he wore out the back of an easy chair. Yet he seemed to see and hear nothing.

The Tippses bought Gene a rowing machine and forced him to row. Then they brought in a stationary bicycle. Gene loathed both machines. His dislike for any kind of exercise was his only obvious emotion.

Sometimes a doctor or relative said that it might be better to place Gene in a nursing home. The Tippses refused to consider it. Their only thought was, "What else can we try?"

They took Gene to neurosurgeons, neurologists, psychiatrists, psychologists. None could help him. They checked him into a Texas rehabilitation center. After two weeks they got a call to come pick him up. It was a waste of time, they were told; Gene would not cooperate with the therapists.

Twice a year, Mrs. Tipps took Gene for checkups to the

family physician, Dr. Charles Randal. Repeatedly, Dr. Randal had to say, "I can't think of anything that can be done for Gene."

In April 1975, Dr. Randal found that Gene had an infected gall bladder. "I should take it out, but with Gene's condition I don't know how he will react to anesthesia. There is a chance that he could die or sink into a deep coma."

Three weeks later, the operation could be delayed no longer. Mrs. Tipps stayed with Gene from the moment he entered the hospital. After the operation, he slept for more than 30 hours. When he awakened, he appeared to be the same as before—withdrawn and indifferent.

Then, about 65 hours after the operation, it happened. Without his being aware that it *was* happening, Gene suddenly escaped from his dark and terrible dungeon. In one flashing instant, at 1:30 a.m. on May 16, 1975, he went from his near-vegetable state to the college student he had been on May 21, 1967.

He stared at his mother, whose head was averted at the moment. He couldn't understand why she looked so much older. "How long have I been in the hospital?" he asked.

It was the first question he had asked in eight years. His mother turned her head. Now it was her turn to stare. "Three days," she answered carefully.

"Three days? I'd better get out of here and back to college. If I'm out more than five days, I get suspended. How long have I been out of school?"

Mrs. Tipps didn't know what to say. For those long years, she had watched for a sign that her son was emerging from the shadows. At times she thought she had detected such an indication, but it was always false—a product of wishful thinking. Now she felt such a thrill as she had never before experienced. She desperately wanted to believe that this transformation was real, yet she was afraid of new disappointment—afraid, too, of what her excitement might do to Gene. So she steeled herself to be matter-of-fact, and said, "Well, son, you've been out of school for quite a while."

"Did the draft board send me my classification?" he asked next.

Now she knew that a change was occurring. She arose and put her hand on his shoulder. "Gene, are you awake?" she asked.

He sat up. "Why, sure, Mother. I've never been more awake in my life."

"Gene," she said slowly, "the last time you were really awake was eight years ago. You were in a car accident and went into a coma."

He heard the words, but they didn't make sense to him. "I can't believe it," he said weakly, trying to think back. He lapsed into silence, then said, "It seems that I was very sleepy for a week or two. I couldn't understand why you and Dad were always trying to wake me up. I just wanted to rest."

Questions bubbled out of him now. But he couldn't absorb the passage of time; to him, 1967 was the present. Asking after Seymour friends and Cisco college students, he shook his head in bewilderment when his mother told him that most of them had married and had children. He learned that the Vietnam war was over, that Lyndon Johnson was no longer President.

He asked for a mirror, and looked into it. He was horrified at the condition of his teeth and wanted an immediate dental appointment. Why was his hair so long? His mother explained that most young men were wearing their hair longer now. Not for him, he averred; he was going back to his crew cut.

"How's that piece of land that Dad bought?" he inquired.

"We had to sell it to pay hospital bills," Gladys answered.

Gene's face clouded over as he caught a glimmer of the truth of the past eight years.

Self-control became excruciating to Mrs. Tipps now. She wanted to go out into the hall and shout to everyone in sight: "My son is awake! My son has come back!" But she still had no way of knowing whether Gene's return was permanent.

The two alternately talked and dozed through the night. In the morning, Dr. Randal was summoned. Gene grinned at him and asked, "What did you do to my head?"

The physician stared at his patient. Nothing in his 30 years of practice had prepared him for this. Neither he nor, later, any of the specialists whom he consulted could offer any explanation of this sudden "reawakening."

"Mother said you took out my gall bladder," Gene went on, smiling. "It might have been a good idea to take it out eight years ago."

Dr. Randal was too surprised to kid with Gene.

After nine days in the hospital, Gene was ready to go home. He put his arms around his parents. "I have an idea of what you've done for me," he said, "but that's over. You don't have to feel sorry for me anymore."

Three months later, Gene was exhaustively tested at the University of Texas Health Science Center. His intelligence checked out as normal. His ability to learn and his willingness to cope with problems were excellent. The examining neurologist found evidence of neurologic dysfunction in his right arm and hand, and in his vision.

Why Gene "left" and why he "returned" still resist definitive medical explanation. A neurologist speculated that the recovery may have resulted from a "biochemical or other metabolic change, possibly related to anesthesia and oxygenation."

Gene reflects, "Where was I for eight years? It's a puzzle. Anyway, what's most important is for me to get on with the business of living."

As he pieces together the history of the lost years, he feels a huge debt to his parents for their patience and devotion. But his mother doesn't want him to try to express gratitude. "It's we who give thanks," she has told her son. "You have come back to us. To us that is a miracle."

And no one can say that it isn't.

The American in Cell No. 5

by Andrew Jones

THE BLINDFOLD and handcuffs had been on him for two days, and when they were taken off he didn't know where he was. The rag was thick with blood from the shotgun-pellet wounds in his face. Although weak from diarrhea, he was able to hold his battered five-foot, six-inch frame erect. He stood there, barefoot, filthy, before several Iranians talking in Farsi.

Suddenly one of them—apparently the No. 2 man—spoke in English. "This is a revolutionary committee, and you will go on trial for killing Iranians. What is your full name?"

"Kenneth Kraus, Sergeant, U. S. Marine Corps," he replied, trying to focus on the interrogator's face. "I didn't kill any Iranians."

"Shut up! Sign this form."

"I won't sign anything."

Guards forced him toward the desk, smeared his fingers with ink and pressed the prints onto a form.

No. 2 continued: "You will go on trial for killing Iranians

19

in defense of the American embassy. The embassy has been taken, the Marines have been shot. The ambassador and all his officers are in prison."

Ken Kraus could not believe this. But he knew it *might* be true. Two days before, on February 14, fedayeen guerrillas had swept into the U.S. embassy in Teheran. Ken had been wounded and taken to the Amir Alam hospital to recuperate. But guerrillas had suddenly charged into his room, pulled the intravenous tubes from his arms and dragged him—shackled, blindfolded, in pajamas and barefoot—to this place.

No. 2 spoke again: "Do you recognize the Ayatollah Khomeini's government?"

"I don't know. I don't understand it." Ken wanted to keep No. 2 talking so he might learn who his captors were and what they wanted.

"Americans are not welcome here," No. 2 said. "We want you all to leave."

"I'll leave right now," Ken replied. "Just show me the door."

"No!" the other shouted. "You are a criminal. You are to be tried. Take him away!"

Guards led him down to a tier of four cells two floors below ground level. This, he would learn, was a dungeon previously used by *Savak,* the dreaded secret police of the ousted Shah Mohammed Reza Pahlavi. He was taken to a cell with the Farsi number five on the door—he recognized the number because as an embassy guard he had taught himself to read Iranian license plates.

By the light of a single naked bulb, Ken could make out pale, wraith-like figures in the bunks around the walls. He climbed onto an empty bunk and pulled a dirty blanket over his body. *What was he doing in this situation?* he wondered. He was 22, with a widowed mother, three sisters, a solid upbringing in the Catholic Church. If his application to Annapolis had been accepted, or if he had taken that college wrestling scholarship instead of joining the Corps, he wouldn't be in this mess. As he took a deep breath to control the choking in his throat, one of the faces spoke: "American?"

Ken said, "Yes, American."

To his astonishment, the cell erupted in laughter as the word bounced from face to grinning face: "American!... American!" They crowded around him, smiling and jabbering. "Me Reza," one said. "Speak English." Next was Ali, who also spoke a little English. One by one they introduced themselves.

From the machine-gun Farsi interspersed with broken English, Ken learned that his cellmates were mostly soldiers and police of the former regime. The significance of this hit him hard: he had been thrown in with people considered criminal scum by the kangaroo-court jurists above. He had the unsettling feeling that they had already been tried and found guilty, and he with them.

Ken Kraus had been in Iran only five weeks, on temporary duty from the U.S. embassy at Nicosia, Cyprus. As anti-Shah agitation escalated from day to day, he and seven other Marines had been flown in to reinforce the 12-man detachment that normally guards our embassy in Teheran. The eight Marines were briefed after their arrival. Most of the insurgents were taking orders from a Muslim religious leader, the septuagenarian Ayatollah Ruhollah Khomeini, an avowed enemy of the Shah, who had been exiled to France. Aligned with the Ayatollah were members of the Marxist-Leninist fedayeen group, and a number of other religious and political guerrilla factions—some not overly scrupulous about how they got their way.

Ken quickly fell in with the duty schedule, standing guard on eight-hour rotation. As the days went by, it became clear that the street situation was deteriorating. There was always the possibility of an assault on the compound, a U.S. symbol in an increasingly hostile land.

Eventually the Shah fled the country and Ayatollah Khomeini returned in triumph. The embassy security force was placed on full alert as armed bands roamed the city streets.

Ken went off duty at 8 a.m. on a snowy February 14. Back in the barracks after breakfast, he suddenly heard a burst of automatic-weapons fire. "They're coming over the walls!" crackled an excited voice on his walkie-talkie. He glanced at his watch. It was 10:26. Grabbing his gear—tear-gas grenades, riot gun and .38-caliber revolver—he raced down the stairs.

Bullets were ricocheting off the compound walls and snipping branches off trees. Taking up his duty post outside the commissary building, Ken spotted a sniper on a roof across the street. He fired a tear-gas grenade and when the smoke drifted away the sniper was gone. From his walkie-talkie came the calm voice of Ambassador William H. Sullivan: "This is Cowboy [his code name]. Do not fire unless your life is in danger."

The compound was now under sustained automatic-weapons fire. Armed Iranians were already inside, and more were scaling the ten-foot walls. Ken ducked into the embassy restaurant, locking the door behind him. Sizing up the situation, he called Ambassador Sullivan on the radio: "Cowboy, this is Bulldog with two other mikes [Marines] in the restaurant. We're holed up here with roughly 20 civilians—five Americans and 15 Iranian kitchen help. What are your instructions?"

Back came some jabbering in Farsi—evidently the guerrillas had captured walkie-talkies—but finally the ambassador's voice came through: "Surrender if you can make contact."

Surrender orders included getting rid of weapons that could be used by the other side. The Marines hid their shotguns in a freeze unit and hammered their revolvers against the cement floor, bending the barrels.

Ken asked an Iranian how to say "Surrender" in Farsi. *"Pasheman,"* she replied. Everyone began chanting, *"Pasheman, pasheman, pasheman...."*

A burst of gunfire from outside blew out a window and shattered a metal container on a shelf directly over Ken's head. At that moment a young Iranian waiter broke toward the kitchen door. Stepping in front of Ken, he caught a second burst, in the chest, from three submachine-gun-carrying fedayeen who crashed through the entrance to the restaurant. He was dead before he hit the floor.

With hands above their heads, the occupants of the commissary were marched outside. The compound was a madhouse of hysterical, gun-brandishing guerrillas, some hooded, leading groups of embassy workers around in the snow, lining them up, searching them. A man neatly dressed in a three-piece suit came up to Ken and asked him in English where he had hidden the "automatic weapons."

"We have no automatic weapons," Ken said.

"I can't control these people much longer," the man said. "Give me your weapons."

Ken led him and several others inside, took his shotgun out of the freezer and handed it to him. The man hefted it and looked at Ken. "This is not an automatic weapon," he said.

"I told you...."

The man interrupted in his own tongue, and one guerrilla struck Ken down with a gun-butt blow to the ribs. As he lay there with his side caved in, Ken saw a man fumbling with his shotgun, trying to figure out how it worked. He was standing 20 feet away and Ken was looking directly up the barrel. "Jesus, I'm sorry," he mumbled. "Please make it quick!" Then the gun went off with a roar.

Huddled against the wall in cell five, Ken recalled regaining consciousness in the hospital. Although his face and upper body had been peppered with shot, he had not caught the gun's full blast, and so had lived. He tried to work out the sequence of events since his kidnapping from the hospital. It was hopeless. He could not tell what day it was or whether, up on the surface of the earth, there was daylight or darkness.

Now the passing hours were filled by talking to his cellmates and playing interminable games of chess and backgammon— with pieces made of floor tiles and playing boards scratched into the exposed cement. At last a guard called for "the American in cell five." The Iranians crowded round to shake his hand. That was the way it happened: prisoners went upstairs to trial and no one in the cells ever saw them again. Either they went free or they were taken up on the roof to face a firing squad.

Ken was taken to a small room and seated before three turbaned officials; three Muslim priests sat along the wall to the left. Another man, seemingly the clerk, announced that this was the "People's Revolutionary Volunteer Court of Khomeini," and that Ken would be tried for shooting three Iranian soldiers at the American embassy.

The questions began: Why was he in Iran? What were his duties at the embassy? Where was he when the attack occurred?

Ken answered everything factually, and denied killing anyone.

After much babbling between the mullahs and the magistrates, the clerk-interpreter said, "We have witnesses who saw you do it. You are a member of the CIA [he pronounced it 'See-ah'] who came to the embassy to train *Savak* agents and terrorist criminals. You took up weapons against the Khomeini government, and you killed three of its soldiers. We find you guilty, and the penalty is death."

Upon hearing the verdict, a strange thing happened to Ken

Kraus. Since his abduction he had been in pain, fear and gut-wrenching uncertainty. Now suddenly all that left him.

Without being conscious of what he was doing, Ken stood up and faced his accusers. In grimy prison rags, barefoot, he began to talk: "Look, I don't know who you people are, but I challenge your right to try me for murder or anything else. I'm an American citizen and I have diplomatic immunity. If, like you say, you're going by Muslim law, then you're supposed to give me rights that are not so different from my own. I have a right to counsel, to an interpreter. You say you have witnesses—where are they? I have a right to question them. You say I killed somebody. I want to see the bullets. I want to see their graves. Where is the weapon I used...?"

The words just came out, plain and simple, as though he had been ready to plead his own case all his life. Amazingly, he felt ten feet tall.

The clerk ranted and the mullahs mumbled for a few more minutes; then the guards took him back downstairs. With cries of joy, the prisoners welcomed his return. But that night, while the others staged cockroach races across the floor, Ken found himself questioning basic premises. *Having lost an embassy, had America quit? Had the embassy staff been jailed or wiped out? And what about his buddies? Marines don't leave Marines to die. Where* was *everybody?* After his cellmates went to sleep, he felt hysteria gaining on him.

All the hours now began to run together. Prisoners were led away and did not return. Ken was taken upstairs for more questioning. At one point he was handcuffed to a chair while two interrogators grilled him concerning communications equipment in the embassy. One of them stood in front of him and grinning ear to ear, cocked a semiautomatic rifle, put the muzzle in Ken's mouth and pulled the trigger. The breechblock slammed home on an empty chamber.

Ken was led to another room. Dazed and only semi-conscious, he was seated in an upholstered chair and given a glass of water. A neatly dressed man with a trim mustache and a gold watch said, "Mr. Kraus, I didn't have any control over what they were doing in that other room. It was very barbaric and animalistic." Ken kept silent.

"I have no desire to see you mistreated," the man continued. "You could be helpful not only to yourself but to us. If you are allowed to live, you could be an adviser to our government.

You have knowledge and training that would be valuable to us. You know how embassies work, and could teach us about security. You would have people to take care of you, a car, a nice home and an office. Does this interest you?"

Ken turned the proposition over in his mind for a moment; then for the second time in his life he began to talk without plan. "I can't do what you suggest. Your country is not my country, your God is not my God. My book says something your book doesn't say—it says that if I try to save my life I'll lose it. If I saved my life the way you want me to, I'd be a traitor. All I want is to go back to the States. I'm scared and hurt and I don't understand what's happening. I didn't kill any of your people and if you kill me I just hope that you can find some justification for, for. . . ."

He broke off. The man glanced at his gold watch, stood up, walked to the door, turned around. He said, "I offered you. . . ."

That night No. 2 came to Ken's cell and told him, "There will be executions on Thursday. You'll probably go with them."

Next morning No. 2 was at the cell door again. He left Ken with two guards. They handcuffed him and opened a door he had never been through before—the door to the stairs that led to the roof. They were halfway up when No. 2 suddenly reappeared and began shouting.

There had been a mix-up. The guards brought Ken down again and this time led him out to the sidewalk. Ken took his first breath of fresh air in seven days. He felt tears coursing down his face as he got into the back seat of a waiting car.

It was a three-quarter-hour drive to Khomeini headquarters, and another hour or so before Ken was on the phone talking to Rick Thomas, the embassy's regional security officer. "You're alive!" Ken shouted at him. Thomas told him everybody was alive, that a car was on the way to pick him up.

Ken arrived at the embassy on Wednesday evening, February 21, one week almost to the hour after his kidnapping. The buildings were scarred and burned, and the facility, although still representing the U.S. government, was under Iranian control. But everyone was alive, and Ken was astounded to learn that he was a national hero—the newspapers and television were all carrying the story of his release, arranged by President

Carter. Since his uniforms had been stolen in the post-surrender looting, he was taken in his prison rags to Ambassador Sullivan's house for a sumptuous dinner.

Afterward, still dazed, he found himself on the telephone with the President of the United States. All Ken could say was, "Thank you, Mr. President!"

Things happened very fast after that. Most of the 7000 Americans in Iran were being evacuated, and Ken flew out with a planeload bound for Frankfurt on Thursday morning. The next day, arriving at Andrews Air Force Base outside Washington, D.C., he stepped out to the music of a drum-and-bugle band and the excited greetings of his family. In a special decoration ceremony, he was awarded the Purple Heart for his wounds and the Navy Commendation Medal for his actions on February 14.

Ken took the accolades in stride. He had lived a very long time in seven days. He was home now, and that was enough.

Cecil Starcher's Bargain With Life

by Joseph P. Blank

HE'S 75 NOW, Cecil Starcher of Spencer, W. Va. He was born deaf. And is mute. And became blind.

He has always loved hard work and has always managed. At age 7, he was caring for livestock on his parents' farm. At 9, he was sent to a state boarding school for the deaf, where he spent most of the next 11 years. As a teen-ager, he was never without summer jobs. At 15, he helped his father build a new house. When his father ran out of money for supplies, Cecil loaned him $50.

In 1938, he built his own house, ten yards from his father's. He built it as he earned money. He never borrowed or asked for credit. That's the way it's been to this day.

In 1935, he married Gladys Billips, who also was deaf. They had a son, Cecil, Jr., in 1938. Gladys died in 1942 after giving birth to a stillborn infant. Some time later, Cecil met Katherine Hedrick, an alumna of the school for the deaf that

27

he had attended. They were married in 1945 and have two daughters, Charlotte and Jeanie.

Cecil has always loved people. On a Saturday, he would walk the few blocks to the main Spencer intersection near the courthouse. There he stood, notebook in hand, greeting dozens of passing friends. If they couldn't guess at what he was trying to say or if he couldn't read their lips, he used the pad for questions and answers. He wanted to know about their families—did a son find a job, was a husband feeling better, did a wife return from a visit to her parents? Then he would sit around the courthouse with old acquaintances, avidly listening with his eyes to conversations.

In 1957, he began having trouble seeing well at night. Then objects became fuzzy in outline. He had to squint and hold the newspaper close to read. An examination by an ophthalmologist revealed that Cecil's retinas were deteriorating and nothing could be done to stop the process.

At the time, Cecil was working in a rubber plant. He soon realized that his failing vision would cause him to make a mistake in measuring the chemical components for a batch of rubber, and he couldn't stand the prospect of failing in his responsibilities. He told his supervisor, "My eyes are going bad. It be best that I leave." He has never forgotten the date: January 11, 1958.

When Cecil went totally blind at the age of 52, he sank into a deep depression. He was no longer able to hold a job. Yet, even then, his pride forbade him to accept aid from the welfare department. The family survived on his monthly retirement check and their savings.

He tried walking into town with a cane, but he couldn't read lips any longer. His old acquaintances didn't know how to finger-talk to him on his hand or arm. He became easily disoriented and had to be guided home. This dependence on others made him decide never again to venture into town. He had lost his only recreation.

He became easily enraged, which frightened Katherine. Fearful that he might harm himself, she hid the .22-caliber rifle that hung on a wall. A physician advised her to have her husband admitted to a state hospital, but she couldn't even think about such an act. When Cecil, Jr., returned in 1960 from Army duty, he was utterly dismayed. How long could his father, given his fierce sense of independence, endure the helplessness, the silence and darkness?

But Cecil Starcher had not yet been broken. That driving desire for self-reliance re-asserted itself. "You could see in his face that something was going on inside him," says Cecil, Jr. "It was that he had decided to grab hold of life."

For progressively longer periods, he left his chair. He asked his wife to get gardening literature from the county agricultural agent. There was a level stretch of land behind the unoccupied house in which his deceased parents had lived. He had in mind planting a variety of vegetables that would keep him busy through the spring and summer, and provide plenty of fresh produce for his family and friends.

In 1961, while waiting for the earth to thaw, he began taking on chores. He learned how to sweep and mop the kitchen floor. He memorized the position of everything in the house. He organized his tool chest so that he could quickly pick out any tool he needed. He changed the washer on a leaky faucet. He ran his hands over all the walls in the house to find cracks, which he then spackled and sanded for Katherine to paint.

In late winter, he began preparing the 4000-square-foot plot for planting. He wouldn't consider asking an acquaintance with a small tractor to till the soil. He wanted to do the work himself. By 8 a.m., he had made his way to the field with his cane, and hacked at the compacted earth with a mattock. Working till seven or eight at night, he dug up brush, weeds and rocks, and raked away the small stones. As the weeks went by, Katherine saw the depression and anger fade from her husband's face. He had returned to the joy of hard work and was proving to himself he was a productive human being.

Under Katherine's direction, he dug holes and set poles firmly into the earth. She then strung wires between the poles; by keeping in touch with the wire, he could dig a straight furrow. He sprinkled seed in the furrows while Katherine set in young plants.

On the road above his hollow, excavation for a house precipitated a landslide that ruptured the rock retaining wall along the brook in front of the Starcher home. Cecil chose not to talk with the builders about repairing the damage. He slowly replaced the rocks and restored the wall by feel. It still stands as firm as the day he completed the job.

In June 1974, Jeanie and her husband, Kim O'Brien, who had been living in Akron, Ohio, decided to return to country living. They moved into the house that had been built by Cecil's father. Ever since her father had gone blind, Jeanie had felt a heavy sorrow for him, but soon this began to be replaced by ever-growing admiration and respect. Early in the morning he was in the garden, tending or picking the vegetables. After an hour for lunch, he was back in the garden, where he would weed for several hours on his hands and knees, feeling the difference between weeds and cultivated vegetation.

He was always looking for work. He would place a ladder against a tree and climb it to saw off low and dead limbs. He would split logs for firewood. He would use a hammer and an anvil to break rocks into gravel-size stone, which he packed into potholes on the long, unpaved driveway.

One steaming-hot day, Kim saw him cutting grass with a sickle on the side of the hill and insisted on helping, despite Cecil's protests. Kim lasted an hour before the sun got to him and he had to take a break. His father-in-law put in another two hours before seeking shade and water.

When Kim began chopping down a large, rotting tree in front of the house, Cecil asked to spell him. Kim, who had not been raised on a farm, had trouble hitting the same spot twice with the ax. But Cecil could swing an ax with his "eyes closed." Each time the ax blade bit into the same niche.

Few jobs daunted him. When the sewer line outside the house got clogged, a town maintenance man opened it up, viewed the problem and hesitated at the messy task. Impatient, Cecil pulled on boots, took a shovel and long poker and cleared out the blockage.

During the O'Briens' first summer in Spencer, Katherine went to visit her mother and oldest daughter, who lived on a farm about 150 miles away. Cecil stayed home to take care of his garden. He appeared to have no anxieties about being alone in his house, but Jeanie asked him to have his meals with her family. He said he'd see.

On the first morning she waited vainly for him, then walked to his house and peered through the kitchen window. She watched him pour water for coffee into a pot and light a burner on the old gas stove. He laid out several slices of bacon in a frying pan and lit another burner. He set a place at the kitchen table with bread, margarine and some hot peppers, which he loves.

After several days, Jeanie realized that if the food shopping was done for him he could take care of himself. She saw him slice an onion more evenly than she could do. He ran his fingers around an apple, touched the soft spots, meticulously peeled it, then remembered exactly where to cut out the bad parts. After tearing his shirt, he asked Jeanie to thread a needle with the proper color and mended the shirt himself.

He did come to dinner quite often. The principal reason was the company of the O'Brien family. Cecil's face glows when he's among people, and his favorite company is the three O'Brien boys: John, 12, James, 11, and Joey, 7. He'll pop corn for them. He'll amuse them by pantomiming stories about the adventures of a big bird, and by blowing into his thumb to make his biceps "inflate."

He and Joey are buddies. The child curls up in his grandpa's lap for hours. Cecil has a weakness for hard candies and doughnuts, and so does Joey. When the child wants a lemon drop, he crosses his grandpa's lips with his index finger. And early in the morning, when taken with a yen for a doughnut, Joey trots across to the other house and leads his grandpa to the refrigerator. The doughnuts are stored on a shelf above it. Grandpa understands.

Occasionally one of the older boys will invite a friend home and introduce him to Cecil. "This is my Grandpa," James will say, with pride. "He can't see, or hear, or talk. But he can do anything."

Of course, Cecil can't "do anything." It just seems that way to his family. And Cecil's view is this: "I'm healthy. I'm strong and in good shape. I enjoy working and enjoy what I have."

While emerging from the despair caused by blindness, he apparently decided to give to living everything of which he was capable. In turn, he has taken from life all that was offered him—the satisfaction he feels at the end of a day of hard work, the pleasure of running his hand over a fine, plump ear of corn, his delight with the touch of Joey's finger on his lips. To Cecil Starcher, it is a fair bargain.

The Boy Who Plunged Over Niagara

by Lawrence Elliott

JUST AFTER 8 a.m. on Saturday, July 9, 1960, James Honeycutt came off the night shift at a Niagara Falls hydroelectric project. Sleep, though, was not on his mind—not on a fine summer morning with a trim new outboard motorboat tied to the dock at Lynch's Trailer Court, where he resided.

Honeycutt was 40, an affable man who had had to leave his family in Raleigh, N.C., when he came north to work. He found the weekends long and lonely. So, after breakfast, he drove to the home of Frank Woodward, a carpenter on his crew. Over coffee Honeycutt sprang his surprise: How would the Woodward youngsters, 17-year-old Deanne and her 7-year-old brother, Roger, like to go for a boat ride?

Deanne, awed by the tumultuous river, which she had seen only once, was reluctant. But with little Roger jumping with glee, and her mother urging her to go along—"You'll have a chance for a swim at Lynch's later"—Deanne changed into a bathing suit, and the three set out.

Soon Honeycutt was easing his green aluminum runabout away from the Lynch dock, his pride and inexperience both obvious in the cautious way he maneuvered clear of other boats. At midstream he turned the sleek 14-foot craft downriver and offered the tiller to Roger. His face grinning above his brilliant orange life jacket, the boy took hold.

Deanne, in the bow, relaxed. If Mr. Honeycutt was confident enough to let Roger steer, what was *she* worried about? When they passed under the Grand Island Bridge, gateway to the American side of the falls, she waved gaily at the cars passing far overhead.

John R. Hayes, a trucker and special police officer from Union, N.J., had crossed the bridge an hour earlier. He and his wife had come to Niagara Falls for the weekend, and now, like the thousands of other tourists, were snapping pictures and marveling at the incredible power of the famous cataracts.

Past noon, they crossed the footbridge to Goat Island, which splits the Niagara into two sets of leaping rapids, its sheer northern end overlooking the awesome cleft into which both the American and the Horseshoe Falls plunge. Downriver from the falls, so far below him that it looked like a toy in a bathtub, Hayes could see a vessel docked under the Canadian cliffs.

It was one of the two *Maid of the Mist* ships that take turns cruising up into the "Shoe." There, within 150 feet of the wet black rocks at the very foot of the Horseshoe Falls, surrounded by wild flying spray and deafened by the roar of the torrent, tourists come face to face with one of nature's great extravagances.

The Niagara River is, in effect, an ever-narrowing trough, draining the North American mid-continent. Plunging north with the overflow from Lake Erie and the three Great Lakes to the west, it drops a precipitous 326 feet in its 36-mile length, flings 823,650 gallons of water a second over the 161-foot falls and swirls through the world's most treacherous rapids before spending its fury in the vastness of Lake Ontario.

Its violence has always attracted daredevils. In steel drums or padded barrels, at least seven stunters have gone over the Horseshoe. Only four survived. Suicides find in the falls the savage end they crave. Scarcely a month passes that one isn't whisked over the brink. Dashed to the rocks below, thrust into wild eddies and currents, their broken bodies have almost in-

variably been cast to the surface at the *Maid of the Mist* landing
exactly four days later.

Jim Honeycutt, again at the tiller, seemed unconcerned as the
little outboard, now four miles downstream from Lynch's and
only a mile or so above the falls, came bouncing past the long
breakwater that evens the river's flow. Deanne, though, was
getting nervous. This was not the broad, friendly river they'd
started out on. It was roiled, leaping turbulently along the
pronounced downhill pitch, breaking white against glistening
rocks. The thunder of pounding water grew louder in her ears.

About this time, a Goat Island sightseeing guide was telling
a group of tourists that the control structure out on the river
was the point beyond which nothing could keep from being
swept over the falls. One tourist gestured at the little green
boat and said, "What about that?" The guide ran for a telephone.
But it was already too late.

With the runabout almost abreast of Goat Island, Honeycutt
finally brought the bow around. For one tenuous moment, the
$7\frac{1}{2}$-horsepower motor beat against the remorseless current,
barely making headway. Then, with a piercing whine, it began
to race futilely; the propeller pin had sheared.

As the boat swept downstream stern-first, Honeycutt lunged
for the oars. Though he pulled frantically, he hardly slowed
the boat's backward rush. He yelled to Deanne, "Put on the
life jacket!"

The girl's fingers were stiff as she laced tight the boat's
only other jacket. In the stern, face suddenly turned white,
Roger called, "Dee-dee, I'm scared." He began stumbling toward her.

"No!" she screamed, terrified that he would tip them over.
"Stay there, Roger! We'll be swimming at Lynch's soon."

"No, we're going to drown!" he cried. But he sat down and,
clinging to the thwart, began to sob quietly. They were in full
rapids now, the water solid white and tearing them toward the
falls. Smashing off a rock, then caught by a vicious rip, the
stern flew straight up.

"Hang on!" Honeycutt cried out, but there was nothing to
hang onto. He and Roger were thrown over Deanne's head.
Then the water snatched at her. She grabbed for the overturned
hull, but it slid from beneath her fingers.

Honeycutt grabbed Roger's arm, fighting to hold the boy's

head out of the water. But the furious currents tore them apart. The rapids wrenched Roger down, spun him around. Then all at once he was free, thrust out over the edge of the falls, dropping through space.

John Hayes saw the boat turn over. He and his wife had been walking toward Terrapin Point, the railed tip of Goat Island that looks out over the lip of the Horseshoe. "Look!" he shouted, racing for the river.

As he ran, he spied Deanne Woodward's vivid life jacket. He dashed upriver, past dozens of stunned tourists, trying to get closer to her. Above the roar of the cataract he heard her crying out for help. He leaned over the guardrail so she could see him.

"Here!" he called out. "Hey, girl! Swim over here!"

Deanne saw him, but shook her head hopelessly. She was unable to make any real progress.

"Try!" Hayes called. He ran downriver to get ahead of her, and leaned farther over the rail. "Try!"

The current was sweeping her inexorably closer to the falls' jagged rim. Hayes stretched his arm out, though the girl was still far beyond reach. Deanne was at the very edge of exhaustion. Her legs ached from being pounded against the rocks. "Help me!" she pleaded with Hayes, the thunder of death a bare 20 feet away. Quickly he climbed over the guardrail. He was only a foot above the rushing water, clinging to the rail with one hand. He cried out, "You got to try, hear? *Try!*"

The sharpness of his voice stirred a last, hidden resource in Deanne. Doggedly she buried her face in the water and pulled once more against its clutch. When she looked up again, Hayes was almost directly above her. Desperately she cast out as she went sweeping by—and caught his thumb. Hayes' hand closed around hers.

His foot wedged behind the rail, the weight of the girl and the awful force of the rapids tearing on his fingers, Hayes thought they would both go over. He called for help. A man broke out of the cluster of spellbound sightseers. Vaulting the rail, John A. Quattrochi, another tourist from New Jersey, leaned down and grabbed Deanne's wrist. For a long moment the three hung on, straining. Then the two men pulled the girl from the rushing water and lifted her over the guardrail.

Deanne Woodward had been just ten feet from the falls,

closer than anyone had ever come before being plucked to safety. As she lay on the ground, she gasped, "My brother! My brother's still in there. Please save him!"

But Quattrochi had seen Roger go over the falls. Softly he said, "Say a prayer for your brother."

Maid of the Mist II, its decks heaving, drenched by spray and surrounded by thunder, was almost to its turning point just below Horseshoe Falls. At the wheel, Capt. Clifford Keech peered into the chaos of white water. When, at 12:52, he spotted a bobbing orange object dead ahead, he craned forward in amazement. He barked into his ship-to-shore phone: "This is Keech. There's a kid in a life jacket floating around up here and—maybe I'm crazy, but I think he's alive!"

Though Roger Woodward was indeed alive—the first human being to survive a drop over Niagara Falls without elaborate protection—his peril was not yet past. He was drifting close to the huge port of an Ontario hydro plant and might yet be dragged into the opening.

The *Maid* came about and bore down on the boy from upstream, using the full reverse power of both engines to hold a position against the driving current. From the starboard bow, mate Murray Hartling and deckhand Jack Hopkins threw a life preserver toward the tiny figure in the water. It fell short. They hauled it in and threw again. On the third try the life preserver bobbed to within an arm's length of the thrashing boy. He crawled up onto it. A moment later, Roger Woodward lay on the deck of the *Maid,* shivering under the blankets piled on him. "Please find my sister," he said. "She and Mr. Honeycutt fell in the water, too."

An emergency launch, responding to Keech's call, searched the swirling caldron for half an hour, but found only the auxiliary gas tank, all that was ever recovered of the boat.

Meanwhile, high up on Goat Island, hundreds had seen the boy in the orange life jacket pulled aboard the *Maid of the Mist.* "They've got your brother," Hayes told Deanne just before she was whisked off to the hospital. "I think he's okay."

"Thank you, God," said the girl, and closed her eyes.

Roger was taken to a Canadian hospital, where an hour later his mother and father came to tell him that Deanne, too, had been rescued. In a few days both youngsters, incredibly uninjured except for superficial bruises, were released.

How did Roger Woodward survive? River men reason that Roger's lightness held him atop the water's surge; that, as he was thrust over the brink, he flew along and down the crest as though going over a slide, thus avoiding the deadly rocks and turbulence at the fall's base. Though he had dropped 161 feet at an estimated 75 miles an hour, his life preserver had forced him back to the surface before he lost consciousness.

But the mighty falls did not go completely unappeased. On Wednesday, July 13, the body of Jim Honeycutt turned up at the *Maid of the Mist* landing. It was four days, almost to the hour, from the moment he was swept to his death.

Farewell to Alcohol

by William McIlwain

I WAS LATE getting to Butner. I had been told to be here at 10:30, but I couldn't see where time made much difference. I got out of bed at nine o'clock, fixed a vodka and orange juice, and drank it while reading the sports pages. I sat for a while by a window, thinking, and drank another vodka and orange juice. Around 11, I decided it was time to go, and I fixed a cup of black coffee and a vodka and orange juice to drink while I shaved and showered.

I had never been to the Alcoholic Rehabilitation Center at Butner (one of three regional operated by the state of North Carolina) or any other comparable institution, and I wasn't sure what I would need. Deciding it would be casual, I packed two bags of sports clothes, my swimming trunks, an unfinished magazine article that I was writing, my typewriter, two tennis rackets and nine books. I wasn't sure whether drunks played tennis, but I would have an extra racket if I found a drunk who did. I got to the center around 2:15, and told the lady at the desk who I was. "Bill," she said, "you're four hours late. You'll have to come back next week."

I almost said, "The hell with it, lady," but something strong made me know I had to get into Butner. If I went away, I wouldn't come back. "Can I get a motel room and get in here tomorrow?"

"Bill, you'll just drink all night, and then we can't let you in."

"No, ma'am. I won't do that. I really need to get in here."

Finally, she said that maybe a person scheduled to report next day might cancel out. I could call in the morning, and she'd let me know.

I went to a liquor store, bought a fifth of vodka, got a motel room, and had a few vodkas and Sprites. I was taking a nap when the lady at ARC phoned to say they'd take me in the morning. That evening, I drank all of the vodka except three drinks. I wanted to have them in the morning before I went to the center.

I woke up sweating and shivering and feeling as if I were choking. In the old days, drinking a fifth of vodka at night wouldn't do this to me, but it did now because I had been drinking a long time. I thought if I could drink a vodka and Sprite, I would quit sweating and shivering, so I drank two. I still felt bad when I drove out and found a restaurant. I had a bowl of Brunswick stew for breakfast, and drank the last remaining vodka and Sprite.

I was scheduled to be at Butner for 22 days. We—the 20 or so in my dorm—included all sorts: a grandmother who drank vanilla extract; a young man who wrote detective stories; Tip Watson (I will not use patients' real names), who constructed a whiskey still when he was 14, sold its output at a nearby sawmill and began drinking it, too; a business executive's wife who had tried three times to commit suicide; Mr. Wellington, a church deacon and "secret drinker," who lost his job in industry after 36 years because "I was drinking beer at night and making mistakes the next morning"; and Mr. Leland, who mumbled, batted his eyes steadily and shook so much that he could hardly lift a cup of coffee to his mouth. There was, perhaps, only one similarity in us all: none of us thought he would ever become an alcoholic.

What kind of program could be put together to deal with

so disparate a group? There was, of course, a rigid schedule we lived by. We had regular housekeeping chores, lectures, avocational classes, group therapy, and compulsory weekly meetings arranged by Alcoholics Anonymous. But, for all of the formal effort put forth by the staff, there may have been equal therapy in our just being together—so many alcoholics studying each other.

You're not talking to a doctor who may be trying to scare you about your liver, or a preacher who is moralizing over you. You're talking to a man who has tried it, and if he says it's impossible to drink even half a beer unless you want to start all over again, you can believe it.

There are other benefits. One is that it's easier to perceive and understand your own flaws and troubles if you see them first in men and women around you, wonder if yours are similar, and then conclude that they are. You see alcoholics kidding themselves, and realize that you've been doing the same thing. Then there are horror cases around you. You look each morning at Mr. Leland, mumbling, eye-batting, shaking, and you think: If I don't stop now, I'll get like Mr. Leland.

That's a negative reason for quitting drinking; a person needs positive ones, too, and I was discovering them each day. Physically, I felt better than I had in at least three years. I didn't wake up shaking, sweating, hot and cold, coughing, snuffling and disoriented. I didn't wake up frightened, wondering what I had done the night before. This is common with alcoholics, and some at Butner had a lot worse time than I did. One man said he would get up in the morning and look quickly around the house to see if he had broken anything. Then he would circle his car, studying it, praying not to find that he had hit something or someone the night before.

How did I become an alcoholic? What were my chances of being able to quit drinking after drinking for 27 years? If I did quit, would I be happy with my life?

In finding answers, I was helped by a number of persons, one of them Dr. Norman A. Desrosiers, the superintendent of ARC. One of the things he said goes to the core of the ARC philosophy: "We're not drying out drunks here. We're treating persons who are using alcohol as a coping mechanism. We must treat the emotional needs." It was his contention that the majority of Americans who drink are trying themselves to treat emotional needs, using alcohol as a handy drug to deal with anxiety, tension, fear, grief, depression, frustration and inhibition. "The term 'social drinker' is meaningless," he said. "If it has any validity at all, it describes a minority of the people who use alcohol strictly at social functions, and at social functions alone."

Statistics on drinking vary, but these rounded-off figures will serve: 130 million American adults drink; of these, 10 to 11 million are alcoholics or bad problem drinkers; that leaves about 120 million who might be considered social drinkers. That's the figure Dr. Desrosiers wouldn't accept. "It is far more likely that the majority of persons who are not yet what we call alcoholic, but who drink, are in reality not *true* social drinkers but rather persons who use alcohol to treat their underlying emotional disorders. It is this population from which the alcoholic population is drawn, and who constitute a vast body of persons who adjust to life with the aid of chemical means."

I accepted that and put myself in that group. Looking back at it, I believe I understand some of what was happening. I was doing my work well, but I seldom felt at ease. Whiskey brought ease, at least some. I drank, and I continued to work well. For a good many years, I succeeded, writing for newspapers, then—at *Newsday*—becoming chief copy editor, day news editor, city editor, assistant managing editor. I felt many days and nights, though, as if I were doing it all with mirrors: not using the *real* skills of a professional, but skills less concrete, even less admirable, perhaps little more than the native cunning and charm of a Southerner who could praise, humor, pamper and reason men and women above and beneath him into doing, finally, what he wanted done.

For at least ten years, I did not drink much each day. On occasion, I would drink for hours, great amounts—the "occasion" being either business or social. Then I had a refrigerator put into my office. I would play tennis at lunchtime, come back and eat a can of cold tunafish and drink vodka and tonic. I would lay off the vodka for a few hours and start again shortly before the 7 p.m. news conference in my office. Later, I quit laying off the couple of hours; I would begin after tennis, drink through the news conference, and then sit and drink a while, thinking, before I began my ride home.

Bill Moyers, then publisher of *Newsday*, spoke to me about drinking so much—gently at first, sometimes in a kidding way, but later in a more concerned fashion. I paid little attention, thinking that Bill would have to accept my drinking and my brilliance; I had helped make *Newsday* one of the finest newspapers in the world, and I had done it while drinking.

I believe now—but didn't then—that I was becoming paralyzed in my job, a drunk figurehead who no longer was making great contributions to the newspaper. Gradually, though, that fear was creeping into my mind, and I grasped at the opportunity when Bill arranged what amounted to an ultra-white-collar firing: my becoming writer-in-residence at Wake Forest University on full salary. My year there (1970–1971) turned out no better than the preceding days at *Newsday*. I drank steadily. Except when asleep, I could not go an hour without drinking. I was accomplishing nothing as a writer. At 45 my life had become worthless. I came to Butner to see if I could turn it all around.

I was told I could leave the next day. (Unless committed by court order, a patient is actually free to leave when he chooses, but the accepted procedure is for the group counselor to approve a patient's departure.) Mr. Wellington and Luther Moore, a quiet sawmill worker, were to leave with me. Neither had a car at Butner. I was to drop them off at their homes and go to Virginia, where I would get a first solid taste of what it was like to be in a room with everyone drinking whiskey except me. That experience would come when I spoke to publishers of a newspaper chain and then, a week later, to editors of the same chain.

As Luther Moore, Mr. Wellington and I stood together that afternoon, talking, I wondered how each of us would fare. I recalled what one AA speaker said: "If you're wondering whether you'll ever be able to drink again, don't bother. You can't. Do you know what one of the greatest dangers is? You leave here, and you get along just fine. I did for three years. You start saying to yourself, 'Maybe I never was an alcoholic after all. I never did drink all that weird stuff that those *real* alcoholics did.' You think you can drink again—and this time control it. You can't. I tried it."

And I recalled the grim statistics: of three patients who complete an alcoholic treatment program, two fail and must return. One succeeds. To myself, I wished us all luck—but if numbers dog us, I wanted to be the one of three.

The two newspaper gatherings in Virginia went well. I arrived at the first one during the cocktail hour, necessitating an explanation as to why I wanted only a Sprite. I had just got out of Butner, I said, a center for alcoholics. No one seemed to care much, one way or the other.

Soon after the Virginia trip, I went to Atlantic Beach, N.C., where I began writing my book *A Farewell to Alcohol*. Eleven years have passed since then. I am now the editor of the Queens edition of *Newsday*. I'm happy, and I don't drink.

David Hartman's
Impossible Dream

---

by Allen Rankin

EVERYBODY WHO KNEW young David Hartman thought he was riding for a fall. Even his own family realized that the time to call a halt to Dave's impossible plans was that September night in 1968—the night before he first went off to college. The four Hartmans were lingering at the dinner table in their Havertown, Pa., home when David, who is blind, broached an old subject with a new intensity. "Dad," he said, "level with me. Do you think I can ever be a doctor?"

Fred Hartman, then an officer in a Philadelphia bank and a very practical man, stalled before replying. It was one thing not to pamper Dave, quite another to let him go on building up for a tragic letdown. What medical school would accept a blind student? The time had come to set David straight. But, wondered the father, how could he give a flat no to a boy like Dave? How could he clamp a ceiling on his dreams? And so, Fred Hartman finally said, "A doctor, son? Well, you'll never know unless you try, will you?"

45

Both he and David grinned. For this was the same response he had always made to David's "Can I do?" queries—ever since the boy, born with defective lenses, had gone completely blind at the age of eight. "Dad," Dave had asked at age ten. "Can I play baseball?"

"Well, let's try it and see," his father suggested, and together they worked out a way. Mr. Hartman rolled the ball along the ground to Dave, who learned to bat and catch it by the whiffling sound it made coming through the grass.

That had begun the family's determined effort to help David become as independent as possible. At times, panicked by darkness, the little boy would cry out, "Mama, I can't stand it!" Then Idamae Hartman, the softest member of the team, would rock him gently in her arms and croon, "I know, I know," until he found he could stand it after all. But his mother also joined the others in making David share household chores; and tired though she was when she came home from her job as a cashier, she read to him nearly every night to broaden his scope.

It was Dave's sister Barbara, however, who steeled herself to be his toughest taskmaster. Even the time he'd left his braille watch upstairs and asked her to retrieve it, she'd said, "Get it yourself. What do you think—that somebody's always going to be around to wait on you?"

So David grew up considering blindness no tragedy—just an exasperating bother—and feeling he could do anything he set his mind to. Then at 13, he announced that he was going to be a doctor and, unable to see the rueful headshakes that greeted this childish proclamation, he began preparing for his career. He insisted on leaving Overbrook School for the Blind, and enrolled at Havertown's public high school. He made good grades, won a place on the varsity wrestling team, and was elected vice president of the student council in his senior year.

Still, as impressive as his accomplishments were, they had always fallen into the realm of possibility. But David's ambition to become an M.D., a psychiatrist, was *not* in that realm, his family believed. So, after seeing him off to Gettysburg College, the Hartmans felt they had not been frank enough with Dave, and they were afraid he was heading for grief.

At Gettysburg, Hartman's faculty advisers tried to reason with him. "Why not settle for something more within your capabilities, like history or psychology?" suggested biology professor Ralph Cavaliere.

Sensing that this key teacher was about to refuse to allow him in his class, David launched into his most persuasive argument. "Look," he said, "I'm no different from anybody else! It's true I can't see, but everybody has some kind of disability. I believe the ones who are the most handicapped are those who don't want to do anything special or challenging with their lives. I want to be a psychiatrist because I happen to believe I'll make a good one—especially in helping rehabilitate people with problems similar to my own. So I want to go to med school, and I'm counting on Gettysburg to get me ready!" From that moment on, Cavaliere was David's staunch ally.

Handsome and well-built, the young blind man strode briskly around the Gettysburg campus with only an occasional searching thrust of his white metal cane. In his sophomore year, Dave kept happening to meet bright, lissome, green-eyed Cheryl Walker. For months he wondered why he was so lucky. Later, after they had become serious about each other, Cheri confessed to him: "I'd see you and run to get in your path—then hope I didn't sound out of breath when I said, 'Fancy seeing *you* again.'"

In the spring of 1972, David was winding up four years at Gettysburg with a near-perfect 3.8 grade average out of a possible 4 points. So far, so good. Ready for the big try, he had applied to ten medical schools.

By early April, eight had turned him down. Then, on the afternoon of April 27, a ninth rejection came from a school he had counted on the most, and Dave was crushed. He and Cheri broke down and wept. It was all over, they believed.

But at the one institution Dave had not heard from—Temple University School of Medicine, in Philadelphia—Dr. M. Prince Brigham, assistant dean in charge of admissions and student affairs, was putting Dave's case most forcefully to fellow admission-board members. "If we were on the Olympics committee," he said, "and a one-legged man came along who was hopping the 100-yard dash in nine seconds, I think we'd have to let him run. By the same token, since David Hartman is already doing impossible things, I think we should see how far he can go."

The other board members agreed. Soon after, Dave received a call from his mother. "There's a letter here I think you'll want to hear." Her voice broke, and his sister Barbara came on the line. "You've done it," she cried. "You've been accepted by Temple!" The news made glorious David's graduation, summa cum laude, from Gettysburg, with the whole student body and faculty standing to cheer him as he marched up for his diploma. He was on his way.

Yet it was a very tense David who enrolled at Temple the following fall. The talking stage was over. He had asked for the heat, the pressure, and immediately he began to get it.

Even anatomy, an introductory course, held special problems for him. By plunging his rubber-gloved hands into the cadavers, David could easily feel the location and shape of the large organs. But to identify smaller, more elusive things like nerve plexuses, he had to use his bare hands. This involved him in a race to learn the necessary before his fingers became numb from the formaldehyde preservative in lab specimens.

Incomparably more difficult was histology, the study of microscopic tissue structures. In this course, Dave had to depend on his teacher's and classmates' descriptions of what *they* saw through the microscope—and on feeling his way through a maze of raised braille-like drawings that his professor prepared for him.

Meanwhile, David began organizing the massive home library he'd need to get through dozens of other formidable courses. Like many other blind college and high-school students, he relied primarily on Recording for the Blind, Inc., to provide free tapes of textbooks. RFB's volunteers taped some 30 volumes for David.

"All for me?" an incredulous Dave asked. Not at all, he was told. The material would also go into RFB's Master Tape Library in New York where it would help other blind medical students, if and when there should be more in the future.

In the spring of his first year in medical school, Dave and Cheri were married. Their honeymoon summer was fairly relaxed, but scarcely had Dave begun his second year of med school when he found himself hopelessly swamped. To try to keep up with six lectures a day, he was taping them *in toto* on one recorder; then, at home, he would replay them and dictate summaries into a second machine. But this system was taking him two hours for every one-hour lecture—a total of 12 hours of homework every day!

It wasn't long before a distraught Hartman, jittery from lack of sleep, called on Dean Brigham. Together they found a solution. From then on, David took notes in class like any other student—except that he whispered them into a tape recorder.

As David started his critical third year working at Temple University Hospital with real patients, real lives, there were still those who had grave doubts about his chances of getting through school. He couldn't read X rays for example; he couldn't examine the ear, eye or mouth without the help of a colleague; he couldn't see the color of skin rashes and had to depend on the descriptions of a nurse or the patients themselves.

But Hartman had abilities that made up for such shortcomings. With his keen hearing he was especially skillful using a stethoscope. With his highly developed sense of touch, he could feel out subtle abnormalities in the chest and abdomen. Most important, he was an excellent listener.

Observed Dr. John H. Martin, in charge of teaching physical diagnosis: "If given the chance to talk about themselves, patients are often very good judges of what's wrong with them. David Hartman, who makes up for his lack of sight by hearing more from each patient, dramatically demonstrates the value of this ancient truth." (David seemed to prove this by getting the highest grade in his class on the final exam in physical diagnosis.)

By the end of his final year, David had made believers of all his doubters—except himself. With most of his academic trials behind him, he was seized with feelings of inadequacy for the job ahead. Everything he'd done so far had been under strict supervision. But soon, he'd be on his own! One night, he poured out his feelings of unreadiness to a fellow student.

"Dave," said the other senior, gripping his shoulder, "I've got 20–20 vision—I can see like an eagle. But you know something? I feel just as scared as you do!"

On May 27, 1976, David Hartman received his M.D. degree. In his view, he had proved the most important thing: that he was no different from anyone else.

There were those, however, who challenged this appraisal. Many professors at Temple had come to agree with Dr. Martin, who declared, "Hartman's not normal—he's super-normal."

One evening a few weeks after graduation, Recording for the Blind celebrated two significant events—its 25th anniversary and the landmark entry into medicine of its most ambitious protégé. In presenting the founder's award to David, RFB's then president John W. Castles III praised him "for exhibiting a triumph of the human spirit." The citation concluded: "With the example of David Hartman before us, we feel renewed faith in the infinite possibilities of all people."

These eloquent words brought a standing ovation for David. But in his brief response, it was some simpler words from the past that David voiced for the consideration of strugglers against obstacles everywhere. "My Dad was right," he said. "You'll never know unless you try."

Today, Dr. Hartman is a private psychiatrist in Roanoke, Virginia. Recently, he was appointed to Virginia's board of mental health and mental rehabilitation.

Unforgettable Richard Tucker

by Robert Merrill

I WAS SCARED stiff that December evening in 1945 as I waited backstage to make my debut at the Metropolitan Opera House in New York. Suddenly, a hand gripped my shoulder. I turned to see a short, stocky figure with intense brown eyes and radiant grin.

"Relax, Bob," said Richard Tucker, who'd made his own Met debut only 11 months earlier. "You're pretty terrific, you know, or you wouldn't be here tonight. Me, too. So let's go out and give that audience everything we've got. They'll love us!"

His confidence braced me. Next thing I knew, Licia Albanese, Tucker and I had sung our way through *La Traviata*. A storm of applause greeted us. Then Tucker was shoving me—a 26-year-old kid from Brooklyn—onto the stage alone to receive an ovation.

Such was my introduction to the man whom top critics would soon call "the American Caruso," and whom *Time* magazine would proclaim the "greatest tenor in the world." For nearly 30 years, until he died on January 8, 1975, at the age of 61, Tucker remained among opera's top stars. He sang 715 performances at the Met, in 30 leading roles.

I was privileged to sing more than 200 performances with Richard, to have him as one of my best friends, and to discover time and again the open secrets of his greatness. To begin with, of course, he had that rare golden-velvet voice which, as a reporter once remarked, sounded as though he were "fresh off the boat from Naples." Because he was quick to agree that he was a wonder of a singer, some people got the impression he was arrogant. But we who knew Richard knew there was nothing vain about him. He was guided by one simple notion: he believed that his voice and the breaks that made him famous were gifts straight from God. "How else," he'd wonder, "could somebody like me have come so far?" His talents, he felt, were simply entrusted to his stewardship, to be shared with as many people as possible.

This explains why Richard Tucker never set foot on a stage without giving his absolute best. And it explains why I, six years younger and inclined sometimes to be a bit easygoing, could not have had a better partner. Not long before his death, I complained, "Dick, why do we have to do so many difficult numbers in our joint concerts? Why don't we program some less strenuous things?"

"Bob," he replied, "people don't come to hear big-time opera stars sing easy pitter-patter songs any more than they come to see big-league ball players bunt. So let's keep going for the home run every time!"

Too many artists think that the world owes them a license to be temperamental, inconsiderate and generally beastly. Not Tucker; he had a king-size concern for others. Down-and-outers knew he would always lend a helping hand. To keep from disappointing an audience, he'd undergo almost any ordeal. Once, scheduled to appear in New Orleans, he found that a storm had grounded all planes. He stayed at Newark Airport for 36 hours, hoping for a break in the weather, then finally took a train to Cincinnati, and from there a plane that got him to New Orleans one hour before the opera. Exhausted, he nevertheless sang flawlessly.

Although phenomenally busy with a schedule that brought him well over $250,000 a year, Tucker couldn't resist taking on charity performances. Admirable enough—except that sometimes he absentmindedly agreed to sing free on nights when he was already booked. In 1972, Richard inadvertently stood up 16,000 paying fans at a Hollywood Bowl gala while singing gratis in Israel!

Richard was an outspoken believer in the American system. "Look what it did for me!" he'd say. His given name was Reuben Ticker, and he was born in a Brooklyn ghetto, the fifth and last child of poor Romanian immigrant parents. The Tickers couldn't afford a radio, much less music lessons. To help put food on the table, Ruby dropped out of high school and became a runner on Wall Street.

But, as Tucker always told it, two "miracles" intervened in his behalf. When he was six, his family had moved to Manhattan's Lower East Side, where a neighbor, hearing Ruby singing in the street, suggested that his parents take him to Samuel Weiser, cantor at the Allen Street Synagogue. Weiser immediately began grooming the boy as a soloist—free voice lessons!

The second miracle happened when Ruby was 20, a $25-a-week salesman of silk linings for fur coats, singing party gigs for $5 bills, and studying to become a cantor. He met Sara Perelmuth, the 19-year-old daughter of a food caterer (and sister of operatic tenor Jan Peerce). It was practically love at first sight. Shortly after their marriage, in February 1936, Sara took her husband to his first opera—and changed his career. Reeling with the music's glory, Ruby decided, "This is for me!"

Six years later, having scrimped to take voice lessons at night, Ruby adopted the stage name Richard Tucker and entered the Metropolitan Auditions of the Air, the Met's annual contest-search for new talent. He sang his heart out, but did not win. The defeat and its aftermath gave him his best talking point in later encouraging struggling young artists. "Never let a failure get you down if you've done your best," he would say. "If you keep trying, *somebody's* going to notice you."

Edward Johnson, then general manager of the Met, remembered Richard's all-out auditioning effort so well that two years later, when he needed a tenor, he sought out Tucker, who had become a cantor at the Brooklyn Jewish Center. So, on January 25, 1945, Tucker made his Met debut in Ponchielli's *La Gioconda*. An hour or so later, taking 16 curtain calls, he was a celebrity.

Richard was among the first singers to prove that you didn't have to be European-trained to become an international opera star. Indeed, a snobbish element at the Met always derided him for being "too American." This clique noted that he was stocky and overweight (so, of course, was Caruso); that he never lost his Brooklyn accent, and sometimes bruised the language he sang in. Also, some felt that his acting left something to be desired. To the last charge, I always felt like yelling, "Even if it were true, you'd be missing the point! Tucker is a great *singer*—and that's what opera is all about."

To protect his voice, Tucker sacrificed a lot. In order not to talk too much before a performance, he'd spend the whole afternoon at a movie. He'd deny himself many of the football and baseball games he loved because, he said, "I can't resist hollering myself hoarse." Most important, he worked up gradually to the more demanding operas.

"A lot of young singers take on the tough ones long before they're ready," he said. "That's why they don't last." To sing Canio, the clown in *Pagliacci,* the throat-racking role that had been Caruso's signature, Tucker waited, painstakingly building up to the part, for 25 years!

Richard claimed he wasn't superstitious; yet he never undertook anything new and difficult without having his wife go through a quaint Jewish custom, the Kayn Ayin Hora. Half pecking, half kissing him on the cheeks, Sara would incant, "Poo-poo-poo," to drive off evil spirits and bring him good luck. The night of January 8, 1970, as Richard waited to perform Canio at the Met for the first time, her Poo-poo-poos were unprecedentedly intense. When the final curtain fell the bravos roared like surf. Later, in the dressing room, even his severest critics—Sara and their three sons—were speechless and weeping from the power of his performance.

Richard was as square as they come, and proud of it. With him, his family was No. 1. His chauffeur-driven Cadillac bore the license plate RST-3, which stood for "Richard and Sara Tucker—and three sons." His favorite spot on earth was with the four of them at their ranch-style house in Great Neck, Long Island, and he turned down many a profitable tour with the explanation, "I'm a father, ya know, and am needed at home right now."

Every year, during the fall High Holy Days and the spring Passover services, he took time off to officiate as cantor at synagogues scattered from Great Neck to Israel. In 1967, when U.S. forces in Vietnam were short of Jewish chaplains, he journeyed to hold services. Twice he turned down invitations to sing in Russia because the Soviets wouldn't agree to two conditions: that he be permitted, when not busy elsewhere, to sing for Russian Jews in their temples; and that all proceeds from his concerts be donated to needy Jews in that country.

But Richard was first and last an American, and a remarkably tolerant one. After all, a "messenger" on business for the Almighty, he felt, doesn't quibble about religious differences among mortals. He was a relied-upon fund-raiser for Catholic schools and charities. A standard fixture at the annual Al Smith Dinner to raise money for charity cases at New York City's Catholic hospitals, Richard would close these affairs—as he closed our concerts—with a whole-hearted rendition of "You'll Never Walk Alone." Moved to tears, Terence Cardinal Cooke, Archbishop of the Diocese of New York, would leap up and hug Richard, and on this highly charged emotional note the dinner would end with floods of additional contributions pouring into the hospital coffers.

Tucker was a man of warm, unpredictable impulses and humor. To ease our tension, we fooled around a lot onstage. I'll always remember how one night, when I was in the middle of a long dying scene, he heckled me by asking, "When are you gonna kick off? I have to catch the 1:40 to Great Neck."

I'll remember, too, a chaotic scene when Dick was learning a new role from his voice coach and, at the same time, dictating letters to a secretary, posing for publicity pictures, conferring with an agent about a concert engagement, and bending an ear to a rabbi who wanted him to sing somewhere else for nothing. I begged him—all his friends begged him—"Dick, slow down!" But he couldn't. "I'll be the first to call it quits," he would promise, "when I can't deliver my best to the public."

That time never came. At an age when most singers are completely washed up, Tucker stayed as powerful as ever. "You keep young," he said, "by learning and doing new things." He continued to learn two entire new operas every year, and in 1973, at the age of 60, triumphed in the new role of the old Jew Eleazar in Halévy's *La Juive*, in New Orleans and in London. He also continued to take his gift to scores of out-of-the-way U.S. towns. "Why," he'd ask, "don't American artists sing and play in Kalamazoo?"

We happened to be in Kalamazoo the day he died. It was a bleak, gray afternoon, but we were having a fine time at rehearsal. About 1 p.m., we finished, and I told him, "I'm going to take a nap."

"I am, too," Richard said, "a little later. Right now I've promised to hear this local girl sing."

It was the last time I saw him alive. While writing a recommendation for the young singer, he collapsed with a heart attack.

Last rites were spoken for him from the great red-and-gold stage of the Metropolitan Opera House—the first funeral ever held there for a singer. Nine months later, his Catholic friends eulogized him at the first memorial service ever held in New York's St. Patrick's Cathedral for a Jew.

Soon, his family and friends organized The Richard Tucker Music Foundation, Inc., an active non-profit organization which continues to aid young singers in their careers. But Richard needs no more durable memorial than the one he assured for himself. For, as a Scottish poet once wrote: "To live in hearts we leave behind is not to die."

My Dark Journey Through Insanity

by Kathleen Walker Seegers

I RAISED the heavy pistol and in a voice tight with panic called out to my husband on the other side of the locked door: "Get away or I'll shoot you!"

I was delusional again. My husband had been urging me to take the little blue pills prescribed by the doctor. Tranquilizers, he said they were, but I was suddenly convinced that he was trying to poison me. I had locked myself in the bedroom armed with the loaded pistol that he kept in his bedside table because of our rather isolated location in the woods of Virginia.

The telephone rang. He answered it in the hall, and I picked up the bedroom extension. It was my aunt. Silently I listened as he explained the situation to her. "That's not true," I broke in. They both then began talking to me, replying calmly to my hysterical accusations, assuring me of their love, gently pressing reason upon me until, after about an hour, I unlocked the door and relinquished the pistol.

This tense scene was the culmination of more than two years

of erratic but gradually deepening depression that accompanied menopause. It was my and my husband's first shattering contact with the strange half-world of insanity.

There was no history of mental disorder on either side of my closeknit, happy Midwest family. I knew that there were mentally troubled people, of course—shadowy nonbeings locked up in asylums. But this sort of thing happened far away and to other people.

I had the usual high-school and college ups and downs. I weathered the early loss of my parents and the death of my fiancé in World War II. Gradually I worked into a responsible and absorbing job in the East as editor of a monthly magazine.

Marriage late in life was a quiet but fulfilling adventure. My writer-husband and I moved into a house he was building in spare time with his own hands. We were profoundly happy. I signed a book contract that allowed me to write at my own pace in between housekeeping, gardening and trips with my husband. We were far from rich, but we had no debts or money worries.

Then, almost imperceptibly at first, this idyllic life began to disintegrate. I grew irritable and contentious over little things, or nothing at all. I had flashes of unreasoning anger. Once when my husband and I were going to a party, he forgot to bring my handbag out to the car as I had asked him to do. I railed at him: "You never pay attention to anything I say!" He looked at me in utter astonishment.

Sometimes I lapsed into laughing jags, chuckling in uncontrolled amusement at such unchuckly fare as the financial pages of the newspapers. Several times I accused my husband of planting some prosaic news story as a joke.

More often I was simply depressed and unhappy. I could not make the simplest decision. Should I go shopping, or clean the closet? I would start a task, then abandon it. I seemed to be on a treadmill to nowhere.

Recognizing that all this was scarcely normal, I began going to a psychiatrist. He fed me tranquilizers and let me talk. But, despite twice-weekly sessions with him, the downgrade grew ever steeper.

Sometimes I completely lost touch with reality. Once I turned to my cleaning woman and said seriously, "Shirley, if you don't want to be blown to bits, you'd better get out of the house before one o'clock. A time bomb is set to explode then."

I found reason for suspicion in everything. One midwinter day, my husband and I were thrown into the near-freezing Potomac when our aluminum skiff overturned in the waterfall below our house. But for his superhuman efforts, we would have drowned. The next day I accused him of causing the accident deliberately in order to get rid of me!

It often seemed that the real me was a spectator—not actually involved, but watching in a detached way. Other times, I felt flashes of guilt for the trouble and expense I was causing my husband, and tried to make it up to him in an outpouring of affection. He came to accept these remorseful tributes warily, as a prelude to renewed hostilities.

Work on my book became sporadic, finally stopped. It eventually became dangerous for me to drive a car, so my husband took me to my sessions with the psychiatrist. Once, on the way home, I demanded that he turn into the driveway of some people we knew only slightly. "But they aren't expecting us," he said, and continued toward home. I lunged in fury at the steering wheel, trying to wrest it from him. He held it steady, so I opened the car door to jump out. He got his right arm around my neck, and with his left hand held the steering wheel while I jerked at it with both hands. Finally, I managed to put the car into a ditch. Now I had him! If he turned me loose long enough to shift into reverse and back out, I could jump out. I felt a glow of real triumph.

He sat patiently, holding me fast until a passer-by stopped and offered help. The stranger backed the car out of the ditch for us.

Not long afterward, the psychiatrist put me into a sanitarium for electric shock treatments. Three weeks later, I came home— subdued and disoriented. I felt sure that the treatments had damaged my brain. Then, four days later, my universe split wide-open: I threatened my husband with the pistol. It was obvious that something drastic had to be done.

Two years of visits to the psychiatrist, plus sanitarium costs, had cut deeply into our financial resources. For the past year my husband's earnings had dropped sharply because of the nearly constant turmoil at home. We did not have the $10,000 or so it would cost to keep me for three or four months in a private hospital. I would have to go to the state mental hospital. It was Armageddon, the Apocalypse, Gethsemane.

I will never forget the day I was committed. Before we got

up in the morning, my husband held me in his arms for a long time. There was nothing to say. Neither of us could guess what lay ahead. It was February, and a blizzard had made the roads impassable for a conventional auto. So we drove the 25 miles to the courthouse in the unheated jeep. With the swirling snow blotting everything from sight, it seemed to me that all life was being obliterated—mine along with the rest.

Fortunately I was in a submissive mood during the committal procedure, holding my husband's hand and answering the judge's questions quietly. "You understand that you are being committed, don't you?" he asked. I nodded silently. "Are you willing to go?" he persisted.

"I don't want to go," I said desperately. "But I want to get well."

The judge agreed to let my husband drive me the 140 miles to the state hospital. I was to be delivered there by ten o'clock that same night.

The snow was coming harder now. I began to get angry. When we saw a motel, I told my husband to stop. He tried to reason with me, but it only inflamed me. "You can't wait to get me to the insane asylum, can you?" I demanded.

Years before, my husband had sung a lot when we were driving. Now he began singing at the top of his voice, so that I could hear him over the noise of the jeep. It worked. I quieted down at once, and as soon as he finished one song I demanded another. As we plowed along the snow-banked highway, he sang almost without stopping—for the entire five hours of the freezing trip.

I do not remember much about the admittance procedure, but my husband said that everyone was very kind. He drove directly back home through the storm, arriving there about eight o'clock the next morning. Later, he told me that those were the bleakest 24 hours of his life.

The bleakest period of my life was just beginning. A pleasant but no-nonsense nurse led me through what seemed miles of corridors and heavy doors, each of which was unlocked by a watchful attendant and then locked again behind us, interposing a barrier between me and the only world I knew.

For the first few days, I sat in my tiny room and brooded. From time to time my apathy was interrupted by the commands of the attendants, who doled out hormones and other pills, and at mealtime herded all patients to the cafeteria.

During those early days, my attention wandered. Unrelated thoughts swirled through my mind like dust devils. One delusion succeeded another. There were several Spanish-speaking doctors on the staff, refugees from Cuba. I became certain that Castro had seized the hospital and grounds as part of his empire, and that I was his prisoner.

Gradually the mélange of horror that was my ward sorted itself out into individuals. The nice-looking, prematurely aged woman in the room next to mine was a friendly alcoholic. Another older, white-haired woman would never raise her eyes from the afghan she was doggedly knitting. A fat girl periodically burst into loud, obscene abuse at no one in particular. An ancient Trinidadian dozed all day, but when roused would sing out in a creaky voice: "When you reach the pearly gates, ask for mercy."

Our monotonous routine was broken by occupational therapy and by an occasional musical-therapy hour. Each patient had a weekly consultation with what seemed an army of doctors and nurses on "staff day." The doctors told my husband, I later learned, that my trouble was an involutional psychosis caused by endocrine imbalance that was likely triggered by menopause. I was given the hormone Premarin, and two tranquilizers, Mellaril and Stelazine, together with small doses of Artane to counteract muscle stiffness or tremor, which are often side effects.

Under this treatment, life seemed to level out noticeably. I had to make none of the nagging little personal decisions that had seemed so burdensome at home. I was told when to eat, when to bathe, when to go to bed. Once a week a bookmobile brought fresh books, and I read everything I could lay hands on. Gradually, my delusions began to vanish, my anxieties and suspicions to fall away.

At the end of a fortnight, my husband, who had been flooding me with affectionate letters, was permitted to visit me for a few hours. A week later, I was given a "grounds card," allowing me to roam freely about the grounds of the hospital. A couple of days afterward, my doctor gave me permission to spend an entire day off the hospital grounds with my husband. We drove over the mountains to a nearby inn, where we had a luxurious and relaxing luncheon.

It seemed much longer, but after just a month I was permitted to go home for a weekend. When my husband and I arrived there, I felt as if I were in heaven. Repeatedly I went to the windows to gaze into the woods or to watch the foaming rapids in the river below. I even tried my hand at a little cooking and housekeeping.

At the end of the fifth week, my husband went with me to see the staff doctors. After a few questions, the chief psychiatrist said to me, "You've progressed so rapidly that you'll probably be ready to leave in another week." My husband and I turned to each other joyously.

For a year and a half following my release, my husband and I visited a local mental-health clinic every six months. With each visit, my drug dosage was diminished, until finally I was told I would need no more medication. Meanwhile, I gradually resumed the active life I had led before my world teetered out of balance.

Once free of the anguish that tormented me for so long, I was filled with a new sense of well-being. Our marriage once more flourished.

I shall never forget my husband's steadfast loyalty during that fearfully trying period. My book has been published. I continue to write, keep house, and garden a little. The whole devastating experience sharpened my appreciation of the world around me. Remembering my wanderings through the nightmare world created by my out-of-kilter mind, I treasure every moment in which I am mistress of my thoughts.

The Cadet
Who Refused to Quit

by Robert S. Strother

AMONG THE 383 new cadets admitted to the United States Military Academy in July of 1932, many were tall, some were handsome, and all were intelligent. Benjamin Oliver Davis, Jr., a likable young man of 19, was outstanding on all three counts. He was a slender six-foot-two, and stood straight as a rifle. He had been president of his class in Cleveland's Central High School, where he was a top student and a good athlete. He was just the kind of bright lad a Congressman likes to nominate for West Point—in every way but one. Ben Davis was a Negro. Not for 50 years had a Negro graduated from the Military Academy.

During Ben's first few days at "The Point," he went through the rugged routine faced by all new cadets. He moved "on the double," saluted anything that moved, stood at rigid attention on the order of any upperclassman, spoke only when spoken to, and included "sir" in brisk response to any question asked. Such hazing was part of a system designed to transform boys into officers. It was tough discipline, but it was dealt out with total impartiality. Ben was confident that he could take it.

Then the blow fell. As young Davis was hurrying to a meeting of his classmates in their barracks one day, he heard the spiteful word: "Nigger." From that day on, no cadet spoke to him. He was being given "the silence." His classmates were trying to force him to quit.

Davis had expected it. He had been reared on Army posts. His father, Benjamin O. Davis, Sr., had enlisted in the Spanish-American War, and three years later won a competitive examination for a commission as a second lieutenant. Young Ben had often heard his father quote the words spoken by President Theodore Roosevelt when he signed the precedent-setting commission. An aide had murmured that the candidate was a Negro. "Bully for him," said T. R. "Only one thing counts—he has *qualified* for the place." And he dashed off the bold signature that was to hold the position of honor in the Davis family's Army quarters throughout Ben's childhood.

Now his father was a colonel, the only Negro line officer in the Army, and young Ben was determined to follow in his father's footsteps. "I decided that first month at West Point that I would *never* quit," Davis said.

Throughout the long, hard winter on the windswept plain above the Hudson River, Cadet Davis endured the silence. The West Point pace is swift and merciless. Drills and classes are crammed into a hectic day beginning at first formation—for 6:30 breakfast. There are 10 to 15 men in each class section; everyone recites in every subject every day. Searching examinations are held at frequent intervals, and the student's class standing is posted weekly. In young Ben Davis's class many plebes failed and were dismissed. Davis began to move up in his class standing.

When plebe year ended, Davis was the hero of the "recognition" ceremony. Upperclassmen crowded around to shake his hand and to congratulate him on the courage with which he had survived the ordeal. It looked, for a few days, as if his worst troubles were over.

Then, inexplicably, the silence began all over again. With a few heart-warming exceptions, it lasted for three more years.

But so did Ben Davis. He lived with the hurt, and concentrated on his studies so effectively that when June Week rolled around in 1936, he stood 35th in his class of 276. By graduating near the top, by proving he could "qualify" with the best, he had blazed a trail. Other Negroes have graduated since; Negro cadets today are treated exactly like their white classmates.

By October 1940, Ben was a captain, and three months after Pearl Harbor he was graduated from the Advanced Army Training School. In May 1942 he transferred to the Army Air Corps, was promoted to major and then to lieutenant colonel and put in command of the 99th Fighter Squadron. Within months he was leading that fine outfit in aerial combat in North Africa, and on into the Sicilian campaign.

Late in 1943, Colonel Davis organized and took charge of the 332nd Fighter Group of the 15th Air Force in Italy. In January 1944 his men shot down 16 German aircraft over the Anzio beachhead. The 332nd was an all-Negro unit, an elite outfit that boasted the highest percentage of college graduates in the armed forces. Its main job was to protect our bombers from enemy fighter planes, and it succeeded so well that in 200 escort missions it never lost a bomber to enemy fighters. Ben Davis led many of the missions personally, and commanders of the bomber squadrons escorted paid the highest tribute to his leadership. "When Ben was in charge, there was no better fighter outfit anywhere," one of them said.

Most bomber crews never saw the pilots of the 332nd except in the air. The fields were widely scattered, and there was little visiting between them. An involuntary visit in December 1944, however, had interesting results. A B-17 squadron returning from a raid into Germany ran into thick weather and had to land on the 332nd's runways.

Colonel Davis welcomed them in. "It was a funny way to be integrated," says Col. Thomas J. Money, who was then adjutant of the 332nd. "We had flown escort for them several times, but they knew us only from a distance. By the time they had drunk our beer and used our razors for the three days the bad weather hung on, we were friends. We got lots of letters from those boys later on."

When reporters asked Colonel Davis to comment on the segregated status of the 332nd and "Negro rights," he replied that integration would come in time. Meanwhile, because the 332nd *was* an all-Negro group, he pointed out, it was winning recognition in a way that would be impossible if its pilots were distributed throughout the service.

"We can't have it both ways at once," he said. "For now,

this is working out all right. Our job is to help win the war. If we don't win, nobody will have *any* rights to worry about."

Colonel Davis emerged from the war with the Silver Star for gallantry in action, the Legion of Merit, the Distinguished Flying Cross, and the Air Medal with four Oak Leaf Clusters. "He didn't get them in spite of being a Negro, or because of being a Negro, but because he earned them," said Gen. Nathan F. Twining, wartime commander of the 15th Air Force and later chairman of the Joint Chiefs of Staff.

The Air Force became a separate service after the war, and was the first to achieve complete integration. Now Colonel Davis, moving steadily up the service ladder, faced a new challenge: he was placed in command of white officers and troops, many of them from the South, in posts in Asia, Germany and the United States. In all of them he made warm friends.

"There was never a moment's trouble," said Gen. Laurence S. Kuter. "Nobody who worked with Ben thought of him as a Negro. He is an Air Force officer of the highest type, highly intelligent, an articulate man whose bravery in combat matched his courage in living above the level of race prejudice. His example played a great part in making the integration of the Air Force a success."

Davis went through the Air War College and became chief of the fighter branch in the Pentagon. But new weapons and new planes were coming into use, and he saw that he needed more training to keep pace with new tactical possibilities. He won assignment to the advanced jet-fighter gunnery school, passed with high marks, and was given command of the 51st Fighter-Interceptor Wing in Suwon, Korea.

The Air Force was accustomed by now to finding that Colonel Davis could handle any job he was given, and the next move made him director of operations and training for the U.S. Air Force in the Far East, with headquarters in Tokyo. This led to his big break. He was named commander of the Air Task Force 13 in Taipeh, Taiwan, and promoted to brigadier general. Thus, in 1954, just 14 years after his father had become the United States' first Negro brigadier general, Ben Davis Jr., was commissioned to the same rank.

By 1959, Davis had been named deputy chief of staff for the U.S. Air Forces in Europe, and had become a major general. Then, in April 1964, after distinguished service as director of Manpower and Organization in Air Force headquarters in

Washington, he 'was nominated by President Lyndon B. Johnson for promotion to lieutenant general. It was another "first" for a Negro in the armed forces of the United States.

Inevitably, Ben Davis, Jr., was asked his views on the equal-rights campaigns. "I would like to think that I'm playing a part by doing my job to the best of my ability," he said. "Congress has passed laws that guarantee Negroes first-class citizenship. But people deeply submerged economically, educationally and socially need a hand to help catch up. At the same time, we must be determined to help ourselves; we must *qualify* to take advantage of the opportunities provided; we must be ready to make the most of the assistance that people of goodwill always offer.

"Opportunities do exist today, and tomorrow there will be more. Everybody at one time or another, however, is tempted to drop out, to fail to qualify. To avoid this, the slogan 'We shall overcome' should include the strongest kind of resolve to master the skills or professions that can win a useful place in American life. When Negroes do stick it out and when they do qualify for better jobs and greater responsibility, I hope that no lingering trace of prejudice will block them from the chance they've earned. That's about all anybody can ask."

The promotion ceremony, conducted in the Pentagon, was simple. In the presence of the top brass of the Air Force, Gen. John P. McConnell, chief of staff, pinned the three-star emblem on one of Ben's shoulders, and Ben's handsome wife, Agatha, stood on tiptoe to pin the stars on the other. The staff officers, many of them friends of long standing, pressed forward to shake his hand. As a white colonel on General Davis' staff remarked, no promotion in recent years seemed to have caused so much satisfaction and pleasure in the Pentagon.

President Johnson sent his congratulations and word of a new assignment. Lt. Gen. Benjamin O. Davis, Jr., 52, was named chief of staff of both United States and United Nations forces in Korea. The shunned cadet of 1932 had come a long way. So, too, had his race.

He Would Not Die

by Lawrence Elliott

TECHNOLOGY HAS DEVISED a whole spectrum of ingenious communications and navigational aids for men who work in the sky. Yet, on a bitter-cold day in February 1967, every one of them failed bush pilot Robert Gauchie, leaving him with only his own human resources to pit against the overpowering violence of the Canadian subarctic.

Gauchie was 39 years old, a solidly built native of the far north. With his wife, Frances, and three daughters he lived in Fort Smith, in Canada's Northwest Territories. In ten years he had logged 6000 hours of the toughest flying there is—hauling freight, fire fighters, trappers, whoever wanted to go anywhere in that wild and empty land.

At 10 a.m. on February 2, having left a group of government inspectors at the village of Cambridge Bay, just inside the Arctic Circle, Gauchie took off alone in his single-engine Beaver. The temperature had gone to 60 degrees below zero the day before, and he had to use a firepot to preheat the frozen-solid engine. He hoped to make Yellowknife, 525 miles to the south, by 3:30, and Fort Smith the next day.

Shortly after noon, he encountered a driving snowstorm. About to set an instrument course, he found that neither his turn-and-bank indicator nor the artificial horizon was working. Quickly he descended to 200 feet, and in the enveloping whiteness he flew by sight over the treeless, windswept barren lands. Finally, he spotted a stretch of blue ice and clattered down to wait out the storm, his skis rattling on the rough lake ice.

Arctic blasts of 50 below zero shook the aircraft. In the icy metal cabin, Gauchie climbed into a sleeping bag and pulled three others over him. He wore mukluks, three pairs of heavy socks, two sweaters and a fur parka. And still he shivered uncontrollably through the long afternoon and night.

When the sun rose on a clear and frosty morning, Gauchie preheated the engine and was soon flying south again. Then his compass failed. The weather worsened, with tiny ice crystals in the air threatening to turn into deadly whiteout, the milky ice fog that obscures land and horizon. He was running low on fuel. Gauchie began radioing what he thought to be his position, asking anyone to "come in." But there was only the crackle of static in his earphones. Finally, a Royal Canadian Air Force Albatross out of Yellowknife responded weakly: "I read you. Suggest you land and activate your SARAH so we can home in."

SARAH, a Search And Rescue transmitter with a self-contained battery, and CPI, a Crash Position Indicator, have led rescue planes to many a lost pilot. Gauchie had both devices.

"We'll have you out in a couple of hours," the Albatross said.

That was the last human voice Gauchie would hear for 58 days.

Just south of the treeline, he found a narrow lake sheltered by a scraggly tree growth along its shoreline, and set down there. For a moment he sat, listening to the whipping rush of the wind. Then he depressed the switch on the SARAH. Nothing happened. Stunned, he pushed it again and again. Nothing. And it was the same with the CPI switch.

Bracing himself, he climbed out on the icy skin of the fuselage—lightheaded in the intense cold—and crept to the wingtip, to break the glass on the CPI. Still nothing; no hum, no buzz—only the endless racing of the wind. Unable to believe that both emergency radio beacons were inoperable, Gauchie got his tool kit and, crouched down on his heels while feet and toes grew numb, he worked for three hours—until dark—trying to activate them. But they remained mute.

Back in the cabin, he tried broadcasting again—over both the high-frequency and the very-high-frequency transmitters—"Mayday! Mayday! This is CF-IOB from Cambridge Bay to Yellowknife. Do you read?" There was no response. It was incredible: everything he relied on—navigational instruments and every piece of radio equipment on board—had failed.

He checked through the survival kit. There were a few packages of dried food, a pound of cube sugar, chocolate—enough to last 10 or 12 days if he was careful. He had bought 80 pounds of arctic char for his wife on one of his stops, but the fish were raw and frozen stiff. He found flares, a rifle, five packages of wooden matches and an ax.

Gauchie crawled into the sleeping bags. Toward morning he fell into a fitful sleep.

Next morning, the temperature gauge read 54 below zero. Clouds of loose snow billowed across the lonely lake. Gauchie judged that the Beaver was 400 yards from the near shore: a plane passing overhead ought to have a good chance to see it. But would there be a plane? He was off the main air routes, and the primary search area, based on his flight plan, would probably be about 100 miles to the southeast.

He drained some of the remaining gasoline into the plumber's pot he used for preheating the engine. He placed it under the battery, lighted a fire, then tried the radios again. "Mayday. Mayday . . ." There was no response.

It occurred to him that if he could chop a small tree and prop up the trailing antenna with it, he might improve his reception just enough to bring in a signal. He trudged toward shore and came back to the plane breathless and weak, but dragging a sapling. This he stuck in the snow some 50 feet behind the tail. The antenna, which was supposed to crank out of its reel on top of the fuselage, wouldn't budge. He spent the rest of the day prying the wire free, inch by inch, until it was long enough to wind around the sapling. But the radio gave only the same echoing, voiceless hum. Totally spent, he ate a sugar cube and went to sleep.

The next two days were hardly more hopeful. Gauchie used

the rest of his gasoline trying to keep the battery alive—melting ice to make soup at the same time—but by the third day even the fruitless hum from the radio had faded. Once, when the wind went down, he walked out on the lake and tramped out an SOS in the snow, each letter 150 feet tall. But in half an hour the surface had drifted smooth.

That night, Gauchie felt a tingling numbness in his feet. He took off his mukluks and socks—and sagged back in horror. Three toes on his left foot and two on the right were dead black. He gagged at the stench, remembering instantly the hours he'd spent hunkered down working on the radio beacons, meanwhile cutting the circulation to his feet. He knew that if gangrene started up from the frostbitten toes, he could be dead by morning.

The RCAF began organizing the search for Robert Gauchie just a few hours after he was overdue at Yellowknife. A two-motor Albatross took off at first light on February 3, retracing his anticipated flight path, but found nothing. Next day, a second Albatross and a DC-3 were assigned to the mission. And because, in crisis, all of the vast Northwest is like a single small town, a veritable squadron of private aircraft joined in.

In Fort Smith, each time the telephone rang, Frances Gauchie said a prayer that it might be news of her husband's rescue. A pretty woman with a hopeful outlook, she had great faith in her husband's skill and resourcefulness. But she needed all her nerve as day after day passed with no sign of promise.

After 12 days of the most intense effort, the RCAF was ready to give up. In a land that is huge and empty beyond belief, the searchers had painstakingly swept 292,000 square miles. To some, the silence of Gauchie's SARAH and CPI indicated a crash so hard as to shatter both, which meant little hope for the fragile human aboard. Temperatures had plunged again to a record 60 below, and there had been fierce storms. All agreed that no one could survive for long in this harshest of winters. Still, when Gauchie's wife pleaded for a few more days of effort, the searchmaster agreed.

The official search was called off February 17. But the people of the Northwest Territories refused to give up. They collected money to pay a few bush pilots to continue the search. The little planes, hampered by terrible blizzards, logged another 100 hours. But by March 1, when Gauchie had gone unreported 26 days, the last hope of finding him alive was abandoned.

Reluctantly Frances spoke to her priest about a memorial service, though she could not yet bring herself to name a date.

Bob Gauchie knew, almost to the day, when the main rescue effort would end. He had flown many such sad missions himself, looking for a single dark speck in the endless white wilderness.

His frostbitten toes hurt, and he knew that the pain would worsen when they started thawing. Still, they had not yet turned gangrenous. He unwrapped and inspected them each day, and kept the ax handy. He would try to amputate them at the first sign of blood poisoning.

The cold never let up, and Gauchie spent most of his time in the sleeping bags. The metal skin of the plane was no real protection against the cold, but it did shield him from the wind, which shook the little Beaver and sometimes threatened to send it skating across the lake. Though Gauchie ate only an ounce or two of his emergency rations each day, his supply was half gone by the eighth day, and almost completely gone by February 16. He tried to eat some of the frozen char, but his stomach rebelled.

The temptation to give up was enormous. Everything that happened, each of those awful malfunctions, seemed to be telling him that he'd finally had it, so why struggle? But he did struggle, angrily unwilling to concede anything to this enemy, the vast land.

Somewhere he found a ballpoint pen, and tore a page from his logbook to begin a diary, in case he was not found alive. The severe cold had frozen the ink, and the pen refused to work. But on the 15th day, when the weather warmed, the pen made a fitful line on the paper. Writing with mitts on, Gauchie began his diary—really a long letter to his wife and children:

> I am sorry, Mickey, that I could not attend your first teen birthday, but I was sure thinking of you. Patti, I'm sure you will make a wonderful nurse. Lynda, your mom will need your help now, as she has a lot of responsibility placed upon her. And now, my darling Fran, if this is the final gun I want to tell you that you were the greatest event in my life.

The weather stayed mild for several days, but Gauchie knew that the cold was not over. His toes had become a gruesome sight, splitting and festering. The pain grew steadily more intense.

He worried that the unending silence would beguile him into some rash act. "I have never been in a place of such infinite quiet," he wrote. "No sound, no birds, wolves, foxes or anything. Just me and the wind."

He remembered seasoned bush pilots who had violated the basic laws of survival by wandering away from a downed plane, and been lost. Now, alone in the limitless landscape, he knew how a man could let himself be deluded into thinking that just waiting was useless, that he had to *do* something, strike out for somewhere. But, with a kind of fury at his fate, he fought off such fantasies. And, every day or so, he forced himself to down a bit of the frozen char.

On February 20 his loneliness was suddenly broken by a pack of wolves on the lake. There were more than a dozen of them, and they circled the Beaver without fear, tugging playfully at the trailing antenna. Later, they staked out the lake in a great half-circle, and Gauchie guessed that they might be waiting for caribou. He readied his rifle—raw meat couldn't be any worse than raw char—but though a few caribou appeared at the far end of the lake, they came no closer. They and the wolves soon disappeared.

On the afternoon of February 28, hope flared dizzyingly. Just past 4:30, in the red twilight, the rising, falling sound of the wind slowly turned into the steady drone of an airplane engine. Incredulous, Gauchie listened for an instant, then bolted out of the sleeping bags, snatched up the flare gun and tumbled into the snow. Less than 2000 feet above him was a red Beaver. Trembling, Gauchie fired a flare straight up, watched it burst into pale color in the sun's glare. The Beaver continued on its inexorable course. He fired a second flare, but it was already too late. The burst went off well behind the unwavering little aircraft. Gauchie stood there as it disappeared.

Torturing himself with what might have been, he didn't sleep all that night. Next day, he gathered his waning strength and forced himself out on the lake, once again trudging out SOS and HELP signals. And once again the wind obliterated them.

On March 5 his toes thawed. The pain maddened him, racked his whole body, and for eight hours he drifted in and out of delirium. At least once he had the bindings off and the ax ready, then he fell back exhausted and finally slept. His spirits slumped to lowest ebb:

> Terrible cold week. Not much time for rescue now. I hope I can make peace with God. I love you girls. Pen won't write. Please pray for me.

He had used the last of the emergency rations, and the sugar as well. Now, all he had left was a bare shred of hope. This he clung to, ferociously, knowing that when *that* was gone, he would be, too.

On March 12, toward evening, two planes flew over the lake within an hour of each other, but neither noticed the flares that Gauchie frantically fired aloft. He hoped that with the lengthening days there would be more planes. And there were— as many as two in one week. None saw him. He kept the flare gun handy, but there was no more he could do now. His toes would no longer stand the sustained effort of stamping out another signal in the snow.

On March 16 he wrote:

> For my meal today I licked the inside of an onion-soup bag. That's living, isn't it!

He began reciting the simple prayers of his boyhood, the only ones he knew. On March 28, the 54th day, he wrote in the diary:

> I know now I must be found within a week if I am to survive. I forced myself to eat some fish so I may have some strength return. Well, honey, at least you'll know that I tried to come back to you.

On March 30, the thermometer crept up to zero, and Gauchie's inexhaustible spirits rose again. It occurred to him that, if he could drain only a bit of hydraulic fluid from the plane's landing gear, he might be able to improvise a wick and cook bits of fish over the fire. With near-frozen fingers he coaxed a little fluid from the line, found some gauze for a wick, and lighted it. It worked! He held a fish over the small flame, watching the edges soften and brown. Then the whole length of the gauze ignited, fire flaring, and Gauchie had to put it out. But he had some warm food.

On April 1, at a little past 6 p.m., Gauchie was crawling into the sleeping bags when the now-familiar and maddeningly hopeful sound came again: the wind's high-pitched whine deepening into the steady murmur of an aircraft engine.

He threw back the covers and fumbled with the door latch. The plane—a red turboprop Beaver—was right overhead. He fired the flare gun, all breath caught in his throat. The Beaver flew straight on. Gauchie felt the will seep out of him, but then he looked up again and saw the angle of the Beaver had changed. It was growing larger. It was turning back!

Bush pilot Ronald Sheardown and co-pilot Glen Stevens were to have left Yellowknife for a mining camp near Coppermine at 2:30 that afternoon, but mechanical difficulties delayed them until after four. So it was that, near sunset, they were over Samandré Lake when Stevens happened to catch a reflection of the sinking sun on what might have been glass. It was only the briefest flash, and it vanished even as he stared at it.

"Did you see anything?" he asked Sheardown.

Sheardown hadn't, and for another minute he held his red turbo-prop on course. Then something—he will never know what—made him put the plane into a steep turn and drop to 2000 feet. And in the next moment both men saw a dark figure moving out from an aircraft that was barely visible in the snow. Two flares lighted the lowering sky beside them.

"That's Bob Gauchie!" Stevens cried out in utter astonishment. "My God, Gauchie's alive!"

It was the sheerest chance. The low-hanging arctic sun, which never rose high enough to reveal the downed Beaver itself, was, at 6:10 p.m., at precisely the right angle to flash off its windshield just as Sheardown and Stevens flew by. Had they left Yellowknife ten minutes sooner, they would have seen nothing.

The turboprop circled the lake, landed, then taxied toward the ghostly figure. Sheardown recalls, "He stood there with that blue suitcase, like a man waiting for a bus."

Bob Gauchie was a man who had just thanked his God. Ahead of him lay long hospitalization, during which he would lose all five frostbitten toes, then weeks of treatment. But he was alive! After an incredible 58 days—longer by far than any other man known to be missing in the northern winter had ever survived—he was alive. Now, in the moment of rescue, with the same determination that had so long sustained him, he drew himself tall and began limping toward the turboprop—a haggard creature with shaggy hair, one foot wrapped in dirty canvas, and a bearded, emaciated face lighted by a shining grin.

"Hello," Gauchie said. "Do you have room for a passenger?"

The Family That Wouldn't Give Up

by John G. Hubbell

LATE IN 1978, communist Vietnam was engaged in a brutal and lucrative extortion racket, evicting those who did not meld into its socialist Utopia, confiscating their property. Ethnic Chinese were required to pay the government $1500 to $2000 to leave the country. Those who could not ransom their way out were being "resettled" in "New Economic Zones," which were nothing more than concentration camps. But hundreds of thousands were paying for the chance to risk their lives at sea in small boats in hopes of finding better lives elsewhere.

Among those "boat people" early in 1979 were the three children of Nghiem Ton That. His oldest child, Nam Tran, whom Nghiem called Nina, was 14; his son, Phung Anh, nick-named Tony, was 12; and his youngest daughter, Thanh Ngoc, or Millie, was 10. The children had been separated from their father since he left Vietnam four years before. They had been living with Nghiem's mother and sisters, and would be accompanied on their perilous journey by one of the sisters, 24-year-old Thao, who had been adopted as an infant by his family.

Nghiem was in Minneapolis, anxiously awaiting their arrival. He had been sent there in February 1972 by the South Vietnamese Confederation of Labor to study industrial relations at the University of Minnesota. Missing his children in Saigon terribly, he was especially moved by a newspaper article about the Children's Heart Fund, which provides open-heart surgery for indigent Third World children. The Fund's office was in the Metropolitan Medical Center, only a block from his apartment.

In a compassionate act that would profoundly affect his future, Nghiem arrived at the Fund's office and offered his spare-time services. During the next two years, he made himself invaluable as an interpreter, companion to patients, and liaison between the hospital and children's families in Vietnam.

His studies completed, in August 1974 Nghiem returned to Saigon to become a labor official—and to a joyous reunion with his children.

By the time Nghiem left Minneapolis, he and the Fund's executive director, Merna Bahman, were close friends and they greatly missed each other.

The following spring, they met again. With South Vietnam falling to the communists, Merna had rushed to Saigon in hopes of extricating several children scheduled for surgery in Minneapolis. She was unable to make contact with any of the children, and joined 38 people associated with the Children's Heart Fund, including Nghiem and his family, to fly out of the doomed city.

In the unbelievable chaos, Nghiem was separated from his family and forced to leave his children behind. As an outspoken anti-communist, he knew that remaining would have meant imprisonment or death. But the emotional wrench was almost more than Nghiem could bear. Someday, somehow, he would bring his family to safety in America.

Back in Minneapolis, Nghiem spent 18 months helping to resettle other refugees. Eventually, he found a well-paying job, and, through a brother who had escaped to Paris, was able to send thousands of dollars home for the children's support. (Mail moved easily between France and Vietnam.) Yet, as the months of separation turned into years, Nghiem longed for his children. In some forlorn moments, he despaired of ever seeing them again.

His consolation and support was Merna Bahman. Shy, soft-spoken but with a will of steel, she had seen the impossible happen too often in children's heart surgery to be anything but an optimist. She and Nghiem were married in May 1978. From then on, she thought of his children as her own, and yearned for them as he did.

In November 1978, word reached Nghiem and Merna that the children could be brought out—for a price. But Nghiem was frightened by news accounts of the travail of the boat people. Untold numbers were dying at sea. Then he learned that girls only a year older than Nina were being drafted for military duty in Cambodia. In January 1979, he sent word for his sister Thao to bring the children out.

Thao, Nina, Tony and Millie left Vietnam by boat before dawn on April 5, 1979, bribing officials to obtain the false papers needed to identify them as ethnic Chinese. The boat captain's price for taking them out was $10,000, to be paid when he delivered the family to safety.

There were 138 men, women, and children on the 40-foot craft, *HF-001*. A Vietnamese police boat led them from Long Xuyen to the Gulf of Thailand. As they approached international waters, the police warned that the seas were full of pirates, and offered to escort the refugees to Malaysia for $100 each. But they feared that the police would take their money and then lead them back to the prison Vietnam had become. They decided to take their chances with pirates.

Toward noon the next day, two ships bore down on *HF-001*. No one thought anything was amiss until the two small fishing vessels, flying Thailand's flag, brought their bows together to prevent the refugees' boat from moving ahead. Aboard each boat were ten men, armed with knives and axes. These pirates robbed Thao of $1000 in gold, and other refugees lost gold, money and jewelry. Nina managed to save one $100 bill by tucking it inside her bra. After about two hours, the pirates sailed off with their loot.

The refugees were thankful that there had been no killing or raping. But their relief was short-lived. By mid-afternoon, more pirates caught up with them, threatening to ram *HF-001* if it failed to stop. All the adult refugees were made to strip. Every piece of clothing was searched, every body inspected, every cranny of the boat ransacked. The pirates took everything they could find, leaving the boat with only one engine.

When the pirates' leader announced their intention to rape some of the women, the captain warned them that, while the unarmed Vietnamese had not resisted robbery, they were not likely to stand by while their women were violated. To the refugees' trembling relief, the pirates departed.

Bad luck continued to haunt *HF-001*. On one engine, the going was slow through the blazing sun. The next afternoon, the engine quit, leaving *HF-001* adrift. That night, howling winds drove mountains of water at the boat, tossing it about like driftwood. The refugees cried, prayed, frantically bailed water. After an interminable time, the storm passed. Miraculously, no one was lost.

Spirits soared when the dead engine was revived. Six days after the start of their journey, the refugees sighted Malaysia.

A Malaysian naval vessel, *Sri Langkawi*, came out to escort *HF-001*. Thao and the children cheered and hugged one another. The Malaysians took the refugees aboard and fed them. Then they were put back aboard *HF-001* and told they'd be towed to a refugee camp.

HF-001 had been towed for about two hours when the refugees were startled by a surge of speed. Soon their boat was fishtailing wildly, taking on water, wallowing. Thao screamed and shouted to the wailing children to hang on. Faster and faster they went, on and on, *HF-001* constantly seeming about to capsize. Clearly, the Malaysians were intent on losing the entire boatload!

When the towline broke and a party from *Sri Langkawi* boarded *HF-001* to fix it, some of the refugees knelt to plead that they not be towed at such high speed. *Sri Langkawi* slowed the pace, but kept towing *HF-001* seaward for two nights and a day. Finally, the towline was detached, and another party came aboard to smash *HF-001*'s compass and sextant. An officer explained that this was to ensure that the refugees would not be able to find Malaysia again. "If you survive," he told them as he left, "write your relatives and friends in Vietnam and tell them that if they come to Malaysia they will be shot on sight."

Becalmed, *HF-001* drifted on a watery oven of a sea for two days. Luckily, an Indonesian naval vessel found the Vietnamese and summoned a police boat to tow them to the island of Letung. The Vietnamese refugees had been ten days at sea, and were sunburned, starving, parched, exhausted. Many of the women and children, including Thao and Nina, had to be carried ashore. Soon, all were fast asleep on a dock.

When the refugees awakened, the islanders had set up a stand at the end of the dock where they now offered to sell back to the nearly penniless refugees every item of value that they had left aboard their boat—every piece of clothing, anything that might be of any use whatsoever as a survival tool.

Finally, the refugees were left on Tulai, a small coral island with palm trees and poisonous snakes—and already a temporary home for 300 refugees. There was no food or water there, no shelter, tools or medicine. Dysentery was rampant, and the beaches were soon awash in excrement.

For about ten days, Thao kept reminding the children that Nghiem would come for them soon, that everything would be all right. Then they stopped talking about him. To one another, the children confided that they did not expect to see their father again.

In Minneapolis, Nghiem was frantic with worry. He hadn't heard anything of his children and sister in 46 days, since word had reached him on April 6 that they had already departed Vietnam. He and Merna were distraught and sleepless. Yet all they could do was hope and pray. Then, on May 22, Nghiem received a letter.

It was a small miracle that the letter, postmarked Surabaya, reached him. Apart from the foreign name on it, the zip code was wrong and the address was now a parking lot. The postman could have delivered it to the dead-letter office; instead, he had left it at the nearest building, the Metropolitan Medical Center. No one in the mail room had heard of Nghiem. But, knowing that the Children's Heart Fund dealt with many Asians, a mailroom employee rerouted the letter there. He had no idea that the fund's director was Nghiem's wife.

Nghiem opened the letter. It was from I. Jacob Jambow, who signed himself, "Indonesian Sailor." A woman from *HF-001* who had befriended Thao and the children had pleaded with him to contact Nghiem. The sailor wrote that he had seen members of Nghiem's family in Indonesian waters. Although robbed by pirates, they were okay. Would Nghiem please "collect them." Somewhere in the sprawling Indonesian archipelago, his family needed him.

Within 48 hours, Nghiem and Merna had begun their long odyssey against seemingly impossible odds. Bureaucracy bedeviled them from the start. They waited a day and a half in San Francisco for Indonesian visas. Then the Indonesian consul played with his dog for more than an hour before telling them the entry visas had been granted. They were received coldly at the U.S. embassy in Jakarta. The vice consul assured them that it would take up to eight weeks to locate the children, and wondered aloud how he could be expected to get his work done if everyone came looking for relatives. He suggested a hotel and said he would be in touch if he learned anything.

But at the office of the United Nations High Commissioner for Refugees in the Indonesian capital, Nghiem and Merna were greeted warmly. Eric Morris, an American eager to do all he could for the refugees, opened his files to them. Because the files were alphabetized, it was possible to scan the lists of registered refugees quickly. No luck.

Morris explained that because thousands of refugees were flooding in every day, information couldn't be kept current. "If your children are on one of the islands," he said, "the only way you are going to find them is to go there." He was planning to visit some of the islands the next day, and suggested they meet him in the island city of Tanjung Pinang, over 500 miles to the north.

On May 31, they caught a dawn flight. In a U.N. office at Tanjung Pinang, they vainly scanned thousands more names.

A boat for Morris was to leave that evening for Letung, administrative headquarters for the refugee camps in the vicinity. The Indonesian official in charge of the trip at first denied Nghiem's request to be taken aboard. Later, moved by Merna's tearful pleas, he relented.

After an overnight trip, they anchored off Letung. Nghiem and Merna were told they had 1½ hours to try to learn which island their family was on, find them and get back aboard. A boat took them ashore. Reaching a small office, they scanned more lists.

Suddenly, Merna screamed. She had found the names! Thao and the children were on Tulai, a few miles distant. They rushed back to the dock and paid a boat owner to take them there.

The short trip was one of the longest Nghiem and Merna ever made. They could not speak, dared not even look at each other. At last they waded ashore into an enormous crowd. Thinking that Nghiem and Merna were U.N. representatives, refugees crowded about them, begging for help, giving them letters to mail. Nghiem shouted pleas for information about his children and sister. Some in the mob knew the children and ran to get them.

It was Nina who arrived on the beach first. A path opened through the crowd to her father, and they stood staring at each other. She had grown taller, but was incredibly thin for 14; she weighed less than 70 pounds. At first her eyes seemed dull, almost lifeless; then they were alive with recognition. She fell into his arms, sobbing. Nghiem sat on the ground with her in his arms, rocking her.

Then came Millie, squealing and hugging Nghiem until he thought his heart would break. Ten years old, she weighed only 38 pounds. And then Tony, smiling and crying and trying to be a man about it all, a 12-year-old who weighed less than 60 pounds. And finally Thao, who had shepherded them across 1000 miles of ocean.

The children had met Merna in Saigon and turned to her now, as she had long dreamed they would, as though she had always been their mother. With only minutes to spare, the reunited family made it back to the boat.

But the reunion was short-lived. Although the children could be granted entry permits to America, our immigration policies made no provision for adopted brothers or sisters. So, as Nina, Tony and Millie departed for America with their parents, heart-broken Thao was forced to remain behind in another wretched refugee camp.

Back home, Nghiem and Merna enlisted the aid of Minnesota's Sen. David Durenberger and Rep. Bill Frenzel in unraveling the red tape that held Thao in bondage—and they told their story on TV. Finally, in October, word came that Thao could rejoin her family in the United States.

Nina, Tony and Millie are already strong enough in English to attend public school—and have developed a typically American liking for hamburgers and malted milks. Merna continues to direct the Children's Heart Fund, and Nghiem has formed his own company to make printed circuit boards.

But for this family who wouldn't give up there is no entirely happy ending. They cannot forget the hundreds of boat people still scattered in miserable encampments throughout Southeast Asia—not properly cared for, and often unwanted by reluctant host countries and free-world nations alike.

Merna and Nghiem feel frustrated that they have been able

to do no more than mail the 6000 or so letters pressed upon them by desperate refugees at Letung and Tulai. They know only too well that while nations delay and bureaucracies dawdle, people are dying.

Only One Came Back

By Øystein Molstad-Andresen

IT WAS A glowering evening—March 21, 1973—when the 20,787-ton Norwegian freighter *Norse Variant* eased out of the harbor at Norfolk, Va., bound for Glasgow, Scotland, with a cargo of coal. From the bridge, Capt. Jens-Otto Harsem could barely tell where the wind-streaked sea ended and the sullen sky began. Yet captain and crew had a good feeling about their ship, despite the weather. Storms had been routine that winter, but the freighter had always shrugged off the North Atlantic's worst moods.

Below decks, as the *Norse Variant* plowed ahead, 23-year-old ship's mechanic Stein Gabrielsen began stowing the food and drink that he had purchased for a birthday celebration. A shipmate would be 25 the next day, and Stein planned to surprise him.

Thursday, March 22, dawned cold and raw. The wind shrieked out of the north, and huge seas bore down on the freighter, exploding heavily against her bows. Inside, the 29-

man crew had to brace against bulkheads to keep from being tossed about like dice in a cup. Stein realized the celebration must wait; the going was simply too rough.

Around 10 a.m., *Norse Variant* ran headlong into an enormous wave that thundered down on her bow and smashed the forward hatch. No. 1 Hold began to take on water as waves kept sweeping across the deck. Although pumps were handling the problem, Captain Harsem decided to return to Norfolk for repairs.

Another great wave struck about an hour later with such devastating force that the welds holding the forward crane to the deck zippered open, and the seas poured into Hold No. 2. Now, under almost continuous battering of wind and water, *Norse Variant* started to come apart. With leaks erupting, the ship grew increasingly nose-heavy. The radio officer began signaling the U.S. Coast Guard for assistance, giving *Norse Variant*'s course and position.

The lifeboat alarm sounded at 1:45 p.m. Grabbing his life jacket, Stein rushed to the afterdeck where the crew was gathering. *Norse Variant* was now wallowing like a harpooned whale. Captain Harsem ordered: "The life rafts! Throw them overboard and jump after them! The Coast Guard will pick you up." Almost as he spoke, two monstrous breakers crashed amidships, plunging the freighter under huge masses of water. In a matter of seconds, *Norse Variant* was gone.

Stein found himself fighting the suction of the sinking vessel as it dragged him downward toward the Atlantic floor. After what seemed an eternity, the pull weakened. Lungs near bursting, Stein struggled to the surface, boosted by the buoyancy of his life jacket. *Keep calm,* he told himself, amazed at being alive. *Save your strength. The men on the rafts will pick you up.*

He hung limply in his life jacket, trying to catch his breath in the almost unbearably cold water as waves lifted, then dropped him. Each time he was swept up to a 50-foot crest, he scanned the sea around him for his shipmates. *There must be others,* he thought. Then he spotted a raft. *There they are!* He struggled toward it and heaved himself aboard. It was empty.

As Stein tried to pull his thoughts together, waves showered sickeningly over the pitching, tossing raft, threatening to wash him back into the sea. Hurricane-force winds were driving needles of sleet and spray into his face. Stein determined to cling to hope. *The Coast Guard is out looking. It will be only a few hours.*

The Coast Guard *was* looking. *Norse Variant*'s distress signals had been picked up at 12:28 p.m., and the search was under way even before she sank. All through the rest of March 22, rescue planes crisscrossed the storm-swept sky, while Coast Guard cutters plowed the heavy seas. But no clue to *Norse Variant*'s fate could be spotted. The Atlantic, it seemed, had swallowed the ship whole.

Meanwhile, clinging to the ropes inside the reeling raft, Stein was grateful that he had put on his windbreaker under the life jacket. Like a diver's wet suit, it gave some protection from the cold. He had just learned to parry the tossing effect of each wave by shifting his weight when, suddenly, a churning breaker drove him deep beneath the surface, chewed up the raft and spat it out in little pieces. Again Stein fought to the surface, and there bobbed helplessly in the mountains and valleys of the seething sea.

Once more now, he began scanning the horizon at each opportunity. *Incredible!* Over there, a few hundred yards away, a second empty raft was bucking! He fought his way into its path, hauled himself aboard, tied its lifeline securely to his left arm and settled back to wait. *Hang on,* he kept telling himself. *It won't be long now.*

Shortly before nightfall, Stein heard a welcome sound above the roaring of the wind. *A plane!* He grabbed a rocket flare from the raft's emergency compartment and—with numbed fingers working in maddeningly slow motion—managed to release the safety and fire. As the drone of the plane grew steadily weaker, in desperation Stein fired another rocket—his last one. But the plane was gone. The young seaman was alone once more with the pitching raft and the roar of wind and sea.

Several hours later, a ship's searchlights appeared, sweeping wide arcs through the murk. Stein waved his arms, shouting vainly into the howling wind, "I'm over here! Can't you see me?" But the searchlights blinked off, and the ship churned past only a quarter-mile away.

At least they're looking, he consoled himself. *There will be another chance.* He settled down to parrying the seas and keeping himself awake.

* * *

Next morning—Friday, March 23—Stein was exhausted. His feet were blue and numb, and he knew he had to get the circulation going in his legs. Sliding into the water and holding tight to the side of the raft, he began slowly kicking until he felt a measure of warmth returning. Still worried about the condition of his legs, however, he tried to wrap them with the tattered remains of a canvas shelter. It was a mistake. A mighty wave capsized his craft again and hurled Stein beneath it, his feet imprisoned in the canvas.

Kicking and clawing frantically, he managed to free himself, only to find his life jacket so buoyant that it trapped him against the raft's floor like a bubble caught under ice. His air almost gone, he pushed up with all his strength and barely managed to squeeze out from beneath.

Late that afternoon, the storm dealt its cruelest blow. An immense breaker—a great, gray monster the size of a five-story building—thundered down on Stein. The turmoil of raging water tore away his life jacket, snapped the lifeline and sent the raft swirling out of reach. Once more he made a desperate swim—and barely got back aboard.

By dawn Saturday, Stein was almost ready to give in. It had been nearly two full days since he had last closed his eyes. *How pleasant it would be to stretch out in the raft and drift off to sleep,* he thought. *No, Stein. If you doze, you are finished. Hang on just one more day.*

Saturday, the storm at last began to taper off. But, as the hours dragged on, the ocean remained empty. Stein began to wonder: *Could the search have been called off?* His muscles ached; his eyes were swollen and nearly blinded by the driving spray. And now his throat was too raw to swallow any of the raft's emergency rations. He felt giddy from lack of sleep. His strength was ebbing fast.

That morning, the search was continuing full-scale. At Coast Guard headquarters in New York, a computer had calculated wind and current and mapped out the area most likely to contain survivors. Coast Guard and Air Force planes were to search a grid of 12,600 square miles that day, but engine trouble forced one plane back early. When the last aircraft returned to base,

2200 square miles had been left uncovered—precisely where Stein Gabrielsen was fighting his battle against the sea.

As daylight faded that Saturday, the temptation to sleep was overwhelming Stein: *Even if you freeze to death, there are worse ways to die.* The word brought him to his senses. *Don't be a fool,* he kept repeating. *You are not going to die.* Somehow, he managed to stay awake another night.

On Sunday morning, the seas were calmer. The exhausted seaman decided that it was finally safe to allow himself the luxury he had not dared yield to for almost three days. He closed his eyes and dozed off.

Minutes later, at 9 a.m., the roar of a jet plane jolted him awake. It streaked by, several thousand feet above, and disappeared. *How could they miss again?* he asked as he gazed with frustration at the empty horizon.

The men aboard Air Force HC-130 had been out for nearly three hours when—at 9:06 a.m., Sunday, March 25—co-pilot Lt. Ronald Balleu spotted something off to starboard. It passed out of sight behind them before he could tell what it was. On the return pass, it was clearer: an orange bubble shining like a tiny beacon on the empty sea. It was unmistakably a life raft.

"My God, there's someone in there!" screamed Balleu. The entire crew jammed into the cockpit as the pilot, Lt. Cmdr. Edward L. Weilbacher, brought the plane down for a closer look. They could not believe their eyes. Not only was there someone there, but he was very much alive, jumping up and down. Balleu dropped flares to assure the war-dancing figure that he had been seen, then radioed his base. Within minutes, the nearest vessel, an oil tanker half an hour away, had set course for the little raft.

Meanwhile, a plane from the 54th Aerospace Rescue and Recovery Squadron at Pease Air Force Base in New Hampshire arrived overhead. Two frogmen bailed out, carrying plastic-wrapped medical equipment, blankets and a radio transmitter. They splashed down a few dozen yards from the raft. Then, as they clambered aboard it, Stein, who a minute before had been dancing for joy, went limp as a rag. "He's okay," they radioed to the plane circling overhead. "It's unbelievable."

There was something Stein had to know. "Have you found

any others?" His voice was so hoarse it was barely audible. "I'm sorry," one of the frogmen answered gently. Stein lay back and closed his eyes.

For nearly 70 hours Stein Gabrielsen—alone in a stormy sea without sleep, food or drink—had survived conditions that no man should have been able to survive. In an incredible feat of human endurance, he had struggled against screaming 75-mile-an-hour winds and 50-foot killer waves. He had endured freezing temperatures, snow, sleet and hail. Amazingly, there was no frostbite. He was dehydrated, cut and bruised, but that was all. After a few days' rest, he would be on his way home to his native Norway. For Stein Gabrielsen, the long ordeal was over.

My Fight for America's First Birth-Control Clinic

by Margaret Sanger

ON THE CRISP, bright morning of October 16, 1916, in Brooklyn, N. Y., I opened the doors of the first birth-control clinic in the United States. I believed then that this was an event of lasting social significance for American womanhood.

Three years before, as a professional nurse, I had gone with a doctor on a call in New York's Lower East Side and watched a frail mother die from a self-induced abortion. The doctor previously had refused to give her contraceptive information. The mother was one of a thousand such cases; in New York alone I had heard there were 100,000 abortions a year.

That night I knew I could not go on merely nursing, allowing mothers to suffer and die.

My studies in Holland, where birth-control clinics had been operated so successfully for 38 years that they were granted a royal charter, had qualified me to give contraceptive instruction. My sister, who was also a nurse, could assist me.

But the New York State penal code declared that only a

physician could give birth-control information—and then only for the prevention or cure of disease. Always this had been held to mean venereal disease. I wanted the interpretation broadened to protect women from ill health as the result of excessive childbearing and, equally important, to give them the right to control their own destinies.

As I was not a physician, I would have no legal protection if I gave birth-control information to anyone. But I believed that if a woman must break the law to establish a right to voluntary motherhood, the law must be broken.

I chose the Brownsville section of Brooklyn. Dingy and squalid, it was crowded with hard-working men and women whose poverty provided sufficient reason for giving birth-control information. An enthusiastic young worker in the cause came from Chicago to help me. Together, one day in early fall, we tramped the Brownsville streets, through a driving rainstorm, to find the best location at the cheapest terms. "Don't come over here." "We don't want trouble." "Keep out." These and other pleasantries were hurled at us as we visited rooming houses, hoping for welcome.

Finally, at 46 Amboy Street, we found a friendly landlord, a Mr. Rabinowitz, who had two first-floor rooms vacant at $50 a month. We bought furniture as cheaply as we could, and Rabinowitz himself spent hours painting until the rooms were spotless and snow-white. "More hospital-looking," he said.

We had about 5000 handbills printed in English, Italian and Yiddish. They read:

MOTHERS!
Can you afford to have a large family? Do you want any more children? If not, why do you have them?
DO NOT KILL, DO NOT TAKE LIFE,
BUT PREVENT:
Safe, Harmless Information can be obtained of trained Nurses at 46 AMBOY STREET, near Pitkin Avenue, Brooklyn.
Tell your Friends and Neighbors.
All Mothers Welcome

With a small bundle of these notices, we fared forth in a house-to-house canvass of the district.

Would the people come? Nothing could have stopped them!

My colleague, standing at the window, called, "Do come and look." Halfway to the corner they stood in line, shawled, hatless, their red hands clasping the chapped smaller ones of their children. All day long and far into the evening, in ever-increasing numbers they came, over a hundred the opening day. Jews and Christians, Protestants and Roman Catholics alike made their confessions to us.

Every day the little waiting room was crowded. Women came from the far end of Long Island (the press having spread the word), from Connecticut, Massachusetts, Pennsylvania, New Jersey. They came to learn the "secret" which they thought was possessed by the rich and denied to the poor.

My sister and I lectured to eight women at a time on the basic technique of contraception. Complete case histories were kept; they were vital if our work was to have scientific value.

Tragic were the stories of the women. One told of her 15 children. Six were living. "I'm 37 years old. Look at me! I might be 50!" There was a reluctantly pregnant woman who had borne eight children, had had two abortions and many miscarriages. Worn out from housework and from making hats in a sweatshop, nervous beyond words, she cried hysterically, "If you don't help me, I'm going to chop up a glass and swallow it tonight!"

I comforted her as best I could, but there was nothing I would do to interrupt her pregnancy. We believed in birth control, not abortion.

But it was not altogether sad; we were often cheered by gayer visitors. The grocer's wife dropped in to wish us luck, and the German baker whose wife gave out our handbills to everybody passing the door sent us doughnuts. When we were too pressed with work to go out for a meal, Mrs. Rabinowitz would call to us, "If I bring some hot tea now, will you stop the people coming?"

On the tenth day a well-dressed hard-faced woman pushed her way through the group of patiently waiting women and, striding into my room, snapped peremptorily, "You, Margaret Sanger, are under arrest. I am a police officer."

Three plainclothesmen from the vice squad promptly appeared. They herded our women patients into line as though they were the inmates of a brothel. Women began to cry; the infants in their arms began to cry. The clinic soon became a bedlam. The raiders confiscated our 464 case histories and our pamphlets.

It was half an hour before I could persuade the men to release the poor mothers. Meanwhile, the event had brought masses of people spilling into the streets. Newspapermen and photographers joined the throng. White-hot with indignation, I refused to ride in the Black Maria. I insisted on walking the mile to the court, marching ahead of the raiders, the crowds following.

I spent the night in the Raymond Street jail, in a cell so filthy that I shall never forget it. The mattresses were spotted and smelly. I wrapped myself in my coat, fighting roaches, crying out at a rat which scuttled across the floor. It was not until afternoon that my bail was arranged. As I emerged from the jail I saw the woman who had threatened to swallow glass; she had been waiting there all that time.

I went back at once and reopened the clinic, but now the police made Rabinowitz sign eviction papers on the ground that I was "maintaining a public nuisance." Again I was arrested. Riding in the Black Maria this time, I heard a scream as we rattled away. It came from a woman wheeling a baby carriage. She left it on the sidewalk and rushed through the crowd crying, "Come back! Come back and save me!"

But as I reached the depths of despair and public humiliation, something like a miracle occurred. Help and sympathy sprang up on all sides. Legal aid was proffered. Doctors rallied to our aid. A group of sympathetic and wealthy women in New York formed a Committee of One Hundred for our defense. Sympathizers even held a mass meeting in Carnegie Hall.

My trial began in Brooklyn on January 29, 1917. About 50 mothers came to court. Timid and distressed, they smiled and nodded, trying to reassure me. Mingled with them were the smartly dressed members of the Committee of One Hundred.

The vehemence of the prosecution surprised me; for to me there seemed to be no argument at all. The last thing in my mind was to deny that I had given birth-control advice. I had deliberately violated the law. But my lawyer, Jonah J. Goldstein, was trying to get me off with a suspended sentence.

One by one the Brownsville mothers took the stand. "Have you ever seen Mrs. Sanger before?" asked the district attorney.

"Yess. At the cleenic."

"Why did you go there?"

"To ask her to stop the babies."

"Did you get this information?"

"Yes, dank you, I got it. It wass gut, too."

For days the legal arguments went on.

At last, one wintry day, Judge John J. Freschi banged his fist on the desk. "All we are concerned about is the statute!" he exclaimed. "As long as it remains the law," he asked my attorney, "will this woman promise here and now unqualifiedly to obey it?"

He turned to me. "What is your answer, Mrs. Sanger? Yes or no?"

The whole courtroom seemed to hold its breath.

I spoke out, as emphatically as I could: "I cannot promise to obey a law I do not respect."

The tension broke. Women shouted, clapped. The judge demanded order. When it came he announced, "The judgment of the court is that you be imprisoned for 30 days."

A single cry came from a woman in the corner: "Shame!"

The next afternoon I was taken to the Queens County Penitentiary in Long Island City. The prisoners—prostitutes, pickpockets, thieves—had somehow heard about me and birth control. One asked me to explain to them about "sex hygiene." When I sought permission to do so, the matron said, "Ah, gwan wid ye. They know bad enough already."

But I persisted and got my way. I also taught some of the girls to read and write. And I kept up with my own writing, planning ahead the birth-control movement. The next step? To appeal the case, of course, to carry it to the highest court possible.

I was released on March 6. No experience in my life had been more thrilling. When I stepped through the big steel-barred doorway, the tingling air of outdoors rushed against my face. In front of me stood my attorney, my friends and co-workers, their voices lifted in the martial strains of the "Marseillaise." And behind, in the windows of the penitentiary, were the faces of newly made friends, and they too were singing for me.

The case of the Brownsville birth-control clinic began its journey through the courts. Then, on January 8, 1918, came the momentous decision:

The New York Court of Appeals sustained my conviction, but Judge Frederick E. Crane's liberal interpretation of the law had the effect of permitting physicians to give contraceptive information to a married person for "health reasons." "Disease" was now to include everything in the broad definition of the word. No longer need doctors fear loss of license for imparting such information. This opened the clinics, as well as doctors' offices, to women for birth-control advice almost everywhere in the United States.

How I Designed an A-Bomb In My Junior Year at Princeton

by John Aristotle Phillips and David Michaelis

THE FIRST SEMESTER of my junior year at Princeton University is a disaster, and my grades show it. D's and F's predominate, and a note from the dean puts me on academic probation. Flunk one more course, and I'm out.

Fortunately, as the new semester gets under way, my courses begin to interest me. Three hours a week, I attend one called Nuclear Weapons Strategy and Arms Control in which three professors lead 12 students through intense discussions of counterforce capabilities and doomsday scenarios. The leader is Hal Feiveson, renowned for his strong command of the subject matter. Assisting him are Marty Sherwin, an authority on cold-war diplomacy, and Freeman Dyson, an eminent physicist.

One morning, Dyson opens a discussion of the atomic bomb: "Let me describe what occurs when a 20-kiloton bomb is exploded, similar to the two dropped on Hiroshima and Nagasaki. First, the sky becomes illuminated by a brilliant white light. Temperatures are so high around the point of explosion that the atmosphere is actually made incandescent. To an observer standing six miles away, the ball of fire appears brighter than a hundred suns.

"As the fireball begins to spread up and out into a mushroom-shaped cloud, temperatures spontaneously ignite all flammable materials for miles around. Wood-frame houses catch fire. Clothing bursts into flame, and people suffer intense third-degree flash burns over their exposed flesh. The very high temperatures also produce a shock wave and a variety of nuclear radiations capable of penetrating 20 inches of concrete. The shock wave levels everything in the vicinity of ground zero; hurricane-force winds then rush into the vacuum left by the expanding shock wave and sweep up the rubble of masonry, glass and steel, hurling it outward as lethal projectiles."

Silence falls over the room as the titanic proportions of the destruction begin to sink in.

"It takes only 15 pounds of plutonium to fabricate a crude atomic bomb," adds Hal Feiveson. "If breeder reactors come into widespread use, there will be sufficient plutonium shipped around the country each year to fashion thousands of bombs. Much of it could be vulnerable to theft or hijacking."

The class discusses a possible scenario. A 200-pound shipment disappears en route between a reprocessing facility and a nuclear reactor. State and local police discover only an empty truck and a dead driver. Two weeks later, a crude fission bomb is detonated in Wall Street. Of the half-million people who crowd the area during the regular business day, 100,000 are killed outright. A terrorist group claims responsibility and warns the President that if its extravagant political demands are not met, there will be another explosion within a week.

"That's impossible," a student objects. "Terrorists don't have the know-how to build a bomb."

"You have to be brilliant to design an A-bomb," says another. "Besides, terrorists don't have access to the knowledge."

Impossible? Or is it? The specter of terrorists incinerating an entire city with a homemade atomic bomb begins to haunt me. I turn to John McPhee's book *The Curve of Binding Energy,* in which former Los Alamos nuclear physicist Ted Taylor postulates that a terrorist group could easily steal plutonium or uranium from a nuclear reactor and then design a workable atomic bomb with information available to the general public. According to Taylor, all the ingredients—except plutonium—

are legally available at hardware stores and chemical-supply houses.

Suddenly, an idea comes to mind. Suppose an average—or below-average in my case—physics student could design a workable atomic bomb on paper? That would prove Taylor's point dramatically and show the federal government that stronger safeguards have to be placed on the storage of plutonium. If I could design a bomb, almost any intelligent person could. But I would have to do it in less than three months to turn it in as my junior independent project. I decide to ask Freeman Dyson to be my adviser.

"You understand," says Dyson, "my government security clearance will preclude me from giving you any more information than that which can be found in physics libraries? And that the law of 'no comment' governing scientists who have clearance to atomic secrets stipulates that, if asked a question about the design of a bomb, I can answer neither yes nor no?"

"Yes, sir," I reply. "I understand."

"Okay, then. I'll give you a list of textbooks outlining the general principles—and I wish you luck."

I'm tremendously excited as I charge over to the physics office to record my project, and can barely write down:

> John Aristotle Phillips
> Dr. Freeman Dyson, Adviser
> "How to Build your Own Atomic Bomb"

A few days later, Dyson hands me a short list of books on nuclear-reactor technology, general nuclear physics and current atomic theory. "That's all?" I ask incredulously, having expected a bit more direction.

At subsequent meetings Dyson explains only the basic principles of nuclear physics, and his responses to my calculations grow opaque. If I ask about a particular design or figure, he will glance over what I've done and change the subject. At first, I think this is his way of telling me I am correct. To make sure, I hand him an incorrect figure. He reads it and changes the subject.

Over spring vacation, I go to Washington, D.C., to search for records of the Los Alamos Project that were declassified between 1954 and 1964. I discover a copy of the literature given to scientists who joined the project in the spring of 1943. This text, *The Los Alamos Primer,* carefully outlines all the details of atomic fissioning known to the world's most advanced scientists in the early '40s. A whole batch of copies costs me about $25. I gather them together and go over to the bureaucrat at the front desk. She looks at the titles, and then looks up at me.

"Oh, you want to build a bomb, too?" she asks matter-of-factly.

I can't believe it. Do people go in there for bomb-building information every day? When I show the documents to Dyson, he is visibly shaken. His reaction indicates to me that I actually stand a chance of coming up with a workable design.

The material necessary to explode my bomb is plutonium-239, a man-made, heavy isotope. Visualize an atomic bomb as a marble inside a grapefruit inside a basketball inside a beach ball. At the center of the bomb is the initiator, a marble-sized piece of metal. Around the initiator is a grapefruit-size ball of plutonium-239. Wrapped around the plutonium is a three-inch reflector shield made of beryllium. High explosives are placed symmetrically around the beryllium shield. When these detonate, an imploding shock wave is set off, compressing the grapefruit-size ball of plutonium to the size of a plum. At this moment, the process of atoms fissioning—or splitting apart—begins.

There are many subtleties involved in the explosion of an atomic bomb. Most of them center on the actual detonation of the explosives surrounding the beryllium shield. The grouping of these explosives is one of the most highly classified aspects of the atomic bomb, and it poses the biggest problems for me as I begin to design my bomb.

My base of operations is a small room on the second floor of Ivy, my eating club. The conference table in the center of the room is covered with books, calculators, design paper, notes. My sleeping bag is rolled out on the floor. As the next three weeks go by, I stop going to classes altogether and work day and night. The other members at Ivy begin referring to me as The Hobo because of my unshaven face and disheveled appearance. I develop a terrible case of bloodshot eyes. Sleep comes rarely.

I approach every problem from a terrorist's point of view. The bomb must be inexpensive to construct, simple in design, and small enough to sit unnoticed in the trunk of a car or an abandoned U-Haul trailer.

As the days and nights flow by, linked together by cups of coffee and bologna sandwiches, I scan government documents for gaps indicating an area of knowledge that is still classified. Essentially, I am putting together a huge jigsaw puzzle. The edge pieces are in place and various areas are getting filled in, but pieces are missing. Whenever the outline of one shows up, I grab my coffee Thermos and sit down to devise the solution that will fill the gap.

With only two weeks left, the puzzle is nearly complete, but two pieces are still missing: which explosives to use, and how to arrange them around the plutonium.

During the next week I read that a high-explosive blanket around the beryllium shield might work. But after spending an entire night calculating, I conclude that it is not enough to guarantee a successful implosion wave. Seven days before the design is due, I'm still deadlocked.

The alarm clock falls off the table and breaks. I take this as a sign to do something drastic, and I start all over at the beginning. Occasionally I find errors in my old calculations, and I correct them. I lose sense of time.

With less than 24 hours to go, I run through a series of new calculations, mathematically figuring the arrangement of the explosives around the plutonium. If my equations are correct, my bomb might be just as effective as the Hiroshima and Nagasaki bombs. But I can't be sure until I know the exact nature of the explosives I will use.

Next morning, with my paper due at 5 p.m., I call the Du Pont Company from a pay phone and ask for the head of the chemical-explosives division, a man I'll call S. F. Graves. If he gives me even the smallest lead, I'll be able to figure the rest out by myself. Otherwise, I'm finished.

"Hello, Mr. Graves. My name is John Phillips. I'm a student at Princeton, doing work on a physics project. I'd like to get some advice, if that's possible."

"What can I do for you?"

"Well," I stammer, "I'm doing research on the shaping of explosive products that create a very high density in a spherically shaped metal. Can you suggest a Du Pont product that would fit in this category?"

"Of course," he says, in a helpful manner.

I don't think he suspects, but I decide to try a bluff: "One of my professors told me that a simple explosive blanket would work in the high-density situation."

"No, no. Explosive blankets went out with the Stone Age. We sell [he names a product] to do the job in similar density-problem situations to the one you're talking about."

When I hang up the phone, I let out a whoop. Mr. Graves has given me just the information I need. Now, if my calculations are correct with respect to the new information, all I have to do is complete my paper by five.

Five minutes to five, I race over to the physics building and bound up the stairs. Inside the office, everybody stops talking and stares at me. I haven't shaven in over a week.

"Is your razor broken, young man?" asks one of the department secretaries.

"I came to hand in my project," I explain. "I didn't have time to shave. Sorry."

A week later, I return to the physics department to pick up my project. One thought has persisted: If I didn't guess correctly about the implosion wave, or if I made a mistake somewhere in the graphs, I'll be finished at Princeton.

A secretary points to the papers. I flip through them, but don't find mine. I look carefully; my paper is not there.

Trying to remain calm, I ask her if all the papers have been graded.

"Yes, of course," she says.

Slowly I return to my room. The absence of my paper can only mean that I blew it.

In the middle of the week, I go back to the physics-department office, hoping to catch the chairman for a few minutes. The secretary looks up, then freezes.

"Aren't you John Phillips?" she asks.

"Yes," I reply.

"Aren't you the boy who designed the atomic bomb?"

"Yes, and my paper wasn't..."

She takes a deep breath. "The question has been raised by the department whether your paper should be classified by the U.S. government."

"What? Classified?"

She takes my limp hand, shaking it vigorously. "Congratulations," she says, all smiles. "You got one of the only A's in the department. Dr. Wigner* wants to see you right away. He says it's a fine piece of work. And Dr. Dyson has been looking for you everywhere."

For a second I don't say anything. Then the madness of the situation hits me. A small air bubble of giddiness rises in my throat. Here I have put on paper the plan for a device capable of killing thousands of people, and all I was worrying about was flunking out.

---

*Eugene Paul Wigner, Nobel Prize-winning physicist.

Niki Lauda's Duel With Death

by Lawrence Elliott

WHEN MARLENE LAUDA arrived at Cologne airport on the evening of August 1, 1976, she expected to meet her husband, world champion racing driver Niki Lauda. Lauda was competing in the German Grand Prix at nearby Nürburgring, but Marlene, whose heart hammered even when she watched televised reruns of races, often stayed away from the track. She and Niki were to meet at the airport after the race and fly home to Salzburg.

Lauda was not waiting for her in the airport lounge. Instead, she was met by strangers who broke the bad news: There had been an accident; Niki was in a hospital at Mannheim, 150 miles away.

Time blurred, and then she was standing in an intensive-care unit looking down at a monstrous mask that bore no resemblance to her husband. The face was brutally burned and swollen to three times normal size; eyes and nose were swallowed up in a balloon of charred flesh. Each frightful gasp from the shriveled mouth seemed to be a final act.

A doctor led Marlene outside. "Will he live?" she asked. The doctor shook his head. The exterior burns might be dealt with, but Niki had sucked flame and poisonous gases down through his bronchial passages. Now the scalded lungs were failing. It could only be a matter of hours.

Marlene, waiting, wept through the night. But behind closed doors, Niki Lauda, who sensed the presence of death in the room, refused to die.

The day had begun with rain, adding an extra dash of danger to the Nürburgring, widely considered the most dangerous track on the Grand Prix circuit. Lauda had lobbied, unsuccessfully, to have that year's race moved to another site. Driving a 12-cylinder, 500-horsepower Formula 1 racing car at Nürburgring, he said, was like trying to land a jumbo jet on a grass strip. Each 14-mile lap snaked through 176 turns and zoomed over countless slopes. Many drivers agree that there is little room for a car in trouble to run off the track safely.

Even without such a track, Grand Prix racing is a devastating test of men and machines. Every year, drivers, crews and cars—as many as 15 for each team—embark on a ten-month odyssey, staging 17 grueling races on four continents. During trial heats, only a few seconds separate the winner from the last qualifying car. And of the usual 25 drivers who start each race, only the first six to finish gain points toward the championship—worth millions to the victor.

The investment is staggering—from the cost of a Formula 1 racer (upward of $100,000) to the toll in lives—for, at straight-away speeds approaching 200 miles an hour, the driver is pushing his fragile powerhouse to its outermost limits. Of the 14 drivers who have become World Grand Prix Champions since 1950, four have been killed on the racetracks.

But nothing could dim the ardor of Andreas Nikolaus Lauda, 28, for fast cars. At age 18, Niki, the son of a Viennese businessman, got his grandmother to put up $3900 for a racing mini-Cooper. Four years later, having raced his way up through the ranks, he took out a $100,000 bank loan in order to join a British racing team and drive a Formula 1 car. In 1974, Lauda signed on with Enzo Ferrari, the dean of motor racing and president of Italy's Ferrari works, and that year he finished fourth among Grand Prix drivers. The following year he captured the championship, and in 1976, going into the German Grand Prix, he had won five of the first nine races.

Despite the rain, a crowd of 300,000 was filling the Nürburgring stands on August 1, when Lauda began the ritual of final preparation. He stuffed both ears with wax and cotton wool. He pulled on a non-flammable sweater and face mask, zipped his flame-retardant jump suit closed and fastened his crash helmet. A few minutes before starting time, the rain stopped and the sun broke through. But Lauda decided to keep treaded "wet" tires on his red Ferrari until the track dried.

Although Lauda's qualifying runs had earned him an up-front starting place, he got off badly. After the first lap, he was in ninth place and pulled into the pits to change to slick, dry-track tires for more speed. That took 60 seconds. Then he came roaring out, leaving swaths of burnt rubber on the pavement, and worked his way up through the gears.

Halfway around on the second lap, something happened. Some say the Ferrari threw a wheel, others that it hit a wet spot; Lauda has no recollection of the moment. But as he came speeding into a rising left turn at 140 miles an hour, his car tore loose from the roadway and went flying into the embankment. The gas tanks split open, and the Ferrari careered back to the center of the track, coming to rest broadside. The first following car swerved left and gave it only a glancing blow. But the next one shot around the curve and, brakes screeching, smashed squarely into the wreckage, setting it ablaze.

Trapped in the cockpit by his jammed restraining harness, Lauda was unable to trigger the Ferrari's fire extinguisher. His helmet had been ripped off, and the flame-retardant face mask was turning black in the intense heat. Other drivers stopped and ran to his aid. One of them, Italian racer Arturo Merzario, dived right into the fire to unbuckle Lauda's six-point seat belt. Then, stepping onto the front of the car, he seized Lauda by the upper arms and pulled him out of the blazing wreck.

Somehow Lauda found the strength to walk away from the inferno. He touched his bloody, blistering face and asked his rescuers, "How do I look?" "Fine," they lied. Then he passed out.

Lauda had been in the flaming ruins of the Ferrari about 45 seconds, inhaling fire and toxic fumes from the burning synthetic parts. As the doctors discovered at Ludwigshafen Hospital, some 90 miles away, where he was flown by helicopter, he had suffered second- and third-degree burns on his face and hands, as well as a crushed cheekbone and three fractured ribs. But the most immediate threat was his deteriorating lungs. That same afternoon, he was transferred to the Mannheim University Clinic, the nearest hospital equipped to deal with pulmonary emergencies.

For the next three days, Lauda hung suspended in a gray void, unable to speak or see, but aware of his wife's presence, of the respirator, oxygen and tubes that tenuously linked him to life. The doctors were astonished at his tenacity. He was stubborn, they agreed, but he was still dying.

At a certain point, Niki felt that his body was beginning to give up in anticipation of blessed relief from pain. But his brain would not yield. He was determined to survive, and he willed his way back from darkness. Even though a priest was called in on Tuesday to give him the last rites, he forced himself to concentrate on voices, sounds—any sensation that confirmed his place among the living.

Hour by hour, the darkness receded. By Wednesday night, he was breathing well enough to be taken off the respirator. The next day he insisted on sitting in a chair, and on Friday, sight and voice restored, he put a bandaged hand on Marlene's arm and walked around the room. From then on, it was Marlene who led him back to life, with love and absolute confidence that he would get well.

That Friday the doctors took him off the critical list, while Lauda continued to work at his recovery. He endured infusions, injections, two complete blood changes and a major skin-grafting operation. The burned tissue was excised from his face and replaced with strips of skin from his upper thigh. Then, barely two weeks after his accident, Niki told Marlene that he was going home to prepare for the Italian Grand Prix at Monza on September 12.

The doctors reluctantly agreed. They told him he required more plastic surgery on his face and that it would be months before he was really well again. But Lauda was ready to get on with his life. The plastic surgery could wait.

"I knew what people would say," Lauda recalls, "that a man with a face like mine should stay in hiding. But that is not my attitude. I have a talent, a profession. And if it turned out that I couldn't handle it anymore, the sooner I found out the better."

Back in Salzburg, Niki began a rigorous conditioning regimen. He ran for an hour every day, did uncounted sit-ups and deep-knee bends and, for the first time since the accident, slept without the shadow of death to goad him awake.

Three days before the Italian Grand Prix, Ferrari publicly declined to accept responsibility for Lauda's decision to race again. But Lauda, already at Monza for the qualifying runs, paid no heed; he had a more pressing concern. Coming to a stretch he ought to have taken flat out, he felt his foot, unwilled, lift from the accelerator. When it happened again, he quit for the day and, as he put it, had a good talk with himself: if he wanted to be a racing driver, he had to be prepared to go the limit.

Six Sundays after the crash at the Nürburgring, Niki drove the circuit at Monza like the Lauda of old. He did not win—he finished fourth—but the huge crowd gave him a rousing ovation. Other athletes had made startling comebacks from severe injury; Lauda had come back from the dead.

But he was to face one more test of courage before the season ended. Having missed two races during his hospitalization and convalescence, Lauda came to the final 1976 race, the Japanese Grand Prix, a bare three points ahead of England's James Hunt, his nearest rival for the title. One or the other would emerge as overall Grand Prix Champion.

On the day of the race, rain and fog shrouded the track at the foot of Mount Fuji. The start was delayed; the drivers debated whether to race at all. Finally, with 55,000 spectators howling for action, they set off onto the wet roadway. Lauda, starting from the second row, drove one lap in blinding spray from the cars ahead, then pulled off the track. He had calculated the odds, carefully and without emotion, and found them too long, too dangerous. He withdrew from the race.

Predictably, there were those who proclaimed that the Nürburgring had finished Lauda. But James Hunt, who stayed and won the championship, understood that Lauda's withdrawal at Fuji was a high order of bravery. "You can beat Lauda if you have a very good day," he said. "To break him is out of the question. He will be back."

He was right. Lauda began the 1977 season by winning the South African Grand Prix, the third race of that year. And he kept winning. When the procession of Grand Prix cars and drivers moved to Japan to close out the season, Lauda was not among them, this time because he did not need to be. He had clinched the World Driving Championship at the U.S. Grand Prix at Watkins Glen, N.Y., three races before the season's end. The man whose indomitable will denied death had come all the way back.

Everybody Likes to Work for Bill Marriott

by John G. Hubbell

ON LABOR DAY, in 1971, President Nixon proudly observed: "America's competitive spirit, the work ethic of this people, is alive and well. The dignity of work, the value of achievement, the morality of self-reliance—none of these is going out of style."

No American better exemplifies that appraisal than the former President's good friend, J. Willard Marriott, a former root-beer-stand operator who has seen his tiny company grow into a more than $2 billion-per-year corporation. Rarely has anyone started with less than Bill Marriott and, by dint of sheer, honest hard work, made more of the opportunity offered by the American system; and shared the resulting opportunities and abundance so generously with those who helped him succeed.

Marriott Corp. prospers in three areas:

Restaurants. Marriott Corp. operates some 900 restaurants directly and franchises more than one thousand. Included are Hot Shoppes and Roy Rogers family-style restaurants, and high-volume, fast-food facilities called Jr. Hot Shoppes and Big Boy coffee shops.

Contract Food Services. In 1982 alone some 80 million Marriott-prepared meals were served to passengers on over 100 of the world's airlines, making the corporation the world's largest in-flight caterer.

Hotels. During 1981, when the hotel occupancy rate was approximately 63 percent, Marriott's hotels were 80-percent full. Marriott has 112 hotels, including 26 franchised inns and has plans to open even more of them during 1982 and 1983. Marriott hotels are located in 82 cities in the United States, Mexico, the Caribbean, Europe, the Middle East, and Central America.

There is an almost tangible mystique about Marriott's company, an aura of certainty among employees that it is, deserves to be and will ever remain No. 1 in its field, and that it will achieve its announced goal of an average 20-percent annual earnings growth. This mystique is rooted largely in the warm personality and sensibly unselfish instincts that have always guided the man in whose image the company is cast.

J. (for John) Willard Marriott was born on September 17, 1900, in Marriott Settlement, near Ogden, Utah, the second of eight children born to Hyrum and Ellen Marriott. His earliest memories are of a clapboard house next to a mosquito-infested irrigation canal, and of the whole family ill with typhoid fever. By the time he was 8, he was earning a man's keep, wearing cowboy clothing that was not a costume, packing a pistol that was not a toy, living off the land and working long, hot summers and longer, cold winters with the Basque shepherds who tended his father's flocks. There were numerous encounters with coyotes and mountain lions, and also a first and last experience with tobacco. (He was chewing a plug one day when a rattler sounded off nearby. The youngster swallowed hard, drew his pistol, got the rattler—and a distaste for tobacco that persists to this day.) When he was 15, Bill took thousands of sheep by train to Omaha to sell them. With this sort of responsibility, self-confidence and business acumen mounted fast.

The close-knit Marriott family was deeply religious, and by the time Bill was 19 he was eager to do his stint as a Mormon missionary. He spent two years in Connecticut and Vermont, seeking converts everywhere he went. This period had a profound effect on him, and would influence the many thousands of lives his own would touch. For the young man acquired a knowledgeable belief in the Mormon message, which enthrones honest work as a cardinal virtue, and insists on energetic independence, thrift, the self-respect that comes from providing for family, church and brothers and sisters in the Faith who have been less fortunate.

Bill got ample chance to help others as soon as he returned home. The bottom fell out of the lamb market. More than 15,000 head of sheep that his father had bought for $14 each had to be sold for $3 per head. Hyrum Marriott went bankrupt, and never really recovered.

As the oldest son, Bill assumed more and more family responsibility. He was determined that he and his brothers and sisters would all complete their educations. Enrolling at Weber College, in Ogden, he worked for the campus newspaper, managed a bookstore and a little theater, and taught high-school English. Though a freshman, he also served as president of the student body. In his spare time—from about 4 a.m. to 7—he studied.

The summer after freshman year, he and a friend earned more than $3000 each selling woolen goods on commission. His impressive performance earned him a chance the following summer to become sales manager for seven Western states. There was no salary, but his percentage of his crew's sales that year came to nearly $5000.

After two years, he transferred to the University of Utah, where he met Alice Sheets, the beautiful daughter of a leading Salt Lake City attorney who was also a Mormon bishop. Spotting her at the student center, Bill decided instantly that someday he would marry her. He shouldered aside a small army of suitors and was engaged to her by the time he graduated in 1926. "Allie" graduated a year later, at 19, with high honors.

With a friend's financial help Bill bought the A&W root-beer franchise for Washington, D.C. Needing a location, he rented half a bake shop in the middle of the city, put up a partition and opened for business the day that Lindbergh flew the Atlantic—May 20, 1927. A few weeks later, he returned to Utah to marry Allie, who immediately became treasurer of the Washington enterprise. "We worked all the time," she recalls. "We'd open at 9 a.m. and usually fall into bed, exhausted, at one or two the next morning."

When autumn air grew crisp, root-beer sales fell off. Bill

decided to sell such hot snacks as chili, tamales and barbecued-beef sandwiches. He spent one entire night removing the big, revolving, orange A&W barrel, installing stoves and counter stools, and painting the door with the legend "Hot Shoppe." Allie says, laughing, "That was typical of Bill. He wasn't willing to waste a day of doing business." With recipes delightedly furnished by the Mexican embassy, Allie became cook and Bill waiter.

Throughout the Depression 1930s, while luxury restaurants failed everywhere, profits mounted in the bright, clean atmosphere of the Hot Shoppe, where emphasis remained on inexpensive, high-quality food and good service. The Marriotts expanded operations and menus, and also brought the drive-in concept to the East. By 1932, there were seven Hot Shoppes in the capital. After World War II, when the country took to the highways as never before, Marriott restaurants began dotting turnpikes from New York to Florida and points west.

As they built their work force (now more than 100,000 people), the Marriotts sought not necessarily experience, but enthusiasm—cheerful people who were interested and *cared* about the service they were providing, and thought nothing of working seven 12-hour days a week. Almost immediately, Bill began dreaming up ways to cut his employees in on the profits. It was in the best Mormon tradition, for it inspired initiative, industry and *esprit*. It was also just plain good business.

Today, Marriott has a hugely successful profit-sharing plan. Employees may contribute between three and ten percent of salary, while the corporation kicks in approximately eight percent of its pre-tax profits after determining that there has been a six-percent increase in their consolidated net worth.

There is also a can't-lose stock-purchase plan. Any full-time employee may elect to have five to ten percent of his salary set aside for a purchase of Marriott stock, at price determined by its value on the first or last day of the fiscal year. If the price is $30 on the first day of the fiscal year and $40 on the last day, the employee can buy at the lower rate. If the stock price declines, the employee may withdraw his money at any time. All he risks is the interest he might have earned in a savings account.

The risk isn't much when stacked against the overall performance of Marriott stock, as this example shows. If you purchase a share worth $16 in 1957, it would be worth $1000 today.

The Marriott company spends in excess of $10 million a year on its training programs, and an employee is almost besieged with opportunities to make the most of himself. The company pays part of the tuition of employees who want to complete high-school diploma requirements or take job-related college or business-school courses.

In addition, Marriott makes extensive use of on-site trainers to teach employees. Some employees come to Marriott's Washington, D.C. headquarters to attend the Food Preparation and Service Class.

Almost incidentally, Marriott's other fringe benefits and pay scales match or exceed those of the rest of the industry. In short, Bill Marriott has fashioned a work force which for 50 years has been characterized by an almost fierce company loyalty.

Sums up one Marriott employee: "If all companies treated their people the way this one does, there would be no employee-relations problems—no need for Social Security, Medicare or anything like that." Indeed, should Bill Marriott's brand of enlightened capitalism ever become widely adopted, there is no telling what altitudes the American economy might reach.

Campy's
Unforgettable Courage

by Howard A. Rusk, M.D.

DURING THE 1950s, before the Dodgers moved from Brooklyn to Los Angeles, I became a real fan. And, to me, the player who stood out among all the rest was Roy Campanella, No. 39. Campy, as we fans affectionately called him, was a canny and scrappy catcher. With a runner breaking off first base to steal second, Campy would spring from behind the plate like a young tiger—all bone, muscle, and concentrated power and control—and fire that ball to second like a bullet. Often the runner hadn't a chance.

And, in those days, the half-black, half-Italian from the Nicetown sandlots in Philadelphia, was probably the best-hitting catcher in baseball. In 1953, one of his best years, Campy set three major-league records for catchers: the most home runs (41), runs batted in (142) and put-outs (807). These achievements, plus a batting average of .312, earned him the National League's Most Valuable Player Award that year. "When I can no longer wear the uniform," he told reporters later, "they might

119

as well bury me, 'cause I'll be dead."

But when I first *met* Campy, less than five years later, he wasn't wearing the uniform, and I knew he never would again. His car had skidded on January ice and crashed into a telephone pole. Campy was thrown under the dashboard and broke his neck. Emergency surgery probably saved his life, but his spinal cord had been severed; he was paralyzed from the shoulders down. As director of New York University's Institute of Rehabilitation Medicine, which specializes in working with the spine-injured and the paralyzed, I was asked to see him.

I'll never forget how Campy looked, lying there in the hospital bed. His tough muscles were still hard, but his body was as unresponsive as stone. He had slight movement in his wrists and could extend and bend his arms but not his fingers. And those anxious eyes, filled with questions about the future.

Sitting on the edge of his bed after examining him, I spoke gently. "Campy, I don't know whether you're going to get a little back, a lot back—or nothing. Only time will tell. We'll start to train you tomorrow, but there's no magic in this. You will have to work harder than you ever have in your life."

"I'm ready," he said.

Next day we moved him into Room 414 at the Institute, his home for the next six months. With agonizing effort, he learned to sit up, first in bed, then in a wheelchair. Then, clumsily, he learned to feed himself with fork or spoon held in a slotted leather wristband. Day after day, he was strapped to a tilt board to promote circulation in his lower extremities. He suffered through torturous periods on the treatment table learning to roll over, and spent exhausting sessions at the weight machines to strengthen his feeble wrists.

Sometimes I wondered if Campy would ever make it. He was a man who loved speed and action and bone-jarring slides to the plate. He needed to catch and throw, and jaw it out with the umpire, and smash a ball over the fence to the roar of the crowd. Did he possess inner resources that he could draw upon to rebuild his life?

The first intimation that he did came one evening as I heard Campy talking on the telephone. "Hello," he was saying. "Is this the Dodger clubhouse? I want to speak to John Roseboro." Then, "John? This is Campy. I've been watching you play on television and, John, you're crowdin' the plate too much." Campy listened for a moment while John talked. Then he said,

"Everybody gets in a slump sometime. But that's no time to feel sorry for yourself. You can't just quit. You got to try all the harder."

I walked on. I knew then that Campy was coming back. He'd dug down, and somewhere found a new kind of courage.

Patiently, he continued his painful exercises, never complaining. Toward the end of the year, the star athlete who could no longer walk had begun to inspire hope and courage in the other patients. He'd talk baseball to them, or he'd get them talking about themselves, or he'd tell them about his own accident, and how he thought his world had come to an end. But it was all different now. Campy believed in his own future, and he made others believe in theirs.

Late that fall, in a wheelchair and a neck brace, Campy was discharged from the Institute. For all the odds against him, he was determined to support his family—his wife Ruthe, their three children, and her son by a former marriage. He started his own radio show, "Campy's Corner," a program of baseball interviews, and accepted a spring-training coaching job with the Dodgers.

Then came another blow. His 15-year-old stepson, whom he loved as his own, was having troubles with the law. Campy was heartsick. There was a second offense, and a third; it was deeply upsetting. He spent long hours with the boy trying to give him the father's love and support that he needed. It was a bad time for both, but it worked.

Campy told me about it later. He'd come into the office for a checkup and I said I'd seen the stories in the papers. For a moment he looked down at his helpless body, imprisoned in a wheelchair. Then he raised his head, smiled a quiet smile, and said the most moving thing I ever heard a patient say.

"You know, doctor, this trouble my boy was in." He spoke slowly, reaching for the right words. "I know that breaking your neck is a tough way to learn a lesson, but lyin' in bed, paralyzed, I learned two things: tolerance and patience, toward myself and everybody else." He hesitated. "That's love—isn't it?"

Not long after, Campy's wife, from whom he had recently separated, died from a cerebral hemorrhage, at age 40. It was a tragic time for Campy. Some years later, he married his present wife, Roxie, and together they kept the family going.

Never once did he let anyone feel sorry for him. He told

me how he and Roxie would go out to dinner, dances and other social events. "It makes me feel great," he said. "I know everybody has problems. But people look at me and get the feelin' that if a guy in a wheelchair can have such a good time, they can't be so bad off, after all."

In the summer of 1976, Campy called me and said he was in deep trouble. Bedsores, a constant problem caused by impaired circulation, were worse than ever. Moreover, he had developed other complications. We put him into intensive care at once. Before we were through, he had to have seven surgical procedures, with skin grafts and dozens of blood transfusions. He stayed with us for more than a year. Most of the time he had to lie flat on his face, in a special frame in which he could be turned over several times a day. Again, he never complained.

One night as I was leaving his room, something made me turn back. "Campy," I said, "here you are, back where you were almost 20 years ago. Yet you still manage to be cheerful, uncomplaining, helpful to others and full of plans. Tell me, what keeps you going?"

"Well," he said, "I go back to the Scripture my momma taught us when we were kids in Philadelphia, the Twenty-third Psalm: 'The Lord is my shepherd; I shall not want.' I say it over and over."

The first time, he said, was right after the accident. With his broken neck, he was already in bad shape. Then he contracted pneumonia. "I was in an oxygen tent, but I couldn't breathe right. The doctor said, 'Campy, the only thing I can do is cut a hole in your throat and insert a tracheotomy tube. It'll help you breathe. But I can't give you any anesthetic.'

"I was feeling so bad, I just thought of Momma, and how she taught us to get down on our knees and say that psalm; and while he operated on me, I kept sayin' it over and over in my head. The next day I was all right. The tube was in. I was breathin' good. There was no pain.

"Roxie and I have taught that passage to our kids, and they have taught it to theirs. I say it every night in bed before I go to sleep. And when I'm out of bed and don't feel right, I say it. So many times it has pulled me through."

When we released him, Campy didn't waste much time getting on the phone. More than anything now, he wanted to go back to work. There might be something in public relations, he thought, with the New York Mets. (As it turned out, there was.)

Some months ago, my office door opened and there Campy was in his wheelchair—cheerful, feeling good again, looking ahead. He told me that he and Roxie were moving to California, where he would begin work in community relations, scouting, and coaching for his beloved Dodgers.

"I'm having a wonderful second life," Campy told me. "I want to tell everybody about it. I want them to remember that when trouble comes, it ain't always bad. Take it with a smile, do the best you can and the good Lord will help you out."

To me, this is Campy—Campy of the fighting heart, the Roy Campanella I'll always remember. His neck was broken, but never his spirit.

Bank Heist
of the Century

by Robert Daley

ON MONDAY MORNING, July 19, 1976, the vault door in the main Riviera branch of France's giant Société Générale in Nice wouldn't open. The mechanism had stuck before, harried bank officials explained to impatient depositors, and would be cleared in a moment. But it wasn't.

By 10 a.m., safe specialists were working on the massive steel door. The mechanism stayed stuck. By noon, the decision was made to smash through the concrete wall beside the door and repair the mechanism from the inside. Masons were called in. At 3 p.m., a small hole was opened up. Workmen peered in.

Within 15 minutes, the bank was swarming with cops. Looking into the vault, they could see safe doors hanging open. Steel grills had been cut to pieces. The floor was strewn six inches deep with paper, most of it valuable: uncanceled checks, bearer bonds, stocks, bankbooks. Out of this paper jutted muddy tools (which would be found to weigh two tons): crowbars, chisels, drills, hydraulic jacks, axes, jackhammers, three blow-torches, 40 flashlights, 31 acetylene and oxygen tanks. It looked like a banquet hall after the gourmands had gone home to sleep it off. The feast, judging from the remnants, had been stupendous.

The vault door barred access not to a single strongroom, but to three interconnected ones. The robbers could be trapped in there, ready to shoot it out. A detective, the smallest man present, stripped to his undershorts and wriggled through the hole.

But the robbers were gone. So, too, it would later be determined, was about $7.2 million, most of it cash, some of it gold ingots and unset jewels kept in 320 safe-deposit boxes that had been cut open.

This was not only the most expensive bank robbery in history, it was also the most artistic. The vault mechanism was not faulty; the door had been welded shut from the inside. The detective's voice suddenly became high and squeaky from astonishment. A tunnel—he had found a tunnel. A portable stove—he had found a stove, plus used food packages, empty wine bottles, and dirty pots and dishes. These people had cooked hot meals! They must have worked in here the entire weekend. Solid-silver heirlooms served as chamber pots.

The welds were chiseled off; the ponderous door swung open. There was a long moment during which no one moved or spoke; these detectives had visited scores of crime scenes, but never one like this. They stared at a taunting message on the wall: "Without Weapons, Without Violence, Without Hate."

The police next turned their attention to the tunnel. The hole was high up in the back wall of the rear strongroom. Chiseled through 18 inches of reinforced concrete, it was little more than two feet wide and about 25 inches high.

A detective was sent into the tunnel. What he saw was a masterpiece of construction. Barely large enough for a man to crawl through, it was nearly 30 feet long, and buttressed every few yards by metal or wooden stanchions. A six-inch-diameter ventilation tube was still in place and an electrical cable lay there, too.

As expected, the tunnel connected with the sewer in the street behind the bank. The cable was a quarter-mile long and led into the parking lot under Nice's main square, where the robbers had wired it into a fluorescent-light fixture. Another trail led to the service road that runs beside an underground river. The gang had driven a panel truck under the crust of the city to within about 400 yards of the bank, and had floated their gear up the sewer from there on rubber rafts.

The detective work to be done was prodigious. There were 4000 lockboxes. That could mean interviewing 4000 people, and checking into the backgrounds of dozens of them. Every present and past employee of the bank, hundreds of them, might have to be checked also, for the robbers had known these strongrooms intimately.

Forty of Nice's detectives would be ordered to contact their local informants and demand: What have you heard in the street? Every detachment of gendarmes in every outlying village would be contacted: Have you noticed anything recently that seemed at all curious?

The tools would have to be traced. The wire also. One does not sell a quarter-mile of electrical wire every day, and whoever sold this wire would have to be found.

The brunt of this investigation fell on the Nice branch of the Police Judiciaire—called the P.J.—the national criminal-investigatory service of France. Their first big break came late in July, when, in response to the P.J. appeal, a deluge of information came in from nearby gendarmeries. Each lead had to be checked out by P.J. detectives, which took weeks. All proved unconnected to the July 16–19 break-in—with one exception.

On July 9, the Plan du Var gendarmes had logged a telephone call about a villa in the village of Castagniers, 11 miles from Nice, which was supposed to be empty, but had strange men in it. Two gendarmes had driven up and checked the names of the five men they found inside. The men said they had been given the villa keys by a friend of the owner and gave his name.

After the robbery, the detectives went to the villa, where one of them noticed a flashlight exactly like other flashlights found in the vault. He saw that the bottom was caked with mud. The light was sent to the P.J. lab in Marseilles, where its mud was compared with Nice sewer mud: identical.

The question was: Did the gendarmerie still have the five names? Yes, five known hoodlums. So, the villa must have been the gang's headquarters.

However, none of the five was a man of stature in the underworld. None seemed capable of organizing such a crime.

The Brain of The Sewer Gang must have been someone else. In addition, there were clearly more than five men involved, perhaps as many as 25. Detectives were sent out to find and tail the five suspects, plus their cohorts.

The police net spread wider and wider. Weeks passed. With so many detectives asking questions, there was increasing danger that The Sewer Gang would take off.

Then it was discovered that two men, Adrien Zeppi, 54, and Francis Pelligrin, 38, had been selling gold ingots to a bank in a Riviera village; the numbers on the ingots identified them as those taken at Nice. Neither Zeppi nor Pelligrin was previously known to the police.

Their arrests would compromise the entire investigation, for their absence would be noticed. The P.J. detectives decided they could wait no longer. At dawn on October 26, the 100th day of the investigation, police in Nice, Marseilles, Paris, Lyons and Corsica rounded up over 30 people, including Zeppi and Pelligrin, and brought them to P.J. offices in Paris and Marseille, where they were held for 48 hours under a legal procedure known as *garde à vue*. During the *garde à vue* the detainee may not be touched, but legal counsel cannot be present and few can withstand the psychological battering and fatigue as detectives try to get admissions. Those who possess guilty knowledge often crack.

The 13 subjects held in Paris were released with no charges filed against them. But in Marseilles, it was another story. At P.J. headquarters there, the lights burned all night, and after 48 hours, seven subjects were brought before an examining magistrate, who indicted six, including Zeppi and Pelligrin, for complicity in the robbery, and sent them to prison.

Considering the size of the roundup, six was not a very impressive haul. A few of these people were carrying uncirculated bills bearing the Nice serial numbers, but no significant loot was recovered. Obviously, The Brain was someone else.

A main center of organized crime in France is Marseilles. Each of the gang leaders there is known to the police. Was one of them The Brain? Each had been investigated by police and rejected.

Was it possible that they were in the presence of a master criminal who was also an amateur, a man unknown to police or criminal circles? By this time, The Brain had begun to attain the stature of myth, even among P.J. detectives.

Suddenly, the P.J. had his name, or hoped it did. But the detectives had almost no proof. They spent 15 hours trying to dredge some up. Apparently, they failed. All the time they feared he would fly. It was amazing that he hadn't gone already. There he sat, like a man without a care in the world. Was he made of marble; or was he perhaps not The Brain at all?

They decided to make the arrest. They would have to gamble that at some point during the *garde à vue* he would crack.

Albert (Bert) Spaggiari, 44, was a photographer who kept a neighborhood shop in Nice. He was known at Town Hall and was sometimes asked to photograph weddings. His wife, Marcelle, nicknamed Audie, was a registered nurse. The couple had a two-room apartment above the shop and they also owned a farm in the Maritime Alps about 30 miles north of Nice.

On October 27, the 101st day of the investigation, the French police arrested Bert. As he was driven away he acted perplexed. Me, The Brain? he said. Why, that's preposterous. The police must be incredibly far off the track. He was a photographer— a chicken farmer on the side. He knew no Sewer Gang. But the detectives had lapsed into silence.

Albert Spaggiari was fingerprinted, photographed, and the *garde à vue* began at 2:30 in the afternoon. Detectives hammered at him. Evening came. Midnight. Dawn.

Soon it was 2:30 in the afternoon again. Bert sat with an ironical smile on his face, blowing smoke rings at the ceiling, shaking his head sadly, saying over and over again: Why don't you admit you've made a mistake?

All this time, Audie had been in *garde à vue* also. That tunnel had taken weeks to dig, detectives told her; you mean you never noticed that your husband was gone all night and that he came home covered with mud?

No, monsieur.

They laughed at her. Marriage is not slavery, she retorted. Sometimes she had patients and did not come home all night. She knew nothing about Bert's business deals.

Audie was transported up to their farm. The house was turned inside out. Nothing. Still searching for the remains of $7.2 million, a squad of gendarmes dug up most of the property. Nothing.

Meanwhile, other detectives were digging into Bert's past. At 19, he joined the paratroops and fought in Indochina. There a military court sentenced him to five years in jail for grand larceny, and Bert returned to France to serve his time. In the late 1950s, he went to North Africa to start a new life, and later joined the right-wing Secret Army, which was struggling to prevent Algerian independence. Bert reportedly offered to assassinate President de Gaulle, but permission was refused. In 1962, he was arrested for complicity in political terrorism and sentenced to another four years in jail. In 1974, he spent three weeks in jail for using fake license plates on his car, and police suspected he had been involved in a bank holdup, although this was never proven. To the haggard interrogators, this information provided some hope and, as the second night of the *garde à vue* began to pass, they hammered at Bert with new vigor.

They told him that accomplices had squealed; they hit him with details Audie had unwittingly disclosed; they hit him with fact, supposition, rumor. Finally, after 36 hours of interrogation, Bert cracked. He began to talk and, once started, he couldn't stop.

Yes, he was The Brain. He had rented a box at the Société Générale two years ago; the idea came to him one day out of the blue. Every time he went down into the vault, he thought of it. On several occasions, finding himself alone, he photographed the place.

He went to Town Hall and procured the sewer plans, then spent six nights scouting out the Nice sewers. He needed specialized tools difficult to obtain, and financial backing to buy them, so he went to a Marseille mob with his idea. The mobsters wanted in. Two teams of ten men each were formed: mobsters on the one side, Bert's political friends on the other.

They worked every night for two months digging the tunnel. Most of the men served as porters, lugging in gear, lugging out dirt. Each dawn they blocked up the tunnel entrance lest some sewer worker find it. On Friday evening, July 16, as soon as the bank closed for the weekend, they were set to move in. But the tunnel aperture was partly blocked by a five-ton armored armoire. They put a pneumatic jack against it and began tilting it forward until they could crawl over the top. Once inside, they welded shut the vault and calked all the ventilator grills so no light or smoke could escape. Then they started to cut open the safes and lockboxes—with Bert handling one of the torches himself.

At 5 a.m. Monday morning, as they were leaving, someone

wanted to scrawl, "Thank you, Mr. Director" on the wall, but this was considered, Bert told the detectives, too banal. They talked it over, and a different message was chosen.

Who were his political accomplices? detectives demanded. Bert would give no name.

Only about five percent of the loot had been recovered so far, including $120,000 found in a safe in a Brussels bank. Where was Bert's share?

He had donated it all, he claimed, to a right-wing political organization called La Catena. His political friends had done likewise. Perhaps the jury would believe him. The detectives did not. They suspected (and it proved true) that they would find no trace of the existence of this Catena.

Detectives would go on hunting for Bert's other accomplices—as this is written, eleven are behind bars—and for the rest of the loot. In court, Bert repeated his confession. The judge ordered him brought to the bank, where he pointed out details that satisfied both the judge and the detectives that Albert Spaggiari was indeed The Brain.

As Bert was led back across the sidewalk toward the van, still smoking a cigar, the crowd cheered him, and someone called out: "Any regrets, Bert?"

Was he counting on the loot's waiting for him when he got out? Or, was he remembering the words on the wall: "Without Weapons, Without Violence, Without Hate."

He looked pleased with himself. He had had a laugh on the world. He smiled. "I regret nothing."

Anatomy of an Illness

by Norman Cousins

EVER SINCE THE publication of Adam Smith's much-talked about *Powers of Mind* in 1975, people have written to ask whether his account in it of my recovery from a supposedly crippling, incurable disease was accurately reported. I had not written about that incident until 12 years later because I was fearful of creating false hopes in other persons similarly afflicted. However, when my case has surfaced in the public press, I feel justified in providing a fuller picture than was contained in Mr. Smith's account.

In August 1964, I flew home from a trip abroad with a slight fever and a general feeling of achiness, which rapidly deepened. Within a week it became difficult to move my neck, arms, hands, fingers and legs. I was hospitalized when my blood sedimentation rate—the speed with which red blood cells settle in a test tube—hit 80 mm per hour, a sure sign of more than a casual health problem. It later reached 115.

I had a fast-growing conviction that a hospital was no place for a person who was seriously ill. The surprising lack of respect for basic sanitation, the extensive and sometimes promiscuous use of X-ray equipment, the seemingly indiscriminate administration of tranquilizers and painkillers, more for the convenience of the staff in managing patients than for therapeutic needs, and the regularity with which hospital routine takes precedence over the rest requirements of the patient—all these and other practices seemed to me to be critical shortcomings of the modern hospital.

My doctor did not quarrel with my reservations about hospital procedures. Dr. William Hitzig and I had been close friends for more than 20 years; he knew of my own deep interest in medical matters, and he felt comfortable about being candid with me. He reviewed the reports of the specialists he had called in as consultants—there was a consensus that I was suffering from a serious collagen illness, a weakening of the connective tissue. I had considerable difficulty in moving my limbs and even in turning over in bed. Nodules appeared on my body, gravel-like substances under the skin, indicating the systemic nature of the disease. At the low point of my illness, my jaws were almost locked.

I asked Dr. Hitzig about my chances for full recovery. He leveled with me, admitting that one of the specialists had told him I had one chance in 500. Up to that time, I had been disposed to let the doctors worry about my condition. But it now seemed clear that if I was to be that "one case in 500" I had better be something more than a passive observer.

I asked Dr. Hitzig about the possible cause of my condition. He said that it could have come from any one of a number of causes—for example, from heavy-metal poisoning, or as a result of a streptococcal infection.

I thought hard about the sequence of events immediately preceding the illness. I had gone to the Soviet Union in July 1964, as co-chairman of an American delegation to consider the problems of cultural exchange. In Moscow, our hotel room was on the second floor. Each night a procession of diesel trucks plied back and forth. It was summer, and my windows were wide open. I slept uneasily each night and felt somewhat nauseated on arising. Could the exposure to the hydrocarbons from the diesel exhaust have anything to do with the illness? Moreover, as I thought back on the psychological and physical stresses of my experience abroad, I found myself increasingly convinced that I had had a case of adrenal exhaustion, which lowered my resistance.

From my reading, I knew that the full functioning of my endocrine system—in particular, the adrenal glands—was essential for combating any illness. In his classic book, *The Stress of Life*, Hans Selye shows that adrenal exhaustion can be caused by emotional tension; he details the negative effects of the negative emotions on body chemistry. The inevitable question arose in my mind: If negative emotions produce negative chemical changes in the body, wouldn't positive emotions produce positive chemical changes? Is it possible that love, hope, laughter and the will to live have therapeutic value?

Obviously, putting the positive emotions to work is nothing so simple as turning on a garden hose. But even a reasonable degree of control over my emotions might have a salutary physiologic effect.

A plan began to form in my mind for systematic pursuit of the salutary emotions, and I knew that I would want to discuss it with my doctor. But first I wanted to find out more about my medication. The hospital had been giving me maximum dosages of anti-inflammatory drugs: 26 aspirin tablets a day, and 3 phenylbutazone tablets four times a day. If that medication was toxic to any degree, it was doubtful whether my plan would work. So, with Dr. Hitzig's support, we took tests—and discovered that I was hypersensitive to virtually all my medication. No wonder I had hives all over my body.

When I looked into research in the medical journals, I found that aspirin is quite powerful and warrants considerable care in its use. The medical press reported that the chemical composition of aspirin impairs platelet function. Did the relation between platelets and collagen mean that aspirin, so universally accepted for so many years, was actually harmful in the treatment of collagen illnesses? The history of medicine is replete with instances involving drugs and modes of treatment that were in use for many years before it was recognized that they did more harm than good. Living in the second half of the 20th century confers no automatic protection against unwise drugs and methods.

Suppose I stopped taking aspirin and phenylbutazone? What about the pain? The bones in my spine and practically every joint in my body already felt as though I had been run over by a truck. Yet I knew that pain could be affected by one's attitude.

I could stand pain so long as progress was being made in restoring my body's capacity to halt the continuing breakdown of connective tissue.

But if we dispensed with the aspirin, how would we combat the severe inflammation? I recalled having read in medical journals about the usefulness of ascorbic acid—vitamin C—in combating a wide number of illnesses. Was it possible that it could also combat inflammation by "feeding" the adrenal glands? I had also read in the medical press that vitamin C helps to oxygenate the blood. If inadequate oxygenation was a factor in collagen breakdown, couldn't this circumstance be another argument for ascorbic acid? Also, according to some medical reports, people suffering from collagen diseases are deficient in vitamin C. Did this lack mean that the body uses up large amounts of vitamin C in the process of combating collagen breakdown?

Dr. Hitzig listened carefully to my speculations concerning the cause of the illness, as well as my layman's ideas for a course of action. He said that what was most important was that I continue to believe in everything I had said. He shared my sense of excitement about the possibilities of my recovery and liked the idea of a partnership.

A systematic program for the full exercise of the affirmative emotions as a factor in enhancing body chemistry was indicated. It was easy enough to hope and love and have faith, but what about laughter? Nothing is less funny than being flat on your back with all the bones in your spine and joints hurting. A good place to begin, I thought, was with amusing movies. Allen Funt, producer of the spoofing television program "Candid Camera," sent films of some of his "CC" classics, along with a projector. The nurse was instructed in its use.

It worked. I made the joyous discovery that ten minutes of genuine belly laughter had an anesthetic effect and would give me at least two hours of pain-free sleep.

If laughter did in fact have a salutary effect on the body's chemistry, it seemed at least theoretically likely that it would enhance the system's ability to fight the inflammation. So we took sedimentation-rate readings just before, as well as several hours after, the laughter episodes. Each time, there was a drop of at least five points. I was greatly elated by the discovery that there is a physiologic basis for the ancient theory that laughter is good medicine.

Next, arrangements were made for me to move my act to a hotel room—which, happily, would cost about one-third as much as the hospital. The other benefits were incalculable. I would not be awakened for a bed bath or meals or medication or a change in the bed sheets. The sense of serenity was delicious and would, I felt certain, contribute to a general improvement.

What about ascorbic acid and its place in the general program for recovery? I wondered whether a better procedure than the injection series we had planned would be to administer the ascorbic acid through slow intravenous drip over a period of three or four hours. In this way we could go far beyond the usual 3-g injection. My hope was to start at 10 g and then increase the dose daily until we reached 25 g.

Dr. Hitzig's eyes widened when I mentioned 25 g. He cautioned me about the possible effect on the kidneys, and on the veins in the arms with such a massive infusion. However, it seemed to me we were playing for bigger stakes: losing some veins was not important alongside the need to combat whatever was eating at my connective tissue.

To know whether we were on the right track, we took a sedimentation test before the first intravenous administration of 10 g of ascorbic acid. Four hours later, we took another sedimentation test. There was a drop of nine full points.

Seldom had I known such elation. The ascorbic acid was working. So was laughter. The combination was cutting heavily into whatever poison was attacking the connective tissue. The fever was receding, and my pulse was no longer racing.

We stepped up the dosage gradually, until at the end of a week we had reached 25 g. Meanwhile, I was completely off drugs and sleeping pills. Sleep—natural sleep without pain—was becoming increasingly prolonged.

At the end of the eighth day I was able to move my thumbs without pain. By this time, the sedimentation rate was somewhere in the 80s and dropping fast. It seemed to me that the gravel-like nodules on my neck and the backs of my hands were beginning to shrink. There was no doubt in my mind that I was going to make it back *all* the way.

Two weeks later, my wife took me to Puerto Rico for some sustained sunshine. Friends helped support me in the breaking surf. Within a week I was able to jog—at least for a minute or two. The connective tissue in my spine and joints was regenerating. I could function, and the feeling was indescribably beautiful.

I must not make it seem that all my infirmities disappeared overnight. For many months I couldn't get my arms up far enough to reach for a book on a high shelf. My fingers weren't agile enough to do what I wanted them to do on the organ keyboard. My neck had a limited turning radius. My knees were somewhat wobbly and, off and on, I had to wear a metal brace. But I was back at my job as editor of *Saturday Review* full time again, and this was miracle enough for me.

Is the recovery a total one? Year by year the mobility has improved. I am now pain free and have been able to discard the metal knee braces. I can ride a horse flat out and hold a camera with a steady hand.

What conclusions do I draw from the entire experience?

The first is that the will to live is not a theoretical abstraction, but a physiologic reality with therapeutic characteristics. The second is that I was fortunate to have as my doctor a man who knew that his biggest job was to encourage to the fullest the patient's will to live. Dr. Hitzig was willing to set aside the large and often hazardous armamentarium of powerful drugs available to the modern physician when he became convinced that his patient might have something better to offer. He was wise enough to know that the art of healing is still a frontier profession.

Something else I have learned: Never underestimate the capacity of the human mind and body to regenerate—even when the prospects seem most wretched. The life-force may be the least-understood force on earth. William James said that human beings tend to live too far within self-imposed limits. It is possible that those limits will recede when we respect more fully the natural drive of the human mind and body toward perfectibility and regeneration. Protecting and cherishing that natural drive may well represent the finest exercise of human freedom.

The Rugged Road
to Independence

by Thomas Fleming

THOMAS JEFFERSON AWOKE as usual with the first faint streaks
of dawn. From his second-floor rented rooms, above Seventh
and Market Streets, the tall, redheaded Virginian looked out
over the city of Philadelphia with foreboding. Today, July 1,
1776, he would find out if for the last three weeks he had
wasted his time in the writing and rewriting of a document he
had titled: "A Declaration by the Representatives of the United
States of America, in General Congress assembled."

Doubting the future of the Declaration of Independence seems
almost laughable now. With comfortable hindsight we ask:
Could there really have been any question? The fact is that
history as men experience it is totally different from the way
those who follow them relive it.

Again and again, America has found itself racked by agonizing decision-making. It is so racked today. Thus it may help
to realize that there was the same kind of agonizing over the
decision that created our nation. Standing at his window that

139

July 1, the 33-year-old Jefferson could not be sure that his Declaration was even going to be read, much less ultimately immortalized. The Continental Congress had first to decide whether the very idea of independence was acceptable; only then could the members worry about how to phrase it.

Down at the City Tavern, 26-year-old Edward Rutledge, of South Carolina, was also awakening. His thoughts and feelings were dominated by an inflexible detestation of a declaration of independence. On June 7, when one of Jefferson's fellow Virginians, Richard Henry Lee, had introduced a resolution declaring that "these united colonies are, and of right ought to be, free and independent states," Rutledge had leaped to his feet to heap scorn on the idea. It was, he shrilled, "a blind, precipitous measure." It would accomplish only two things, both bad. It would reveal America's intentions to the enemy, and it would make the unborn nation look "ridiculous in the eyes of foreign powers."

In a manor house five miles outside Philadelphia, an even more powerful foe of independence was arising—43-year-old John Dickinson, political leader of Pennsylvania. A year before, almost single-handed, Dickinson had beaten back a surge toward independence, persuading the Congress to present instead a petition to George III, begging His Majesty to redress America's grievances. Although the king had callously rejected the petition, Dickinson believed that to make a declaration now would be like "destroying a house before we have got another, in winter, with a small family."

Thus Dickinson had joined Rutledge in vehemently opposing the June 7 resolution. After three days of wrangling, the Congress had compromised. It ordered Jefferson to begin drafting a declaration—but there would be no vote on independence until July 1. By then, perhaps, opinions might be closer to unanimity.

Both sides were acutely aware that near-unanimity was called for. John Dickinson had already threatened John Adams, of Massachusetts, one of the most outspoken independence men, with a weapon that could make a mockery of the whole idea of independence. "Concur with us," Dickinson had snapped, "or we'll break off from New England." If powerful Pennsylvania made such a decision, New York, New Jersey, Maryland and Delaware might follow suit. Thus, instead of uniting the colonies, independence might well destroy them.

These and other gloomy thoughts were in the minds of Thomas Jefferson and his fellow delegates as they made their way down dusty Chestnut Street to the handsome red-brick Pennsylvania State House, where Congress was sitting. There, as the tower clock struck nine, tall, elegant, John Hancock strode to the President's chair and gaveled the Congress into session. (Jefferson, with his scientist's curiosity, noted that the temperature stood at 81.5 degrees.)

First came reports from American armies in the field. None of them was likely to inspire a waverer to vote for independence. In the North, the once-proud army that had invaded Canada was in headlong retreat, ridden by disease and dissension. In New York, Commander in Chief George Washington's army of 19,000 was desperately short of ammunition—and a huge British fleet had been sighted off Sandy Hook. In the South, a British army supported by a naval squadron was battering at Charleston. British forces attacking from three directions—and some men of Congress wanted a vote for independence!

By noon the tension in the room was almost unbearable, and the Congressmen gratefully escaped into the State House yard for an hour's recess. On their return, they resolved into "a committee of the whole," under the chairmanship of Virginia's Benjamin Harrison, so that everything said or voted would be unofficial. The purpose was to encourage every man to speak his mind.

Instantly, John Dickinson was on his feet. What was there to gain from declaring independence, he asked. Would it add a single man to the cause? Would it impress the nations of Europe? Or would it make them think that the Americans were blustering windbags, proclaiming as a fact something they had yet to prove against the British armies?

Outside, nature added to the drama of Dickinson's powerful speech. Huge clouds had formed above the city. Now thunder crashed, and lightning streaked the sky. Candles were lighted against the room's sudden gloom.

Dickinson spoke on. A declaration of independence was a declaration of all-out war. Did the members know what that meant? "The burning of our towns. The setting loose of the Indians." War against the richest, most powerful empire in the world. Could America depend on her own people to stand firm in a war "rendered more cruel" by this declaration? "In bitterness of soul, would they not complain against it as madness, rashness?"

In the momentary stillness that followed these ringing words, rain could be heard lashing against the windows. John Dickinson sat down. All eyes in the silent room turned to the stumpy, 41-year-old delegate from Massachusetts, John Adams. Only he could answer Dickinson.

Wearily, Adams rose to his feet. For months he had been living on four hours' sleep a night, serving on more committees than anyone else in Congress, writing endless letters and reports, battling each day on the floor for independence. For a moment he wondered if he could go through with another repetition of "what had been repeated and hackneyed a hundred times, for six months past." But the moment he began, the immense importance of the subject gripped him again, and weariness vanished from his voice. In the pounding, vehement style that had made him one of the dominant voices in Congress, he gave the greatest speech of his career. Of that speech, Thomas Jefferson would later say that it had "a power of thought and expression that moved us from our seats."

How many times, Adams asked, did Americans have to see their humble petitions scorned, before they realized that George III was an enemy? With armies invading from three directions, who could still be deluded by rumors of reconciliation? The hour had come, said Adams, for the people of America to decide whether to submit as slaves or to fight as free men. At Lexington and Bunker Hill, George III had destroyed the loyalty of most Americans forever. A declaration would tell this to the world, win friends, perhaps allies. More important, it would rally thousands of men and women who were temporizing. As for himself, Adams cried, "All that I have, all that I am, and all that I hope for in this life, I am now ready to stake on this resolution. Live or die, survive or perish, I am for the Declaration."

Benjamin Harrison called for a vote. Around the room the ayes and nays went. The results were grim: only nine colonies were in favor of a declaration. Pennsylvania and South Carolina had followed their leaders into opposition. Delaware had split, one to one, thereby canceling its vote. New York had abstained. Four delegations, almost a third of the 13, not voting for independence! Quickly, Edward Rutledge moved that an official vote be postponed until the following day.

A night of frantic negotiation and desperate action began. Thomas McKean, of Delaware, hired an express rider with the fastest horse in Philadelphia to cover the 80 miles to Dover. There he was to find Caesar Rodney, a pro-independence delegate who had gone home on business. If he could be got back to Philadelphia in time, he would swing Delaware's vote.

At the City Tavern, Edward Rutledge debated far into the night with his fellow Carolinians. He was still against a declaration of independence. But he was statesman enough to see that a split of even one colony could be a first step toward disunion and disaster.

New Yorkers, conferring with pro-independence men, admitted that they were in favor of a declaration. But they were under specific instructions from home *not* to vote for independence. They would continue to abstain.

This left Pennsylvania. For sleepless hours, John Dickinson struggled with his conscience. One of his chief Pennsylvania supporters, Robert Morris, had urged him to submit to the will of the majority. But Dickinson, Quaker-bred, could not vote war's suffering on this people, whatever the majority willed. He sent word to Robert Morris that he was staying home from Congress on July 2, and that perhaps Morris should do the same thing. This meant that Pennsylvania's delegation would be reduced to five. Two were for independence, two opposed; one, John Morton, was undecided.

July 2 dawned rainy and cooler. Through the muddy streets the delegates clumped to the familiar chamber. The absence of Dickinson and Morris was instantly noted. But the independence men grimly noted another absence: Caesar Rodney's. Had the messenger failed in his mission? All morning and into the afternoon, President John Hancock delayed the vote with other business. Finally, further delay was impossible.

Name by name, Secretary Charles Thomson called the roll of the delegates. The nine yeas of the previous day caused no suspense. New York politely declared its abstention. Pennsylvania's vote split two-two until John Morton rose, weak from the disease that was to kill him a few months later.

Morton shared John Dickinson's dread of the impending war. Only a month earlier, he had said: "The contest is horrid. Parents against children, children against parents." But now he voted, in a voice tight with anguish, for independence. John Adams had convinced him.

And Delaware? Outside, Thomas McKean had spent most of the day straining eyes and ears for sight or sound of a horseman. As the vote rolled away inside, McKean at last saw what he was praying for. Covered with mud after an all-night ride, Caesar Rodney slid off his horse. Minutes later, he arose in the meeting room to declare, "The voice of my people at home is for independence. I concur."

Now it was South Carolina's turn, and the independence men sighed approval when Edward Rutledge announced that his state was joining their ranks.

In a voice that trembled with suppressed excitement, President John Hancock read the result: for independence—12; against—none. The great decision had been made.

Everyone present in Congress that day, July 2, assumed that thenceforth it would be known as Independence Day. "I believe that it will be celebrated by succeeding generations as the great anniversary festival," John Adams wrote to his wife, Abigail. But he and the others did not reckon with the power of the written word. Little of John Adams' magnificent speech was recorded. Congress, after debating various deletions and additions to Jefferson's Declaration of Independence, voted approval of the edited document on the evening of July 4. And thus Jefferson's brilliant prose has been indissolubly linked in American minds with independence.

Yet some of sturdy John Adams' praise of independence deserves to be remembered by Americans forever. "I am well aware of the toil and blood and treasure that it will cost us to maintain this declaration," he wrote to his wife. "Yet through all the gloom I can see the rays of ravishing light and glory. I can see that the end is more than worth all the means; and that posterity will triumph in that day's transactions, even though we should rue it, which I trust in God we shall not."

The Princess
and the Kidnapper

by Peter Browne

JUST AFTER 7:30 P.M. on Wednesday, March 20, 1974, Princess
Anne of Great Britain and her husband, Capt. Mark Phillips,
emerged from a charity film show in London and settled in the
back of their maroon limousine waiting near St. Paul's Cathedral. As the limousine slid away, no one really noticed a white
Ford Escort edge out from a nearby curb to follow.

At the wheel of the rented Ford was a gaunt 26-year-old
man, Peter Sydney Ball—or Ian Ball, as he called himself.
He was brooding—about the details of the crime he had been
meticulously planning for three years. The previous December,
Ball had flown to Spain and obtained two revolvers from a
Madrid shop: a five-shot .38 and an 11-shot .22. Smuggled
into Britain, the guns, now loaded, were stowed in his car,
along with four sets of handcuffs—two of them linked to form
leg shackles. And tucked inside his jacket was a typed letter
addressed to Queen Elizabeth. Ian Ball intended to kidnap the

Queen's only daughter and hold her for £3 million (some $7 million) ransom.

Inside the limousine, the Princess and her husband chatted with lady-in-waiting Rowena Brassey. Like other royal cars, NGN 1 had neither bulletproof windows nor emergency radio. Such things were considered unsightly; besides, the Queen disliked security fuss.

NGN 1 went through Admiralty Arch into The Mall, the broad processional route that runs along St. James's Park to Buckingham Palace. Beside the chauffeur sat Inspector James Beaton, 31, Princess Anne's appointed "personal police officer." In the holster beneath his suit jacket was a Walther PP Automatic—Princess Anne's sole protection.

It was unlikely that Ian Ball had considered kidnapping the Princess in the heart of London. His plan was to wait for a suitable moment in the Surrey countryside, near her home at the Royal Military Academy of Sandhurst, where her husband is a staff instructor. Ball had been shadowing her every movement for seven days, awaiting his opportunity.

But something had gone amiss. That Wednesday morning, parked near the rear gate of the Royal Military Academy, his white car had caught the eye of a police officer who was investigating a local burglary. When questioned, Ball produced a license in the name of John Williams, an alias. His car was searched. Since nothing was found, there was no reason to detain him.

Badly shaken by the experience, Ball realized that he could not delay much longer. By telephoning the press office at Buckingham Palace, he had learned that Princess Anne would be going to Germany in five days. Racked with indecision, he followed the Princess to London that evening, drawn as by a magnet to any chance of watching her.

As he drove along The Mall behind the royal car and saw Buckingham Palace looming some 500 yards ahead, he realized that within 30 seconds Princess Anne would once more be out of reach. Already it was dusk, with pools of heavy shadow between the Victorian lamps lining The Mall. Suddenly, his sick mind seething with frustration, he cast aside all caution. He could wait no longer.

Ball accelerated and swept past the royal limousine, then

slewed his Ford across in front. Stopping dead, he forced the chauffeur of the royal car to brake hard to avoid a collision.

When the Princess's bodyguard, James Beaton, saw what he took to be an irate motorist leave the Ford and hurry back toward the chauffeur, he got out and started around the back of the limousine to see what was wrong. Ball reached the right front window, in his hand a .38 revolver. "Switch off the ignition," he ordered the chauffeur. Then he went to the rear window and said to Princess Anne: "Come with me. I only want you for two days."

The hideout was ready: a house five miles from Anne's home at Sandhurst. Ball, giving his name as Jason Van der Sluis, had signed a six-month lease on the house, commenting that he looked forward to moving in shortly with his wife. He had equipped it for the Princess with brand-new bedding, towels, alarm clock, even a toothbrush—all bought at stores like Woolworth's to make the purchases untraceable. There was enough food for two people for a week.

On a rented Olivetti typewriter he composed his ransom letter to the Queen: "Your daughter has been kidnapped. A ransom of £3 million ($7 million) is to be paid in £5 notes. They are to be used, unmarked, not sprayed with any chemical substance, unconsecutively numbered." Describing how the ransom money, in unlocked suitcases, was to be loaded into a plane which would later fly to Zurich, Ball instructed: "A police car is to meet Anne and myself at the roundabout just before entering the tunnel into London Heathrow airport, at 7 a.m. It is to escort our car to the aircraft."

Ball pledged that once he was safely in Zurich, and assured of immunity from the Swiss police, Princess Anne would be released. But he demanded documents guaranteeing a free pardon covering the kidnapping and crimes connected with it—including "the murder of any police officers."

Rounding the rear of the royal car, bodyguard Beaton came face to face with a tall, thin figure leveling a revolver at him. Ball fired twice. One bullet scuffed Beaton's jacket; the other smashed into his shoulder and pierced a lung. Beaton realized he had been hit only when, drawing his gun, he felt the strength drain from his arm. His first shot missed Ball. He tried again, using both hands to steady the Walther. The gun jammed.

As Beaton stepped back, working to clear the Walther, chauffeur Alec Callender came up behind Ball and tried to grab his revolver. "I'll shoot you," said Ball, and fired at point-blank range. The chauffeur reeled back into the driver's seat, a bullet in his chest.

Meanwhile, lady-in-waiting Rowena Brassey was scrambling out the left rear door to make room for Princess Anne to escape. But Ball had caught the Princess by the forearm, commanding, "Please get out." To the bodyguard, now on the far side of the car, he shouted, "Drop that gun, or I'll shoot her!"

Beaton had no choice. He put his jammed automatic on the ground.

A bizarre tug-of-war developed, Ian Ball pulling at the Princess with one hand while her husband, Mark Phillips, held her round the waist and leaned across her trying to shut the door. Beaton had climbed into the car, intending to place himself between Anne and her would-be-kidnapper. To distract Ball, the Princess coolly asked him why he wanted to take her, and was told: "I'll get a couple of million."

As Beaton edged forward, Mark Phillips managed to close the door. "Open it," Ball shouted, "or I'll shoot!"

Beaton put his hand up directly in front of the muzzle. The bullet shattered the window and lodged in his palm. Twice wounded, he kicked the door open, hoping to knock Ball off balance. But the ruse failed. And now, for the third time, Ball shot James Beaton—this time in the stomach. Stumbling out, through yellow roses scattered from Princess Anne's bouquet, the inspector collapsed on the pavement.

Perhaps 90 seconds had passed since Ian Ball had swung his Ford in front of the royal limousine. Passersby were gawking, and a tangle of horn-blowing traffic was building up along The Mall. From 100 yards away, Police Constable Michael Hills heard what sounded like an engine backfiring. He saw a knot of cars. As he got closer, he recognized the big maroon limousine and radioed Cannon Row police station that a royal car seemed to have been in an accident. Dodging the traffic, Hills crossed the road. He saw that the limousine's right rear window was shattered, and a man was leaning inside. Someone shouted to Hills, "Get away, you bloody fool. He's got a gun." But the constable stepped forward, gripped the gunman's elbow, and said, "What's going on?" Ball spun around and shot him in the stomach.

Ball had emptied the .38. It was a .22 bullet that clipped the policeman's whistle chain, plowed through a pocket diary, and settled just outside his liver. To Hills, it felt like a hard punch. Ducking behind the royal car, he radioed to Cannon Row: "I have been shot. Royal car is involved. There is a man with a gun. Urgent assistance is required."

At 19, Ian Ball had begun to question his own behavior. Fearing persecution, suicidal, hearing "voices," he sought psychiatric help, and became one of the 150,000 people in Britain diagnosed as schizophrenic. But he refused full-time day help. He drifted through a succession of menial jobs, turned to petty crime and soon had a record. He dreamed of the perfect crime that would make him a millionaire playboy and a success with women.

As his illness took hold, he became more secretive. In September 1972, he was certified sick, suffering from nervous debility and psychiatric depression, and he abandoned his last job to draw £12 (about $30) a week social-security benefit. Living alone in a furnished room in Bayswater, rarely going out, never speaking to anyone, he began to plot the kidnapping.

In The Mall, Glanmore Martin, chauffeur of a privately owned Jaguar, backed his car against the Ford's front bumper to block any escape. Courageously he approached Ian Ball, who stuck a gun in his ribs and snapped, "Clear off!" As Martin turned, he saw the dazed Constable Hills, who had picked up the bodyguard's jammed automatic, intending to shoot Ball. As Hills swayed, trying to steady his aim, Martin led him to the sidewalk, where he collapsed.

Another passerby, journalist Brian McConnell, leaped from a taxi to challenge Ball. Ball swung around and warned, "Keep out of this." McConnell took two steps forward, and was shot in the chest.

A third unarmed member of the public, Ronald Russell, a burly six-foot businessman, now left his car and dashed across The Mall. The kidnapper was hammering at the limousine's door with the butt of his gun. Russell punched him on the side of the head. Ball fired at him and missed. Russell ran to the other side of the car, where the Jaguar chauffeur was tending wounded Constable Hills. "Give me his truncheon," said Russell. Two more shots sounded and, without waiting for the truncheon, Russell doubled back to find that Ball had forced the door and was again trying to pull Princess Anne from the car. With his gun pointed at the Princess, Ball said: "Come on, Anne. You know you've got to come."

"Why don't you go away?" said the Princess, calmly. "What good is all this going to do?"

Like a child given an unexpected scolding, Ball stared at her, momentarily irresolute. Princess Anne seized her chance. She broke free from his grip, moved over and began to climb out the other side of the car. But then, as Ball came round the front of the car, Mark Phillips promptly pulled his wife back. The burly Russell, standing in front of her as a shield, met the oncoming Ball, punched him, and then again—delivering the last blow with such force that he lost his balance and fell headlong.

As he picked himself up, he heard the sirens and approaching police cars. Ball turned and ran.

Jumping out of a police car, trainee detective Peter Edmonds heard Princess Anne call, "Get him!" He spotted Ball, gun in hand, running. He gave chase, and brought him down with a flying tackle. A moment later, five other policemen threw themselves on Ian Ball, one knocking the revolver—which still held five cartridges—from his hand.

It was just seven minutes since the kidnap attempt had begun.

A woman from one of the stalled cars walked over to the royal limousine and saw that Mark Phillips still had a protective arm around his wife. "Are you all right, love?" the woman asked. The royal couple looked up and smiled at her. "Yes, thank you," said Princess Anne. "I'm fine."

On May 22, Ian Ball pleaded guilty to two charges of attempted murder, two of wounding, and one of "attempting to steal and carry away Her Royal Highness, Princess Anne." The trial was brief. A Home Office psychiatrist testified that Ball was suffering from a severe personality disorder, and Lord Chief Justice Widgery ordered that he be detained "without limit of time," and he was placed in a top-security hospital.

In November, the Queen held an investiture at Buckingham Palace. James Beaton was awarded the George Cross, Britain's highest honor for peacetime gallantry. The George Medal went to Ronald Russell and Michael Hills. The Queen's Gallantry

Medal was presented to Alec Callender, Peter Edmonds and Brian McConnell. Glanmore Martin received the Queen's Commendation for Brave Conduct.

In those violent seven minutes in The Mall, Ian Ball brought about something no one else had been able to achieve. Since then, there has been a considerable tightening of royal security. As he told detectives: "There's one good thing coming out of this—you'll have to improve Princess Anne's protection." In that, at least, he was right.

The Real Robinson Crusoe

by Leland Stowe

THE ISLAND, 13 miles long, juts up from the southern Pacific's heavy swell like a defiant fortress, some 400 miles off Chile. For an hour our small fishing craft bobbed along beneath the surf-pounded, naked cliffs thrusting 500 to 1000 feet straight up from the sea. Then, as we rounded a colossal promontory, a wide and verdant valley stretched before us.

"Look!" my companion exclaimed. "There is the cave of the real Robinson Crusoe."

At the base of an immense ledge, about 100 yards back from the shore, was a shadowy aperture scarcely ten feet high. Here Alexander Selkirk, a 28-year-old Scottish seaman, first found refuge after being abandoned in 1704 following a mutinous protest against his ship's unseaworthy condition. For four years and four months he remained a solitary castaway on this remote, uninhabited island. Later, after his rescue, his "strange, surprising adventures" inspired Daniel Defoe's classic novel, *Robinson Crusoe*.

To explore this island had been my dream for 30 years. Now I could clearly visualize Selkirk when, wading up to his armpits, he implored his ship's enraged and taunting captain not to leave him behind on this forlorn and rocky shore. All in vain.

Overwhelmed by despair, Selkirk took stock of his pitifully few possessions: a firelock with powder and bullets; a hatchet, knife and kettle; a small sea chest containing clothes, tobacco, some nautical instruments and a Bible. He was left no food of any kind. (For his fictional character, Defoe cannily provided a wrecked ship from which Crusoe salvaged a wealth of supplies, including seven muskets, barrels of powder and bullets, sugar, rum, a hogshead of bread, bags of nails—even a grindstone and a carpenter's chest.)

Selkirk first took shelter in the shallow cave. But soon his nights were shattered by the terrifying roars of hundreds of sea lions engaged in mating-season battles on the shore. To get away from their fearful bedlam, he scaled the heights above Cumberland Bay, painfully back-packing his sea chest.

Our boat was spearing toward this bay when we spied, halfway up an 800-foot cliff, a white goat maneuvering incredibly along a splinter-size shelf; then, higher still, another. No doubt their ancestors had provided Selkirk with vital sustenance.* As we churned into the broad bay, we saw a mammoth horseshoe of ranges and craggy peaks surrounding a wild amphitheater, which was cleft by two valleys that twisted and tumbled downward onto a narrow beach. Here basks the fishing village of San Juan Bautista, a neat half-mile row of pastel-hued wooden cottages facing a shorefront dotted by boats. Erase these foreground signs of man's existence and you behold Selkirk's exile refuge in all its solitary grandeur.

Establishing his abode on one of these middle slopes, for months Selkirk scanned the ocean daily, watching for sails that never came. As with the fictional Crusoe, desolation engulfed him. He saw "nothing but death" in prospect, and deeply repented his youthful sins—including the street brawls for which he had been publicly rebuked in the church of his native Largo,

---

*After discovering the island in the latter half of the 16th century, mariner Juan Fernández tried to start a colony. It was a short-lived venture, but the goats left behind multiplied, and became a godsend to ships that occasionally put in there for provisioning and repairs.

in Fife. Now Selkirk read the Scriptures and prayed nightly; and, wandering the hills, he sang psalms remembered from boyhood.

Bit by bit, his devotions banished melancholy. He found a burgeoning delight in the splendors about him, and an increasing solace in solitude. With faith rekindled, he constructed two huts from durable pimiento saplings (one for a dwelling, one for a kitchen), placing them where they could be reached only by scrambling over rocks. In the book, Crusoe feared cannibals; what Selkirk feared was detection by hostile Spaniards. (Spain was then waging war with England.)

At first Selkirk was pestered by rats which gnawed his feet and clothing while he was asleep. They had proliferated enormously after coming ashore from ships. Fortunately, cats—liberated by sailors—had done the same, so Selkirk had a solution at hand. As his rescuer, Capt. Woodes Rogers, relates, he "cherished the cats with goats' flesh," making them so tame that they clustered about his huts in hundreds, and soon delivered him from the rats. Delighted by their companionship, he amused himself by teaching the cleverest kittens to dance.

Meanwhile, Selkirk's chief diet consisted of the meat of goats, which he easily shot—just as Crusoe did. Turtles and fish did not agree with him, but he enjoyed the clawless lobsters whose abundance provides the island's present inhabitants with a main source of livelihood. Palm cabbages proved a substitute for bread, and he discovered turnips, radishes and parsnips, planted by privateers decades earlier. Tamed nannies provided him with milk. When his constant forays rapidly tore his limited clothing to shreds, he perforated dried goatskins with a nail, cut strips of thong for thread, and thus fashioned crude breeches, a jacket and a cap.

Selkirk's few ounces of powder were swiftly depleted, but he became a steel-muscled cliff scrambler of amazing agility by running down the goats—barefoot. More than 500 of them, eventually! Captain Rogers records that, later, Selkirk captured several goats daily for his rescuers' barbecues—and far outsped the ship's bulldog. Once, upon seizing a whiskered quarry at a bush-hidden cliff's edge, he plunged with the goat down the cliff and lay unconscious for 24 hours. Despite agonizing injuries, he crawled to his hut. Thanks to an early precaution against possible illness—he had domesticated some goats for an ever-ready food supply—within ten days he recovered.

(*Defoe* had his Crusoe imitate this foresight.)

During the years until Captain Rogers's arrival, only two ships—Spanish frigates—stopped at the island. They came together, and from their crews Selkirk had a hair-breadth escape. He incautiously revealed himself before he was certain of their identity, and the Spaniards shot at the goatskinned hermit, then hotly pursued him. Being far fleeter, Selkirk eluded them, clambered up a heavily-leafed tree—and clung there quaking while his pursuers paused directly beneath him.

What has come to be called "Selkirk's Lookout" is on a lofty saddle between two peaks. It is a gasping two-hour ascent—up steep, rain-gashed gullies, then zigzag through semi-tropical jungles.

Finally, you emerge upon a completely unobstructed hump—the Lookout! To the north, west and southeast the Pacific stretches to far horizons. Here, month after month, the island's prisoner watched for the sails of salvation. But the few ships he sighted furrowed undeviatingly past, ignoring or not noticing his signal fires.

So the years dragged on until, on the afternoon of February 1, 1709, Alexander Selkirk spied two sails thrusting straight toward the bay. Racing down to the shore, he kindled a fire in mad haste. All night he waited. Fearing a trap, the privateers *Duke* and *Duchess* stood at sea until noon, when Captain Rogers dispatched a boat to reconnoiter. Its eight well-armed sailors were dumfounded by the spectacle of a bearded apparition clad in hairy goatskins "and looking wilder than their first owners."

When they brought Selkirk aboard the *Duke,* Rogers found that the castaway "had so much forgot his Language for want of Use, that we could scarce understand him, for he seem'd to speak his words by halves." While the crews spent ten days provisioning the vessels and repairing sails, Selkirk astounded his rescuer with the story of his survival, which was promptly recorded in the captain's log. Rogers appointed Selkirk his second mate—likely the first barefoot mate he ever had. The exile's feet were so calloused that for weeks he could not tolerate shoes.

Soon the *Duke* and *Duchess* set sail northward, marauding. Selkirk was named master of the second Spanish vessel they captured. For 11 more months, Rogers's buccaneers looted ships from Chile to Mexico, amassing booty later valued at £800,000. Then they sailed west, circling the globe on their way home. At last, in mid-October 1711, Selkirk disembarked near London—not as a penniless nomad but in rare affluence, having earned a modest fortune in prize money.

Reaching his hometown, Largo, on a Sabbath morning, Selkirk went straight to the church. The appearance of a stranger in gold-laced finery provoked stares from all sides. For several minutes not even his parents and brothers recognized him. Then suddenly his mother jumped up, crying his name, and rushed into the arms of the son long given up for dead.

But the need for solitude was now embedded in Selkirk's character. He fished alone along the firth, or roamed secluded woodlands, sometimes bursting out with the lament, "Oh, my beloved island! I wish I had never left thee!"

One day he eloped with a neighbor girl, Sophia Bruce, to London. But she could not quell his restless spirit for long. Within two years he joined the Royal Navy. While serving as first mate aboard H.M.S. *Weymouth* a few years later, he died off the coast of Africa, aged 45.

During his London sojourn, two published accounts of his solitary island exile made Alexander Selkirk a celebrated figure. The first, by Captain Rogers in 1712, created a sensation. And the following year, Sir Richard Steele published an essay, after lengthy talks with Selkirk.

Six years later, in 1719, Defoe's *Robinson Crusoe* appeared. It immediately became a best-seller. English readers found striking parallels between Selkirk's adventures and those of Defoe's hero. While Crusoe's island was described as near the mouth of "the Great River of Oroonoque [Orinoco]," off the north coast of South America, no such island exists, and it seems clear that Defoe simply placed his island where it would be beyond identification.

Today Selkirk's isle is popularly known as Robinson Crusoe Island. (Its official name is Juan Fernandez.) The island is reachable by a regular air line service from Santiago, Chile. Although there are very few inhabitants, the island is a popular tourist resort. Crusoe devotees roam the Castaway's haunts—which will never again know the absolute solitude he came to cherish.

When the *Eagle* Landed

by Ronald Schiller

On July 20, 1979, three middle-aged men—a university professor, a museum administrator and an engineering consultant—held a reunion in Washington, D.C. Reporters, scientists, diplomats, the President of the United States, Congressional leaders and 50,000 spectators shared in the tenth-anniversary celebration of one of the most destiny-laden moments in human history: the day man landed on the moon.

Since then, other voyages have been made to the moon, and brilliantly successful unmanned probes have been launched into deep space. Yet no space venture has had the emotional wallop of that initial lunar touchdown over a decade ago. Do you remember how it was, that historic week, when man first touched the moon with a silver finger—and felt the heartbeat of his own world?

THE MEN who made the epic voyage seemed, in many ways, ordinary men—unlikely candidates for immortality. Neil Armstrong, Edwin "Buzz" Aldrin and Michael Collins all were men in their late thirties. They were, and still are, introspective men who cherish their privacy. But they possessed qualities NASA was looking for: exceptional flying skill, intelligence and strength, the capacity to concentrate and absorb information, icy coolness and a gambler's impulse to rise to challenges. They were among the first 30 astronauts accepted for what seemed to many a foolhardy undertaking.

The U.S. flight to the moon would not have occurred when it did had it not been for the Russians. Their early superiority in space—including the first unmanned flight around the moon and the first manned flight in orbit around the earth—goaded President Kennedy in 1961 into pledging to put a man on the moon "before this decade is out."

Now, on July 16, 1969, Apollo 11 was ready to try for the moon. That Armstrong, Aldrin and Collins were the crew was largely a matter of chance. In the system of rotation, modified by accidents and the death of other astronauts, it was simply their turn. Armstrong was appointed commander partly because he had a year's seniority over the others.

Few men ever worked harder to prepare for a mission. For 12 hours at a stretch, they operated command module and moon-landing simulators, worked submerged in water to accustom themselves to weightlessness, and handled countless simulated emergencies on panels with hundreds of instruments. They took crash courses in astronomy, celestial navigation, rocket propulsion, digital computers and lunar geology. Compared with all this, the actual flight came as a welcome relief.

On its launch pad, snorting steaming wisps of vented oxygen, the 3100-ton Apollo 11 looked like a gargantuan living monster, 36 stories high. Its smooth skin concealed 8 million working parts and 91 engines. Thirty-three stories above the ground was the tiny command module *Columbia,* in which the three astronauts lay on their couches listening to the countdown.

No one who saw the liftoff from the launch pad at Merritt Island is ever likely to forget it (there were a million viewers across the river at Cape Canaveral, 500 million on worldwide TV). For a heart-stopping nine seconds, while Saturn V's mighty booster engines built thrust and the nozzles below spewed out flames with an apocalyptic roar, the great rocket did not budge. Then ever so slowly it began to rise on a great pillar of fire—

seeming to pause as it veered slightly to the right to avoid the control tower—then slowly gaining velocity until it was gone from sight.

The first- and second-stage rockets were jettisoned. Tracked by a communications network extending around the earth and above it—from the Manned Spacecraft Center near Houston to key antennas in Spain, Australia and California—the command/service module and the lunar module (housed in an adapter) circled the earth for 2½ hours to make sure the vehicle was moonworthy. Then, its velocity boosted to 403 miles per minute by a refiring of Saturn's third stage, Apollo tore loose from the earth's gravity on trajectory to the moon.

Shortly afterward, three thousand miles from the earth, the command/service module separated from Saturn's third stage and was turned around. At the conclusion of a complicated docking sequence, command-module pilot Michael Collins gently inserted *Columbia*'s pointed probe into the drogue atop the lunar module, ultimately forming a pressure-tight seal. With *Eagle* attached to its nose, *Columbia* continued toward the moon.

One great difficulty the crew encountered on their four-day outward journey was functioning in the cramped, weightless environment. Although the conical capsule's outside dimensions were 12.8 feet in diameter at the base and about 11 feet in height, the men had approximately as much room as they would in a taxi: most of the space was occupied by a floor-to-ceiling instrument panel, storage lockers and the couches into which the men strapped themselves for sleep to keep from drifting around the cabin.

Occupied with checking instruments, copying computer data, and testing systems, the astronauts were so untalkative that Mission Control often urged them to say something "to make sure you're still there." But there were compensations for their quiet and cramped routine. As they flew through the moon's shadow, they could watch the stars blazing in the infinite blackness, marvel at the solar corona—a luminous envelope surrounding the sun—and gaze at the fragile blue earth receding in the distance. The most impressive sight was the moon itself, illuminated by the earth and, at close range, appearing three-dimensional.

On the third day the linked *Columbia* and *Eagle* swung

behind the moon, and for 33 minutes were out of radio contact with tracking stations on Earth. During that interval the astronauts fired their service-module rocket to slow the vehicle and go into lunar orbit.

On the fourth day, during their 11th revolution of the moon, Aldrin and Armstrong donned space suits and crawled through a tunnel for a final checkout of the lunar module before its long separation from *Columbia*. Two minutes before the 13th revolution, after 24 hours in lunar orbit, they were advised by Houston, "We're go for undocking." Forty minutes later the spacecraft emerged from the far side, and Armstrong reported laconically: "*Eagle* has wings."

In the meantime, Mike Collins, in *Columbia*, was cut off from voice contact with the earth and his companions for 47 minutes during each revolution. "Not since Adam has a human being known such solitude," a NASA official remarked.

During the creaking and groaning descent of the ungainly *Eagle*, its computer, taxed from handling the input from many instruments simultaneously, began flashing warnings that it couldn't handle any more calculations. But engineer Stephen G. Bales in Mission Control had prepared for such an emergency and concluded that malfunction could be averted if Mission Control interpreted landing measurements previously handled by *Eagle*'s computer. Without consultation—there was no time for it—he relayed to the crew, "Go for landing."

Meanwhile, another emergency had developed. The autopilot, programmed to set *Eagle* down on a presumably safe landing area in the Sea of Tranquility, was actually guiding it into a crater filled with huge boulders. Hundreds of hours Armstrong had spent in simulators and in test-flying experimental aircraft paid off. Strapped upright at the controls and staring through the window like an old-time streetcar motorman, he took over partial control from the computer and directed the ship toward a relatively clear area beyond the boulders. As the craft moved forward and down, Aldrin's altimeter readings came over Houston's loudspeaker: "100 feet . . . 50 . . . 25 . . ."

"Houston," Armstrong finally called. "Tranquility Base here. The *Eagle* has landed." The quiet announcement shredded the professional calm at Mission Control. People cheered, laughed, cried and applauded.

After about 6½ hours of painstaking preparation, Armstrong gingerly made his way down the ladder. In a moment that had been awaited as long as men had gazed at the heavens and dreamed, he reached out his booted left foot and planted the first footprint on the moon. Then he uttered those famous, eloquent words: "That's one small step for a man, one giant leap for mankind."

After Armstrong had discovered he could survive in the moon's low gravity and would not sink over his head in the moon's powdery dust as some astronomers had predicted, Buzz Aldrin descended the ladder—"making sure," as he announced, "not to lock the hatch on my way out." "Magnificent desolation" was the phrase he used to describe the crater-pocked moonscape.

In the low gravity, the astronauts moved with ease, like windup toys in a kind of slow-motion lope. Although their pressurized space suits made it extremely difficult to bend over, in 2 hours and 20 minutes they set up a television camera; planted and saluted the American flag; unfurled a strip of aluminum foil to trap particles of solar wind; stood at attention to receive a greeting from President Nixon; set up a laser reflector to measure the lunar distance and a seismic unit to record moonquakes and tremors; and collected 46 pounds of moon rocks and soil.

Returning to *Eagle*, they left behind, among other things, over a million dollars' worth of equipment, a disk inscribed with goodwill messages from 73 heads of state, five medals honoring Russian and American astronauts who had died— and footprints. The visible tracks of their boots in the lunar dust will last for a half-million years, until erased by the impact of micrometeorites.

Some 21 hours after the astronauts landed, Houston radioed: "You're cleared for takeoff." "Roger," answered Aldrin. "Understand. We're No. 1 on the runway." The quip hid his nervousness. *Eagle*'s ascent engine had been test-fired successfully more than 3000 times. If it failed to ignite this one last time, the two men would remain on the moon to die as their oxygen supply ran out. But the engine fired, and they were carried aloft, coasting into a low lunar orbit seven minutes later. "That was beautiful!" exclaimed the relieved Aldrin as the lunar module lifted. "Very smooth, very quiet ride."

When *Eagle* docked with *Columbia,* Collins reported, "All hell broke loose." The ships gyrated violently. But the coupling held, and the crewmen set about transferring themselves and their cargo back into *Columbia.* More emotional men meeting after such perilous journeys might have wept or embraced. These men simply shook hands.

Eagle was jettisoned and, after the men had rested, *Columbia*'s big engine was started up again, homeward bound, to splash down in the Pacific 60 hours later.

The astronauts were unprepared for the acclaim that followed. They addressed Congress, received Medals of Freedom, paraded through U.S. cities and toured 23 countries. For a year they were so hounded that they and their families went into seclusion. Says Aldrin, "It was by far the most difficult part of the entire mission."

All three were too restless and conspicuous to fit back indefinitely into the routine in the space program. Michael Collins ultimately joined the Smithsonian Institution in Washington, which he now serves as under secretary. Neil Armstrong resigned to become professor of aeronautical engineering at the University of Cincinnati. Buzz Aldrin had returned to the Air Force, then retired in 1972 and entered a series of private businesses. A nervous breakdown followed. Ultimately, he worked in Los Angeles as an engineering consultant.

Just as the moonshot changed the astronauts' lives, Apollo 11 and five subsequent U.S. moon landings have altered ours. They have expanded our knowledge of and raised new questions concerning the geology of Earth, of the solar system and of the origin of the cosmos. Out of space technology have come billion-dollar industries (transistors, alloys, fabrics), and four broad categories of satellites (called application satellites) of direct economic benefit to man. These include the navigation satellites; the earth-resources satellites that detect air and water pollution, inventory crops, locate new sources of water, minerals, petroleum and natural gas; weather satellites—stations in space that transmit global weather images and other vital data; and the satellites that play an increasingly important part in global communications.

But those of us who watched the first moon landing had no thought of material benefits. What is engraved in our memories is the impact on our spirits, imagination and morale. It opened a badly needed window in the crowded cell of Earth, providing psychological elbow room. Through the window we vicariously share the thrill of those who will continue to explore the unknown—exalting our spirits and renewing our pride in human accomplishment.

We Called Him Duke

by Ronald Reagan

WE CALLED HIM Duke, and he was every bit the giant offscreen he was on. Everything about him—his stature, his style, his convictions—conveyed enduring strength, and no one who observed his struggle in those final days could doubt that strength was real. Yet there was more. To my wife, Nancy, "Duke Wayne was the most gentle, tender person I ever knew."

In 1960, as president of the Screen Actors' Guild, I was deeply embroiled in a bitter labor dispute between the Guild and the motion-picture industry. When we called a strike, the film industry unleashed a series of stinging personal attacks against me—criticism my wife was finding difficult to take.

At 7:30 one morning the phone rang and Nancy heard Duke's booming voice: "I've been readin' what these damn columnists are saying about Ron. He can take care of himself, but I've been worrying about how all this is affecting you." Virtually every morning until the strike was settled several weeks later, he phoned her. When a mass meeting was called to discuss settlement terms, he left a dinner party so that he could escort Nancy and sit at her side. It was, she said, like being next to a force bigger than life.

Countless others were also touched by his strength. Although it would take the critics 40 years to recognize what he was, the movie-going public knew all along. In this country and around the world, he was the most popular box-office star of all time. For an incredible 25 years he was rated at or around the top in box-office appeal. His films grossed $700 million—a record no performer in Hollywood has come close to matching. Yet John Wayne was more than an actor; he was a force around which films were made. As Elizabeth Taylor stated in 1979 when testifying in favor of the special gold medal Congress struck for him: "He gave the whole world the image of what an American should be."

He was born Marion Michael Morrison in Winterset, Iowa. When Marion was six, the family moved to California. There he picked up the nickname Duke—after his Airedale. He rose at 4 a.m. to deliver newspapers, and after school and football practice he made deliveries for local stores. He was an A student, president of the Latin Society, head of his senior class and an all-state guard on a championship football team.

Duke had hoped to attend the U.S. Naval Academy and was named as an alternate selection to Annapolis, but the first choice took the appointment. Instead, he accepted a full scholarship to play football at the University of Southern California. There coach Howard Jones, who often found summer jobs in the movie industry for his players, got Duke work in the summer of 1926 as an assistant prop man on the set of a movie directed by John Ford.

One day, Ford, a notorious taskmaster with a rough-and-ready sense of humor, spotted the tall U.S.C. guard on his set and asked Duke to bend over and demonstrate his football stance. With a deft kick, Ford knocked Duke's arms from beneath his body and the young athlete fell on his face. Picking himself up, Duke said in that voice which even then commanded attention, "Let's try that once again." This time Duke sent Ford flying. Ford erupted in laughter, and the two began a personal and professional friendship which would last a lifetime.

From his job in props, Duke worked his way into roles on the screen. During the Depression he played in grade-B westerns until John Ford finally convinced United Artists to give him the role of the Ringo Kid in his classic film *Stagecoach*. John Wayne was on the road to stardom. He quickly established his versatility in a variety of major roles: a young seaman in Eugene O'Neill's *The Long Voyage Home*, a tragic captain in *Reap the Wild Wind*, a rodeo rider in the comedy *A Lady Takes a Chance*.

When war broke out, Duke tried to enlist but was rejected because of an old football injury to his shoulder, his age (34), and his status as a married father of four. He flew to Washington to plead that he be allowed to join the Navy but was turned down. So he poured himself into the war effort by making inspirational war films—among them *The Fighting Seabees, Back to Bataan* and *They Were Expendable*. To those back home and others around the world he became a symbol of the determined American fighting man.

Duke could not be kept from the front lines. In 1944 he spent three months touring forward positions in the Pacific theater. Appropriately, it was a wartime film, *Sands of Iwo Jima*, which turned him into a superstar. Years after the war, when Emperor Hirohito of Japan visited the United States, he sought out John Wayne, paying tribute to the one who represented our nation's success in combat.

As one of the true innovators of the film industry, Duke tossed aside the model of the white-suited cowboy/good guy, creating instead a tougher, deeper-dimensioned western hero. He discovered Monument Valley, the film setting in the Arizona-Utah desert where a host of movie classics were filmed. He perfected the choreographic techniques and stunt-man tricks which brought realism to screen fighting. At the same time he decried pornography, and blood and gore in films. "That's not sex and violence," he would say. "It's filth and bad taste."

In the 1940s, Duke was one of the few stars with the courage to expose the determined bid by a band of communists to take control of the film industry. Through a series of violent strikes and systematic blacklisting, these people were at times dangerously close to reaching their goal. With theatrical employees' union leader Roy Brewer, playwright Morrie Ryskind and others, he formed the Motion Picture Alliance for the Preservation of American Ideals to challenge this insidious campaign. Subsequent Congressional investigations in 1947 clearly proved both the communist plot and the importance of what Duke and his friends did.

In that period, during my first term as president of the Actors' Guild, I was confronted with an attempt by many of these same leftists to assume leadership of the union. At a mass meeting I watched rather helplessly as they filibustered, waiting for our majority to leave so they could gain control. Somewhere in the crowd I heard a call for adjournment, and I seized on this as a means to end the attempted takeover. But the other side demanded I identify the one who moved for adjournment.

I looked over the audience, realizing that there were few willing to be publicly identified as opponents of the far left. Then I saw Duke and said, "Why I believe John Wayne made the motion." I heard his strong voice reply, "I sure as hell did!" The meeting—and the radicals' campaign—was over.

Later, when such personalities as actor Larry Parks came forward to admit their Communist Party backgrounds, there were those who wanted to see them punished. Not Duke. "It takes courage to admit you're wrong," he said, and he publicly battled attempts to ostracize those who had come clean.

Duke also had the last word over those who warned that his battle against communism in Hollywood would ruin his career. Many times he would proudly boast, "I was 32nd in the box-office polls when I accepted the presidency of the Alliance. When I left office eight years later, somehow the folks who buy tickets had made me number one."

Duke went to Vietnam in the early days of the war. He scorned VIP treatment, insisting that he visit the troops in the field. Once he even had his helicopter land in the midst of a battle. When he returned, he vowed to make a film about the heroism of Special Forces soldiers.

The public jammed theaters to see the resulting film, *The Green Berets*. The critics, however, delivered some of the harshest reviews ever given a motion picture. The *New Yorker* bitterly condemned the man who made the film. The *New York Times* called it "unspeakable . . . rotten . . . stupid." Yet Duke was undaunted. "That little clique back there in the East has taken great personal satisfaction reviewing my politics instead of my pictures," he often said. "But one day those doctrinaire liberals will wake up to find the pendulum has swung the other way."

I never once saw Duke display hatred toward those who scorned him. Oh, he could use some pretty salty language, but he would not tolerate pettiness and hate. He was human, all right: he drank enough whiskey to float a PT boat, though he never drank on the job. His work habits were legendary in Hollywood—he was virtually always the first to arrive on the set and the last to leave.

His torturous schedule plus the great personal pleasure he derived from hunting and deep-sea fishing or drinking and card-playing with his friends may have cost him a couple of marriages; but you had only to see his seven children and 21 grandchildren to realize that Duke found time to be a good father. He often said, "I have tried to live my life so that my family would love me and my friends respect me. The others can do whatever the hell they please."

To him, a handshake was a binding contract. When he was in the hospital for the last time and sold his yacht, *The Wild Goose,* for an amount far below its market value, he learned the engines needed minor repairs. He ordered those engines overhauled at a cost to him of $40,000 because he had told the new owner the boat was in good shape.

Duke's generosity and loyalty stood out in a city rarely known for either. When a friend needed work, that person went on his payroll. When a friend needed help, Duke's wallet was open. He also was loyal to his fans. One writer tells of the night he and Duke were in Dallas for the première of *Chisum.* Returning late to his hotel, Duke found a message from a woman who said her little girl lay critically ill in a local hospital. The woman wrote, "It would mean so much to her if you could pay her just a brief visit." At three o'clock in the morning he took off for the hospital where he visited the astonished child—and every other patient on the hospital floor who happened to be awake.

I saw his loyalty in action many times. I remember that when Duke and Jimmy Stewart were on their way to my second inauguration as governor of California they encountered a crowd of demonstrators under the banner of the Vietcong flag. Jimmy had just lost a son in Vietnam. Duke excused himself for a moment and walked into the crowd. In a moment there was no Vietcong flag.

Like any good John Wayne film, Duke's career had a gratifying ending. In the 1970s a new era of critics began to recognize the unique quality of his acting. The turning point had been the film *True Grit*. When the Academy gave him an Oscar for best actor of 1969, many said it was based on the accomplishments of his entire career. Others said it was Hollywood's way of admitting that it had been wrong to deny him Academy Awards for a host of previous films. There is truth, I think, to both these views.

Yet who can forget the climax of the film? The grizzled old marshal confronts the four outlaws and calls out: "I mean to kill you or see you hanged at Judge Parker's convenience. Which will it be?"

"Bold talk for a one-eyed fat man," their leader sneers.

Then Duke cries, "Fill your hand, you sonofabitch!" and, reins in his teeth, charges at them firing with both guns. Four villains did not live to menace another day.

"Foolishness?" wrote Chicago *Sun-Times* columnist Mike Royko, describing the thrill this scene gave him. "Maybe. But I hope we never become so programmed that nobody has the damn-the-risk spirit."

Seventeen years ago when Duke lost a lung in his first bout with cancer, studio press agents tried to conceal the nature of his illness. When Duke discovered this, he went before the public and showed us that a man can fight this dread disease. He went on to raise millions of dollars for private cancer research. Typically, he snorted: "We've got too much at stake to give government a monopoly in the fight against cancer."

Early in 1979, when doctors told Duke there was no hope, he urged them to use his body for experimental medical research, to further the search for a cure. He refused painkillers so he could be alert as he spent his last days with his children. When he died on June 11, a Tokyo newspaper ran the headline, "Mr. America passes on."

"There's right and there's wrong," Duke said in *The Alamo*. "You gotta do one or the other. You do the one and you're living. You do the other and you may be walking around but in reality you're dead."

Duke Wayne symbolized just this, the force of the American will to do what is right in the world. He could have left no greater legacy.

The Twins
Who Found Each Other

by Bard Lindeman

ON A JANUARY night in 1963, a tall, handsome man of 24 from
Binghamton, N.Y., stepped from a jetliner at Miami International Airport for the most important encounter of his life.
Masking his excitement, he called a greeting to the man waiting
nervously for him. "Hi," he shouted. "I haven't seen you in
24 years!"

The other man, also 24, had been planning this night for
three months. Now he did not know whether to hug the new-
comer or shake his hand.

For Tony Milasi, of Binghamton, N.Y., and Roger Brooks,
of Miami, Fla., are identical twins. Yet, incredibly, they were
meeting for the first time. Separated soon after birth, they had
been raised in foster homes more than 1000 miles apart. At
the airport that night they shook hands self-consciously. "Roger,
I can't believe it," Tony said at last.

In many ways the story of the twins who found each other
is hard to believe. The story starts on May 28, 1938, in Bing-

hamton City Hospital. At 8:31 and 8:36 p.m., Dr. Vincent M. Maddi delivered twin boys born to a young Italian mother and a Jewish father. But in this case the normally happy event was a cause of anguish. There were already two other children in the family, whose weekly income was $15, and the tearful mother explained to Dr. Maddi that she and her husband could not keep the newborn babies; it would be impossible to provide for them.

Dr. Maddi remembered that a neighbor had begged for a child to adopt. He mentioned the twins to her, but she was neither young enough nor strong enough to raise both boys; she had to choose between them. And so "Baby B," the smaller twin, came into the lives of Mr. and Mrs. Joseph Milasi. He was christened Anthony Joseph.

The Milasis lived in an apartment above their small grocery and meat market in Binghamton's predominantly Italian seventh ward. Young Tony attended Catholic schools, was an altar boy at St. Mary's of the Assumption Church, and was graduated from Binghamton Central High School. When he was 12, one of the neighborhood children hurled an accusation which hurt and confused him. "You're not Italian like the rest of us," Tony's tormentor shouted. "Your real father is a Jew."

That night Pauline Milasi told the boy the full story, beginning with the money troubles of his true parents. She also showed him his adoption papers. As to his twin, she said Dr. Maddi believed that he had died in infancy. It was best, she said, that Tony believe this, too.

In fact, "Baby A's" chances for life had not been good. When he was three months old, the city's public-welfare department placed him in a boarding home, where he was badly burned when his crib mattress caught fire. After being hospitalized for almost a year, he was transferred to an orphans' home.

In 1942 Mrs. Mildred E. Brooks, a practical nurse, learned of the sickly, unhappy child. She took the boy, called Roger, to live with her and her husband, Jules Brooks, in Syracuse, N.Y. The Brookses, however, never legally adopted the boy. A year later, Mrs. Brooks and her husband separated. With five-year-old Roger, her 11-year-old son and her mother, she moved to Miami. There she supported the family by operating a beauty parlor.

Roger knew that he was not the true son of Mildred Brooks,

but that was all he knew about his origin. Because the Brookses were Jewish, he sang in the choir at the temple and was introduced to Judaism. When he was 15, a friend of the Brooks family told him that he had a twin. Roger was curiously thrilled. He had once dreamed he had a twin, but Mildred Brooks had told him to put it out of his mind. "I felt Roger would never find his brother," she explains, "so why give him something else to worry about?"

In August 1955, at 17, Roger enlisted in the Air Force. His school grades had not been good, and he thought the service would give him a chance for a fresh start. More important, he believed that he might somehow find his brother in the armed forces.

One night in Japan a soldier approached Airman 2/C Brooks and told him, "I saw you playing basketball for St. Mary's in Binghamton." Roger excitedly wrote down the address of St. Mary's church and sent his photograph there, with a letter telling about his search for his twin.

Three weeks later, a heavy brown business envelope arrived from Binghamton. But the contents proved a disappointment. "They couldn't help me," he says, "but they told me to pray for my lost brother and sent me rosary beads!"

When he left the Air Force in the summer of 1959, Roger went home to Miami and took a job as an office worker with an aircraft manufacturer. In the next three years he worked his way up from $67 to $107.50 a week.

Meanwhile, Tony Milasi's life had paralleled his twin's in a curious way. The same month that Roger enlisted in the Air Force, Tony had joined the Navy. On several occasions during his four-year enlistment, GI's had stopped him to ask, "Haven't I seen you around Miami?" Tony began to wonder if his twin might be alive.

Back home in Binghamton in the summer of 1959, he went to the Bureau of Vital Statistics and asked for information about his brother. The registrar told Tony that, because he was adopted, his file was sealed. "That really put me down," he says.

In January 1962, Tony became a book salesman in Buffalo, and in six months he was promoted to sales manager. One of the door-to-door salesmen he hired that summer was an eager young Bostonian named Mark Frattalone, who worked for the company only a short while before resuming his studies at the University of Miami.

Some weeks later, Roger Brooks went to a roadside restaurant near Miami. One of the busboys approached his table and said, "Tony?"

"I'm sorry," Roger said. "You've got me confused with someone else."

The busboy explained that only a short time before he had worked in Buffalo, N.Y., for a fellow named Tony Milasi, "who looks and *sounds* just like you." The busboy was Mark.

"He was excited," Roger remembers. "If I moved my hands when I spoke he'd say, 'Tony does that! Tony does that!' I made a date to see him the following morning."

Next day, Roger told Frattalone that he had a twin brother whom he had never seen, and Frattalone said, "I'm positive Tony is your brother." Roger, afraid of being disappointed again, suggested that Mark call the company in Buffalo and ask when Tony Milasi was born. He pushed a handful of change across the table. Minutes later, Mark came out of the phone booth and said, "Tony Milasi was born May 28, 1938."

"That's when I was born," Roger Brooks said.

The two drove downtown to the Miami office of the book company that employed Tony Milasi. In a copy of the monthly newsletter, Mark found a picture of Tony. Without a word, he handed it to Roger.

"In that moment," Roger says, "I think I knew that this was my brother. I was proud, but I was afraid, too, that something might go wrong, to keep us from meeting."

Roger turned for help to the Family Service Association, telling his story to social worker Catherine M. Bitterman. She explained that they must first be certain, not only that Roger and Tony were twins, but that Tony Milasi knew he was adopted and was interested in reuniting with his brother.

Miss Bitterman sent a letter to the Family and Children's Society of Broome County in Binghamton, asking for an investigation. The letter arrived on October 15, 1962, and from then on, thanks to the efforts of social worker Zev Hymowitz, things moved quickly. "The whole office was excited by this case," says office director Perry Gangloff. "It was wonderful to see Tony's reaction. He couldn't wait to hear from his brother."

It was arranged that Roger Brooks telephone his twin at 6 p.m. on October 19. When his telephone rang that night, Tony

Milasi grabbed it on the first ring. The operator said, "Long distance calling for Anthony Milasi." Then he heard another voice: "Tony?"

"Roger?"

"I don't know what to say." An awkward pause, then, "How tall are you?"

"How tall are *you?*"

"I asked first."

With this they both began to laugh. They discovered they were both six feet three inches tall, that Roger, at 209 pounds, was a pound lighter, that both wore size-13 shoes and had blue eyes and brown hair parted on the left. After the preliminaries, there was only one point to settle—where to meet.

"I'll come down there," Tony volunteered. "Your weather is better."

Roger took a week's leave from his job to spend with his brother. After the first constraint of their meeting at the Miami airport, the brothers found no difficulty in talking. They were fascinated—and amused—by the extent of their physical likeness. And they were even more delighted at the unexpected similarities of taste and habit they discovered.

Both smoked the same brand of cigarettes. Both used the same aftershave lotion and—more amazingly—the same kind of toothpaste, an obscure brand made in Denmark. And both were fast eaters, long sleepers and light drinkers.

Tested by Dr. Syvil Marquit, a Miami psychologist, the two were found to have almost identical IQ's and great aptitude for clerical work. In personality, however, Tony was much more extroverted and self-assured; Roger was more sensitive and impressionable.

With 24 years to catch up on, the time for Tony to leave came all too soon. In March, Roger visited Tony and the Milasis in Binghamton for 12 days. "Every meal was a Roman banquet," he says, "and I must have met a hundred members of the Milasi family. Tony's friends showed me a kind of friendship that I'd never known."

The story of the twins quickly spread through Binghamton. When the boys walked downtown, people called, "Which twin is the Tony?" One woman came up to them and said, "When I read in the paper how you found each other, I cried."

Roger Brooks decided to leave his own familiar world and

move to Binghamton. In February 1964, when Tony married a Binghamton girl named Shirley Gaydos, Roger was best man.

But the central fact of the lives of both Tony and Roger is that they had succeeded in finding each other. For by doing so, each, in a sense, found a missing part of himself.

Back From Drugs: The Triumph of Johnny Cash

by Floyd Miller

HE STOOD on a peak of the Ozarks at sunset, a tall, craggy man, feet planted wide, hands clenched at his sides. He had grown up in and around these mountains, hunted the woods, fished the streams. Now he found the familiar place threatening; his nerve endings felt raw and exposed. A chipmunk turned a twig—the sound seemed thunderous. A gentle breeze drove needles into his bare arms. His heartbeat accelerated with unnamable fear. The tall man was deep in amphetamine psychosis.

He had started taking amphetamine pills five years before, when his career seemed to demand more energy than he could produce. He had no misgivings at the time; they were "just pep pills," and he planned on using them only intermittently. But soon it was every day. Then he found he had to counter their effects with barbiturates (sleeping pills) to get a few troubled hours of sleep each night. Gradually the dosage increased until now he was consuming a staggering amount.

This trip to the mountaintop had been made in the hope that the wilderness would somehow heal him. He was one-quarter Cherokee Indian. Perhaps he would find within him old echoes, some ancient ancestral wisdoms. But if present, they were not powerful enough to counteract the drugs which filled him with delusions.

As darkness settled, he methodically swallowed two more pills, climbed into his jeep and waited. As the amphetamines seeped into his already drugged mind, some new power seemed liberated within him; he stopped being an ordinary man and became godlike. Nothing could hurt him!

He put his car into gear and started down the narrow road carved out of the mountainside.

Suddenly he shifted into neutral and stood up, steering only with his fingertips. The car gathered speed; as it approached each sharp turn the headlights shone futilely into the black abyss that dropped away hundreds of feet. Each time, he spun the wheel, the tires screamed—and the road reappeared. He courted death, defied it. Twice the right front tire spun in space, but each time the left one held, enough to bring the hurtling car back onto the road. Neither time did he make any move to brake the car—nor would he. He had pledged himself to this test to prove that he was invulnerable, beyond death.

At last the car rolled onto the flat at the foot of the mountain. Soaked with perspiration, trembling, he shut his eyes and rested his forehead on the steering wheel. He had proved nothing. Now paranoia crept into his fevered brain, and statements made by friends and business associates suddenly took on dark significance. They were plotting against him, determined to ruin his career. He felt sick at his stomach. He swallowed two more pills.

As he approached the town, he saw posters carrying his name in large letters: JOHNNY CASH. This was the spring of 1967, and he was fast becoming a popular country and western singer. He was booked into the local auditorium this evening; already he was 30 minutes late. The place was sold out. It gave him savage pleasure to think how his associates would sweat if he didn't show up!

For the next hour he drove aimlessly through the town's back streets, keeping watch for a police car. Surely they'd alert the cops that he was missing. Oh, there'd be hell to pay! Finally, the pleasure of laying up trouble for himself drained away. He drove to his motel, swallowed sleeping pills and went to bed.

Some time later he awakened to stare up dully at several worried faces. Everyone spoke at once.

"What happened to you, Johnny?"

"The crowd almost took the place apart—4000 people!"

"They're gonna sue us."

"We had to refund all the money."

He gave them a long, bleak look, then said, "I was sick." He turned his face to the wall.

Born in 1932, Johnny Cash grew up in a family that didn't know it was poor. Their 40 acres of cotton in Dyess, Ark., required the sunup to sundown labor of father, mother, four sons and three daughters. Yet there was no feeling of privation; rather, there was that strength and sense of well-being that comes from hard labor (even as a boy, Johnny could pick 350 pounds of cotton in a day), simple joys, and deeply held religion.

After high school, Johnny went to Detroit to take a job in an auto plant, but could not endure the routine and confinement. He enlisted in the Air Force and spent three years in Europe. Discharged as a staff sergeant in 1954, he returned to Arkansas to try and settle down on a farm. But he was not the same man who had left home—he had discovered music.

In the barracks in Germany he had learned enough basic chords on the guitar to accompany himself while he sang, in his rough voice, the songs he had heard in the Arkansas jukeboxes—about salvation, about railroads, cowboys, loneliness, whiskey, about home and mother and unrequited love. These were old standards, but this man brought something new to them—a fierce poignancy that welled up out of his own scowling personality.

So Johnny Cash began to sing for a living. His voice rang with conviction, and his popularity quickly spread. But with public attention came new pressures for which he was unprepared. He had to deal with people whether he liked them or not; regardless of his mood, he had to sing, every day for weeks ahead; he was occupied with rehearsals, performances, recording dates, travel schedules—all immutable. There was even less freedom than he'd had working in a Detroit factory. Soon the need for solitude became so great that he could endure it only by taking pills—a few at first, then more and more. Often, drugged, he acted irrationally. People began to avoid him; his promising career started to disintegrate.

There was a deep gentleness in him, but when a man of dark aspect acts eccentrically he seems menacing. On a summer night in 1967, he was driving wildly around Lookout Mountain in Georgia when his jeep flipped over, throwing him clear. As he regained consciousness, he began wandering, totally lost. Time and again he fell. The underbrush tore his clothes and whipped and lacerated his face and arms. At last he saw the lighted window of a cottage. He stumbled toward it.

A woman opened the door. When she saw this bloodstained, inarticulate man lowering there, she screamed, slammed the door and ran to the telephone. Soon a car with flashing red roof-light arrived, and a solid man got out, his belt heavy with gun and bullets. The hysterical woman talked of a rapist lurking close by. At this moment, a figure staggered into the beam of the headlights. The woman gasped and pointed. The sheriff ordered the man to turn, spread his legs and lean his hands against the car.

After frisking him and finding no weapon, the sheriff asked, "What happened to you?"

"My jeep turned over."

"Where?"

"I don't know," Johnny said.

The sheriff put him in the car, and they began a silent trip to town. Johnny's mouth was dry; his hands trembled uncontrollably; sweat ran down his back and chest. The thought of confinement was pushing him to the edge of panic. He had been jailed before—once for three days in El Paso for trying to smuggle amphetamines across the Mexican border, and by the end of that time he had been almost climbing the walls.

At the sheriff's office he sat in a straight chair across a desk from his captor. "I know who you are," the sheriff said. "You're too good a man to be destroying yourself. You've got influence on the kids around here. That's a pretty rare thing, for kids to listen to an adult. So what are you going to tell them? That life is so pointless and cheap they might as well throw it away?"

Humiliated and resentful, Cash stared at his clenched hands. He desperately needed some pills, but he dared not reach for the emergency supply he had hidden on him.

"I could lock you up," the sheriff continued, "but I'm not going to. I'm going to take a chance on you, for the kids' sake. I'm betting you're not going to let them down."

Moments later, Johnny was outdoors. He took a long, shuddering breath of relief and reached for the pills. To hell with the kids. To hell with the sheriff. He swallowed the pills to banish them all.

But they refused to be banished. That night, despite sleeping pills and pep pills, they haunted him.

Late one night several weeks later, Johnny called an old friend, a prominent Nashville doctor. "I need help," he said.

The doctor had received several such calls from Cash over the years. Each time he had arranged for hospital admission; each time the terrors of confinement had driven Johnny to disappear.

At Johnny's house, the doctor found his friend distraught. In a quavering voice, Cash kept repeating, "I've lost control of my life."

"For the moment, yes."

"For five years!" Cash flared at him. "For five years I've been doing crazy things, as if I was somebody else. I can't sleep, I can't work, I can't face the kids who come to hear me sing and ask me for autographs. I can't even stop taking the pills that are driving me crazy." Then, in an agonized whisper, "Do you know what it's like to despise yourself?"

"What are you going to do about it?" the doctor asked.

Cash shut his eyes. "I'm going to quit," he said. "Starting now." His meaning was clear—no hospital confinement. He would do it on his own or not at all.

In a distant voice, Johnny asked, "What's it going to be like?"

"Pure hell," the doctor replied.

The flicker of a smile crossed Johnny's face. "I'm familiar with the place."

The doctor summoned Cash's family and a few intimate friends. Johnny was not to be left alone at any time, day or night. Braced as they were, these volunteer nurses were unprepared for Johnny's agony. He paced the floor in torment. He could not sleep, or keep food down. Sweat soaked his clothes. His mouth was so dry that he had to sip water constantly to keep his lips from adhering to his teeth. He trembled, not only from chills and fever but because his nerves, tissues and muscles, suddenly freed of drug controls, were on a rampage.

"Johnny," the doctor said after a week, "you belong in the hospital."

Cash slowly shook his head. His eyes were glazed with suffering, but through cracked lips he whispered, "I'll make it."

He made it. He went through hell and came out on the other side.

That was in 1967. Since then, Johnny Cash has remained a top performer in Country Music, selling hit records and drawing big crowds at personal appearances. His income is about four million dollars a year. Liberated from drugs, he now knows who he is and what he truly and clearly thinks about life. Some of his opinions are unpopular in various quarters, but he speaks them loud and clear.

Cash has a special affection for men in jail, and he speaks out against the brutalities they endure. He fights for justice for the American Indian.

Johnny Cash is his own man. He has been through the fire, and has come out fused and solid.

Beethoven and the Boy

by Robert Magidoff

IT WAS the evening of November 25, 1927. Chubby 11-year-old Yehudi Menuhin, dressed in knee pants, had just arrived for his appearance as a violin soloist with the New York Symphony Orchestra in famed Carnegie Hall. On his way from the stage entrance to the artists' room he saw a large fire ax hanging on the wall. "What's that for?" he asked a guard standing nearby.

"To chop the heads off the soloists who don't play well," was the reply.

"And how many heads have you already cut off?" asked Yehudi.

"Oh, quite a few," said the guard with a friendly wink.

There were those in the audience that night who expected the young Menuhin head to roll. Foremost among them were the music critics. For it had been announced that the boy would play the Beethoven violin concerto, which the critics regarded as nothing short of sacrilege. They felt that this difficult masterpiece should not be attempted by anyone except the most mature artist; that it was impossible for a child's small hands, no matter how well trained, to execute the intricate fingering.

As a matter of fact, a simpler number—the A-major Mozart—had been suggested when Yehudi first received the invitation to appear with the New York Symphony. "But I've waited so long!" young Yehudi said to his father. "I'll play the Mozart as an encore, but I must do the Beethoven first. *Please* make them let me."

"I'll do my best, Yehudi," his father said gently. He did not tell the boy that word had already come from Fritz Busch, the famous German who was to conduct that night, that he refused even to consider the Beethoven. The conductor's reply to all arguments was, "One does not allow Jackie Coogan to play Hamlet!"

One day, however, Yehudi's managers arranged for him and his teacher, Louis Persinger, to have an audition with Busch in the latter's hotel suite. The conductor displayed a studied coldness toward his young soloist. He was provoked by Yehudi's insistence on playing the Beethoven concerto, and he happened to dislike all prodigies. He had been a prodigy himself, and shuddered at the recollection. Moreover, at this concert he was giving the world première of a new work by his brother Adolph, violinist and composer, and he'd never forgive himself if this small boy ruined the evening.

As the audition of the Beethoven concerto was about to get under way, Persinger made a start toward the piano. Busch, however, sat down at the instrument himself. Calm and purposeful, Yehudi lifted the lid of his violin case, laid back the green velvet shield and handed the violin to Persinger to be tuned (his small hands were still too weak to twist the pegs into position). Busch smiled sardonically and plunged into the final part of the orchestral introduction. Yehudi adjusted his instrument, raised the bow and released the first measures with their broken octaves so feared by violinists.

As the boy played on, Busch signaled to Persinger to replace him at the piano. The conductor retired to the corner, his whole bearing betraying excitement and unbelief. Suddenly he interrupted the music and threw his huge arms around Yehudi. "You can play anything with me, anytime, anywhere!" he cried. Yehudi impatiently disentangled himself and continued to play.

Busch kept him there for more than an hour, going over

various passages and practicing in particular the pauses so significant in Beethoven. Later, at Yehudi's first rehearsal with the orchestra, even the completely conquered Busch was amazed to find that the boy had not overlooked a single point.

At the end of that first rehearsal, the musicians accorded Yehudi a standing ovation and Busch made an amazing announcement: contrary to all general rules at the time, he had decided to shift the concerto soloist to the concluding half of the program. "No orchestra and no conductor could compete with the overpowering effect of this, Yehudi's first appearance," he frankly admitted in his autobiography. "Not a creature in Carnegie Hall would have had ears for any music whatever after Yehudi had played his last bar."

Carnegie Hall was packed to the roof and charged with expectation on the evening of November 25. When Busch appeared on the stage after the intermission, he was greeted warmly, but all eyes turned toward the entrance on the left from which would enter the boy whose story had so excited the public imagination. There was an outburst of applause when he came out, chubby and awkward in white silk blouse and black velvet knee pants. Showing no trace of self-consciousness, he took his place near Busch, acknowledged the applause with a jerky nod of the head and, businesslike, handed his beloved Grancino to the concertmaster to be tuned.

There was a breathless silence in the hall when the kettle-drum announced the opening of the concerto, followed by the clear, lyrical voice of the woodwinds. Yehudi stood unruffled, so absorbed in the music and seemingly oblivious of his part in the performance that some people feared he would miss his entrance. But, with only seconds to spare, he adjusted the thick, black pad which dangled from his violin, placed the instrument under his chin and raised his bow. At the great singing tone that filled the hall there was a gasp, an exchange of amazed glances, a slight stirring—and then the hush of complete absorption.

It was only during the Joachim cadenza, when the soloist remained alone to face its exacting technical and intellectual challenge, that the audience once more became aware of the absurd size of the violinist. Now listeners reflected on his pure intonation and sense of rhythm, and marveled at the fingering, the trills, the perfect coördination between spirit and muscle. Unable to contain their excitement and amazement at the end of the cadenza, the audience burst into applause, threatening to stop the performance. Supported by Busch and the orchestra, Yehudi returned them to Beethoven with all the authority of a veteran.

It remained only for his incredibly graceful execution of the finale to complete a performance that was followed by an unforgettable ovation. People shouted and yelled, many with tears in their eyes, while the men in the orchestra rose and joined in the noise.

At this point Yehudi's extraordinary aplomb left him, and he suddenly looked like the bewildered small boy he was. Catching sight of Persinger in the wings, he dragged him onto the stage, pointing at him and applauding. Persinger finally managed to disengage himself, and vanished, but still the applause went on. Yehudi had to appear on stage in his overcoat finally, cap in hand, before the audience would let him go.

Even the music critics, forgetful of deadlines, had stayed on to applaud the young violinist.

Next morning Olin Downes wrote in the New York *Times:* "I had come to the hall convinced that a child could play the violin no more effectively than a trained seal. I left with the conviction that there is no such thing as an infant prodigy but that there *is* such a thing as a great artist who begins at an early age."

Time, and Yehudi Menuhin, have vindicated that judgment.

Motl Weiss
and the Golden Land

by Theodore Marks

YES, MOTL WEISS is dead. If you are trying to jog your memory—don't bother. Motl Weiss was no chief of state, no general of the armies, no superstar. No great scientific achievement was his. You will find him in no *Who's Who*. Motl Weiss was my father-in-law, an ignorant, superstitious, old Jew-American citizen.

So Motl Weiss was born about 1890 (who knew the exact year or date?) and brought up outside Ostilla, a small village in a part of Russia that today is Poland. He had no education other than the short time at Hebrew school, learning by rote the necessary Hebrew to become *bar mitzvah* at the age of 13. After all, teachers cost a chicken, and a chicken was to eat.

When the time came for army service, he went off to serve. And the truth is, he didn't mind. It was an adventure. They fed him, his uniform was warm, and they paid him. And the captain of his company, thank God, didn't allow the men to treat the Jew soldiers too terrible.

Motl Weiss saved his kopecks and rubles, and when his time was up, he went home. A matchmaker was called; a match was arranged; he got married.

Rumors had filtered back to the village about America, "The Golden Land," where a living could be made, men could live with their heads up, and there was no threat of a *pogrom*. So Motl left his new wife, already gagging with morning sickness, and started for America.

Consider the nerve, the *chutzpa,* the sheer stupidity of this young man of 20, journeying to a strange country thousands of miles away, unable to read or write in *any* language, much less speak the new one, having no skill or trade.

Was this any less heroic than the labors of Hercules? Was this any less epic than *The Odyssey?* More, I say, because this was no bigger-than-life hero. Motl Weiss was a *schnook,* a *schlimazel,* a patsy, a dumb kike immigrant.

His small bankroll was conned away by a smooth-talking acquaintance aboard ship. (Did I have to tell you?) He got through Ellis Island and on to Milwaukee with a loaf of bread and a piece of sausage given to him by the Jewish Agency. He arrived days later, half-starved, penniless—alone, and lost.

He scavenged from the refuse barrels behind Berkowitz's Bakery, and finally spent the first freezing night in paradise sleeping on the floor of an abandoned house at 4th and Cherry Streets.

The next morning, all the stories of the new world came true. There on the front steps of the house next door were a bottle of milk and a bag of rolls. Motl Weiss ate and drank and started off to make his way.

After two days of wandering about the city and returning to his house at night, paradise was wearing thin. On the third morning, the rightful owner of the milk and rolls was there to greet him with hollering and cursing.

So he ran down the street, shivering in the raw wind off Lake Michigan. Then he heard a voice (not unlike Moses before him). "Motl, Motl Weiss!" It was Pinchus Kimmel from home—a boy who had gone to school with him and had left for America two years before.

Pinchus took Motl home with him, and laid out a banquet of a meal. Motl ate until it hurt. And yet, when Pinchus turned away for a moment, Motl stuffed a chunk of bread in his pocket. (Say, listen, tomorrow is another day, no?)

Pinchus insisted that he spend the night. And the next day he bought Motl Weiss a new outfit from cap to shoes. He took him to the foundry where he worked, and talked the foreman into hiring him, and found him a rooming house. (Motl would remember him as long as he lived, and when Pinchus Kimmel died Motl remembered him always in his prayers for the dead.)

Motl Weiss worked 12 hours a day, six days a week, for $7 a week, saving his money to bring his wife, Brooche, to America. He trusted no one, so his crumpled dollars went into his pants pocket, and the sweat of his body from the blazing forge threatened to rot his soggy mass of bills. He saved on the price of food by eating the free lunch at the saloon. He worked. He slept. And finally he went to Ulevitch, the man who arranged these things for the Jews in the ghetto, and he sent a ticket for Brooche and his baby daughter.

Brooche and the baby came, and he found a couple of rooms, and he worked. Brooche looked at the rooms, and the working 12 hours a day, six days a week, and the wretchedness of the ghetto, and she said, "Where is the golden land? At least before I could see grass and breathe the air, and not be a slave among strangers. I am going home."

But, before she could leave, the Great World War began, and travel to Russia was suspended. So Motl Weiss worked, and he got four rooms in a better house. The time came when he was called to the army for his new country—but, thank God, the war ended.

By now, Brooche had learned to speak a little English and the strangeness of America was not so strange. "So," she said, "we are here already, so we'll stay. But listen, Motl. Things are very bad at home. Maybe we could bring my sisters to America?" So Motl Weiss worked, and they saved, and they bought a ticket for Bella. And for Sarah, and for Ida. Motl and Brooche fed them, and clothed them, and helped them get work and husbands.

Well, do you know what happened? This man, Motl Weiss, had a breakdown. The doctors said he must quit the foundry. Now, how do you like that? He learned a skill, and they said it was killing him.

So he said, "I will get a horse and a wagon, like others I know, and peddle fruits and vegetables." And he did it. He did it without being able to read a street sign. Many times he got lost, and how do you ask directions of strangers who don't understand your heavy accented, limited few words of this language?

One day Brooche looked at some rotting tomatoes and said, "Motl, some days you don't sell everything, and you lose money. So why don't you change, and peddle instead junk? That doesn't spoil?"

And he did it. He learned what was iron and what was brass, and the price he could get from Bremmer at the junkyard for papers and rags and mattresses. He made himself a route, and he got regular customers who saved their junk for "Max." (Oh, yes, he had cards printed—for he couldn't write.)

Motl Weiss moved to a nicer apartment. And he and Brooche raised two daughters, and he went through the Depression of the 1930s and he never took a penny of charity—or welfare. He paid his rent and bills when he said he would. And he gave to charity.

When World War II came, he was too old to go, but he bought some war bonds. When the city grew too large and he could not make a living with his horse and wagon, he got a truck and learned to drive it (never over 20 miles an hour). And he and Brooche became citizens, and voted.

And every morning Motl Weiss got up at 5:30 to make sure he arrived at Rabbi Twerski's temple at seven o'clock for the public services. And the proudest day of his life was the moving day, when Rabbi Twerski built a new temple on the west side of Milwaukee, and Motl Weiss carried the rabbi and the sacred scrolls from the old temple to the new—in his truck.

Now, I don't want you to get the wrong idea. Motl Weiss was not a rigid orthodox Jew. He liked ham—so he ate it. He worked on Saturday—he was a practical man. But he was a real practicing Jew who believed in his God and his fellow man. The temple was not only a place of worship but, even more, a social gathering place where he could gossip, learn the news and enjoy the companionship of men who spoke his language.

Well, every story must have an end, no? So Brooche died, and this was a great loss. And Motl had a heart attack, and the doctors said no more peddling. He sold his truck. And this was a great loss. He couldn't get out to the temple. And he grieved. And finally Motl Weiss died. He left a small insurance policy that almost covered the burial expenses, and a $75 war bond that had matured to $100. That's how rich Motl Weiss got in America—the golden land.

So shake hands, Motl Weiss, and say *shalom* to the other *menchen* in your new temple: to Ben Franklin, and Albert Einstein, and George Washington Carver, and Abe Lincoln, and the Kennedy brothers, and Pinchus Kimmel, and Franklin Roosevelt, and Martin Luther King. And then tell them— We're still working on the golden land!

"The Wire Is My Life"

by Joseph P. Blank

HELEN WALLENDA began urging her husband Karl to retire from the high wire in 1970 when he was 65 years old. She was afraid for his safety. "There are other things you can do," she implored.

"Look, honey, let me do it as long as the good Lord lets me," he answered in his German accent. "He's up there with me." Before stepping out on the wire, the greatest high-wire performer in circus history always popped a piece of hard candy into his mouth ("It keeps me from getting nauseous") and said silently, "God, please. . . ."

"How will you know when the good Lord tells you to stop?"

"When He leaves me, I'll know," Karl said.

Karl Wallenda was born in 1905 into a Magdeburg, Germany, family that had been acrobats and trapeze artists for three generations. At six, Karl was performing in the family show. Five years later he was doing stunts in beer halls. His best act was stacking three chairs and doing a handstand on the top chair-back.

In the early 1920s Karl met a high-wire walker named Louis Weitzmann who taught him to walk the wire. Weitzmann designed an audience heart-stopper that would use Karl's handstand prowess. With a balancing pole, Weitzmann would walk to the center of the wire. Karl would follow, with a hand on Weitzmann's shoulder for balance. Weitzmann would bend low at the knees. Karl would climb his back to a handstand position on his shoulders, and Weitzmann would then stand erect. The innovative stunt and its variations were quickly booked throughout central Europe.

Two years or so later Karl formed his own troupe with his older brother, Herman, and a young woman. She was the high-mounter who balanced on Karl's shoulders or on a bar yoked between Herman and Karl as they walked across the wire. When she left the act, Karl placed an ad for a replacement. The only reply was from Helen Kreis, a teen-ager who turned out to be a natural on the wire—graceful, confident, gritty.

In 1927 The Great Wallendas were invited to perform in Havana. The highlight of their show was a three-tier act: Herman and a young man named Joe Geiger were the under-standers. Karl stood in a chair on the pole yoked between them, with Helen mounted on his shoulders. John Ringling caught the performance and offered Karl a contract with "The Greatest Show on Earth." Karl signed.

One audience-thrilling feature of The Great Wallendas' act was the absence of a net under the 40-foot high wire. While a flying trapeze act *must* use a net because missed catches are not unusual, Karl believed that a net was dangerous for The Great Wallendas.

Flyers practice falling and know how to land on their backs to help avoid injury. But it was impossible for a four-person act to practice falling. Bodies would strike bodies on the net, and the cascade of balancing bars, bicycles and a chair could kill or injure. The net offered no security. It was better to rely on skill and quick-thinking in an emergency.

Karl was 23 when his troupe opened in New York's Madison Square Garden in 1928. As the Wallendas stepped out on the ¾-inch wire in their deerskin slippers, the band music muted and salesmen stopped hawking their wares. After the 15-minute performance, the audience broke into loud applause, feet-stamping and whistling. The troupe was dismayed. In Europe such a display is the same as being booed. They took a quick bow and fled. The noise continued until the ringmaster told Karl, "We can't go on with the next act until you take your bows." "But the whistling?" Karl asked. "That's appreciation," the ringmaster explained.

Karl always tried to give the audiences a new feat. In one, Helen perched without a bar on Karl's shoulders as he stood on a chair balanced on a bar across the shoulders of two men on bicycles. In another, Herman stood on a bar yoked between two under-standers and Karl did a handstand on his shoulders. But the act that established the Wallendas as truly special was the seven-person pyramid. Conceived by Karl in 1947, it was to bring the family triumph and tragedy.

The pyramid consisted of four under-standers, the first and second pair yoked together by shoulder bars. Karl and Herman, also yoked, were the second level of the pyramid, balanced on the two first-tier bars. Then a top-mounter, either Helen or her younger sister, sat and stood in a chair balanced on the second-tier bar.

The troupe started practicing on a wire three feet high, then 12 feet and finally at about 40 feet. Karl harped continually on precautions. "Never drop the pole. Make it a part of your body. It is your security. If you drop the pole you endanger your life and the lives of everybody else on the wire."

"On the wire you concentrate," Karl repeated. Concentration enabled the seven-person pyramid to stave off the unexpected. Once, the wire suddenly slackened about six inches. All the balancing poles see-sawed precariously, but every person kept his erect position and the pyramid held firm. In outdoor performances the pyramid survived cloudbursts and unpredictable gusts of wind.

Helen, who married Karl in 1935, retired from the circus in 1959, but agreed to tour with him during the summer months. But being a spectator was different from being a part of the act: she couldn't take the anxiety and suspense, and would remain fearfully in her quarters praying during a performance. After two summers she told Karl she would stay home.

He telephoned her every day. Then, on returning home, he tried to help with household chores. Helen wished he wouldn't. "As graceful as he was in air, so was he clumsy on the ground," she recalled. "He couldn't put up a picture hook without banging his thumb. Once he was painting a wall and he fell off the ladder and broke two fingers."

In January 1962, The Great Wallendas took their famous pyramid to the Shrine Circus in Detroit. During the second night's performance, the pyramid moved out smoothly at the command of Gunther, the last under-stander. At mid-wire, it paused dramatically as Jana, the top-mounter, rose to her feet on the chair, balanced between Karl and Herman. Then the 1300-pound pyramid continued its slow, even pace to the terminal platform. About 15 feet from the end of the wire, Dieter Schepp, the front under-stander, suddenly stopped and his pole inexplicably wavered. Karl called out in German, "What's the matter?"

Schepp cried, "I can't hold any longer." The pole slipped from his grasp and he toppled 35 feet to the arena floor (he would die later that night). Karl, who had been standing on the bar yoked between Schepp and Dick Faughnan, fell, striking and grabbing the wire as his leg got twisted between the wire and a guy line. Faughnan, Karl's son-in-law, fell to the dirt-packed concrete (he died 35 minutes later), followed by Karl's adopted son Mario, the third under-stander (he suffered a spinal injury that would paralyze him for life from the waist down). Gunther, the last under-stander, kept both his pole and his balance. His father, Herman, crashed into the wire, gashing his head but managing to clutch the wire with both hands. Jana fell, striking Karl in the back with an impact that he thought would split him in two. She grabbed his leg as he caught her arm.

Gunther took a step to Herman, "Are you all right, Dad?"

"Yes, I can make it to the platform. Help Karl."

Gunther stepped over his father's hands, and managed to reach Jana's other arm. The two men tried to pull her to the wire, but they had little strength left and even her 100-pound weight was too much for them. "Don't drop me," Jana pleaded. Gunther yelled for a net, but circus hands could find only a tumbling mat.

"They'll catch you," Gunther told her.

"No!" Jana screamed as she plummeted, feet first. She landed on one side of the mat, tearing it from the hands that grasped it. Her head struck the arena floor, causing a mild concussion.

Karl was hospitalized with a hairline crack in his pelvis, a double hernia and bruised ribs. Herman required only a patch on his gash. Of the seven in the pyramid, only Gunther escaped injury.

The day after the accident Herman, Gunther and a backup performer climbed the ladder for the evening performance. Karl wept as he watched them on television in his hospital room. On the following morning he was running a fever of 102° and hurt all over, but he asked his doctor to discharge him. "I feel like a dead man on the ground," he told Helen. "The wire is my life."

Grief was more bearable for him on the wire than on the ground. Karl gave a performance that day and concluded his act with a chair-stand on the shoulder bar between his brother and nephew, deliberately making the chair wobble to bring gasps from the spectators. He took his bows, then walked out of the arena, crying.

As Karl moved through middle age he became increasingly popular as a "skywalker," a solo act in which he walked long cables between buildings and across sports stadiums. In 1970, at the age of 65, he contracted to do a 1000-foot walk, more than 700 feet above Tallulah Gorge in Georgia. About 30,000 people paid admission.

Climbing to the wire was a strength-sapping effort in itself. Then Karl hefted the 35-pound pole, looked across the gorge and stepped out. He trembled during the first few steps, then committed himself. Midway he stopped, slowly bent his knees, lowered the pole to the cable and did a headstand. A thunderous ovation echoed through the gorge.

Since the cable had about a 60-foot slack, the second half of the walk was uphill, and the pole grew heavier by the second. But Karl was grinning when he completed the 20-minute walk. Helen embraced him and silently vowed never again to watch him perform. His manager, Stephanie Shaw, also embraced him—and poured him a martini.

In early March 1978 Karl and three protégés—his 17-year-old granddaughter Rietta, Farrell Hettig, 22, and Phillip Gikas, 25—went to Puerto Rico to join the Pan American Circus.

The three young performers adored their 73-year-old mentor. Rietta had fallen in love with the wire at age three and asked her grandfather—whom she affectionately called *Vati*—to teach her. Ten years later she was performing professionally. Farrell had trained and performed with Karl for seven years. Phillip had joined the troupe a year earlier and San Juan was to be his debut.

During the second week of the booking, the circus management asked Karl to do a skywalk between two resort hotels as a promotional stunt. Karl readily agreed.

But Stephanie Shaw was concerned. This walk seemed particularly hazardous. The wire would be strung between the 10th floors, 120 feet above the street, and there was no way to measure the updraft—or the gusts of wind from the sea. When Stephanie couldn't talk him out of it, she asked Helen to intervene.

Helen flew to San Juan and asked Karl to cancel the publicity walk. "Why do it Karl?"

"I gave my word to a man I've known a long time."

"But it's windy out there. I'd rather you break your word than your neck."

"Helen, it's just a breeze. I've made longer walks in worse winds."

Helen sighed and gave up. On Tuesday she and Karl roamed around Old San Juan, hand-in-hand. "They were like young lovers," Phillip remembers.

About 10:30 the following morning a crowd began gathering in the street. Helen accompanied Karl to the hotel room where he would begin his walk. She sat stiffly on a couch, away from the window. She would not watch. Rietta and Phillip watched from the street. Farrell went to the room where the walk would terminate. Karl checked the wind. It was about 12 m.p.h. on the ground, with much higher gusts.

Shortly after 11, Karl, carrying a 33-pound, 24-foot pole, stepped out on the wire. The crowd quieted. He took five steps forward, then hesitated. The gusts were picking up. He took one step backward, paused, then decisively moved forward.

About midway the wind ballooned his shirt and whipped his trousers. After another some 15 steps Karl bent his knees as if to reduce his profile to the wind. Rietta saw the balancing pole waver and knew that Karl's situation was perilous. She shrieked. "Sit down, *Vati*, sit!"

Karl bent his knees as if to take the sitting position, then grimaced as his feet slipped from the wire. He grabbed for the wire with his right hand and momentarily caught it. But he held on to the pole with his left hand. *Never drop the pole*. Then the wind turned the pole, pulling him from the wire. As he plummeted to the street he grasped the pole in both hands in the professional elbows-crooked wire-walking position.

Helen heard a commotion from the street and froze as she recognized cries of anguish and horror. Then there was a pounding on her door and she heard Rietta cry, "Let me in, let me in!"

Helen slowly opened the door. She looked at her granddaughter, and said, "He fell."

"Yes."

"He's dead."

"Yes." Rietta clutched Helen in her arms. "Say something, *Mutti* [grandmother]," Rietta cried. "Cry." But Helen couldn't. The time for tears and loneliness would be later. Now, there was only paralyzing shock.

The three protégés decided to do the matinee that day. Each knew that it was what Karl would have wanted. He strongly believed that "the show must go on."

"Doing the matinee was our way of saying that we loved him," Phillip said. After the performance Rietta, Farrell and Phillip took bows to a standing ovation. When they straightened up, their cheeks were glistening.

Karl's death did not surprise Herman and Gunther. It was a piece of sad news that they expected to hear some day. "It was the way he wanted to go," Herman said.

When Gunther told his six-year-old daughter, Lisa, she said, "But Uncle Karl had a long and good life, didn't he?"

Until his very last minute.

The Man
Who Will Not Forget

by Joseph P. Blank

AS THE CHIEF JUDGE recapitulated the defendant's crimes, the two outwardly most impassive listeners in the crowded court-room in Düsseldorf, West Germany, were the accused, former *SS Hauptsturmführer* Franz Stangl, and Simon Wiesenthal, a private citizen who had tracked Stangl for 20 years and was responsible for bringing him to justice. At the opening of the trial, seven months previously, the prosecutor had declared, "Stangl is the highest-ranking official of a death camp that West Germany has ever been able to try."

In his 2½-hour review on that cold December 22, 1970, the judge said, "The defendant, as commandant of the Treblinka extermination camp in Poland, supervised the murder of at least 400,000 men, women and children." The judge's words gave new life to an ugly piece of history that many people wanted to forget. Stangl, who had defended himself with, "I only did my duty," stood at attention to hear his sentence: Life imprisonment.

Wiesenthal, a bulky man of 220 pounds with gray, thinning hair, a gray mustache and bright alert eyes, strode quickly from the courtroom. In the corridor he stopped by a waste container, opened his wallet and extracted a picture of Stangl that was tucked between photographs of his wife and daughter. He had kept it as a constant reminder of Stangl's innocent victims. Now, silently, Wiesenthal tore up the picture.

He felt no elation: "Stangl's sentence meant nothing to me. It was purely symbolic. No punishment could be equated with the enormity of the crime. The important thing was that guilt had been established, and justice done."

Starting the trip back to his three-room Documentation Center in Vienna, Wiesenthal had already forgotten the trial. He still had more than 300 active cases of wanted mass murderers in various stages of investigation. His files contained thousands of other names that might never get any attention.

"It's a job I'll never finish," he reflected recently. "I'm now 74. I'll just go on with the work, one way or another, until I stop breathing."

Since May 1945, when he was freed from the Mauthausen, Austria, concentration camp by the U.S. Army, Wiesenthal has been gathering evidence against the men and women responsible for history's most awesome crime—the Nazi extermination of six million Jews and several million Gentiles during World War II. He has located more than 1100 of these criminals, an achievement that makes him unique as a sleuth. And he has done this, except for a year immediately after the war when he worked for U.S. war-crimes investigators, as a private citizen, without any legal authority, financed only by small contributions from individuals across the world and his earnings from lectures and writing.

Wiesenthal works with only the help of one or two part-time secretaries who handle his world-wide correspondence. In the beginning he had a staff of 30 volunteers and poorly paid part-time assistants. Gradually, these men and women left for the peace of normal careers and family life. Even today, however, a message from Wiesenthal will set a nun in Australia, a rabbi in South Africa or a lawyer in New York on the track of a wanted man.

Simon Wiesenthal never *wanted* to give his life to this grimmest of all detective work. Before the war he was a young, successful architect in Lwów, Poland. After he and his wife were reunited in late 1945—each had believed the other was dead—they talked about their lives.

"Everybody in our families has been killed," Wiesenthal told his wife. "I can't go back to my profession. How can I build houses until I've done what I can to see that people are safe in them? I can't forget the millions who were murdered. I am alive. Being alive puts a debt on me. Justice must be done."

Wiesenthal was initially motivated by revenge, but he soon realized that his passion was destructive and futile. He tried to explain it to a Jewish partisan leader who wanted his files "so that we can exterminate them as they exterminated us."

"No, no," Wiesenthal replied. "We will not be like them. We will use the law. If you kill them, the world will never learn what they did. There must be an accounting. There must be testimony in court, a record for history."

Although Wiesenthal argues passionately against every such call for eye-for-an-eye vengeance, when a death-camp survivor weeps over witnessed horrors, Wiesenthal weeps, too, and that man or woman's experience becomes part of his experience. "At times," he says, "it is hard for me to separate in my mind what happened to me and what happened to others."

This soul-deep empathy has sustained him in his lonely work, but it has also driven him to illness and terrible insomnia. At night, scenes of Nazi atrocities used to kaleidoscope endlessly through his mind. Visiting a physician, he was told, "I can't do anything for you. You need distraction from your work. A hobby."

Wiesenthal had always been idly interested in the stamps on his mail that came from scores of countries. So, he took up stamp collecting—he's now an expert philatelist—and learned to lose himself in the art and history of stamps. It was a hobby that was to prove inadvertently instrumental in locating Adolf Eichmann, the demon of death who directed Hitler's whole campaign to annihilate the Jews.

Wiesenthal's patient search for this criminal began in 1946. Although Eichmann's personal dossiers had been destroyed on the eve of Germany's defeat—there were no fingerprints, no photographs—sleuthing unearthed Mrs. Eichmann, living under her maiden name, and her three children.

Neighbors understood that she had divorced Eichmann. Wiesenthal didn't believe it. She was rigidly suspicious of all strangers, and to him this wariness meant that she was in some kind of contact with her husband. Then, in 1948, he learned that she had requested the courts to declare her husband officially dead. To support her claim she presented an affidavit from Karl Lukas of the Czechoslovakian Ministry of Agriculture, who swore that he had seen Eichmann dead in Prague on April 30, 1945.

"I was sure that Eichmann had plotted this move," Wiesenthal recalls. "If he were declared legally dead, all governments would quit their search for him and he would be free."

Wiesenthal and a few of his part-time volunteers leaped into action. Within two weeks they had proof that Lukas was married to one of Mrs. Eichmann's sisters; they also produced sworn statements from an SS officer and other witnesses who had seen Eichmann alive after April 30. The court promptly threw out Mrs. Eichmann's petition. Eichmann remained "wanted."

Although two prewar photographs of Eichmann turned up, the hunt was dead-ended. Then, at Easter 1952, Wiesenthal lost his only "contact" with his quarry: Mrs. Eichmann and her children vanished. She had been issued a passport under her maiden name. "Eichmann felt safe enough to have his family join him," Wiesenthal figured.

One evening 18 months later Wiesenthal was discussing stamps with a fellow collector. "A beautiful stamp just came from Argentina on a letter from an old acquaintance," the man mentioned. "He's a former *Wehrmacht* officer now training Argentine troops. Talks about meeting people from Germany." Then he read the letter aloud. Wiesenthal was stunned by two sentences: "this awful swine Eichmann who ordered the Jews about. He lives near Buenos Aires..."

The Eichmann case was alive! The very next day, Wiesenthal sent this information, together with copies of the old photographs, to the Jewish World Congress in New York and the Israeli consulate in Vienna.

In late 1959, the Israeli government wrote him that it had located Mrs. Eichmann and her three children living with a German named Ricardo Klement in Buenos Aires. Two Israeli agents visited Wiesenthal to review the history of the case. "Klement has to be Eichmann," Wiesenthal told them. "There's no other reason why Mrs. Eichmann would leave her home here and sneak away with the children to Buenos Aires."

"We must be certain. We can't make a mistake in identification. We need a picture more recent than those old shots you sent us."

A few months later, Wiesenthal read that Eichmann's father had died, and he recalled the early years of his search when he would frequently pursue tips about Eichmann's presence—only to have the man always turn out to be Otto, one of Eichmann's four brothers. The resemblance between the two must have been striking.

Wiesenthal found the Eichmann family burial plot in Linz, Austria, and carefully examined the terrain for a hundred yards around it. Then he traveled to Vienna, where he hired two photographers and told them, "I need pictures of everybody attending this funeral. But you must not be seen." He sketched possible hiding places for them.

Five hours after the ceremony, Wiesenthal studied blowups of the brothers' faces. They very strongly resembled one another—and the prewar photographs of Eichmann.

Later, armed with a magnifying glass, he pointed out to Israeli agents the similar head and facial characteristics. "Let your imagination age Eichmann in accordance with the way his brothers look today, especially this one, Otto," Wiesenthal instructed. "What you see in your mind's eye is probably a very good likeness of this Ricardo Klement."

On May 23, 1960, Eichmann was arraigned in Israel. From Jerusalem, Wiesenthal received a cable: "Congratulations on your excellent work." Tried and convicted, Eichmann was hanged on May 31, 1962.

Wiesenthal never can anticipate the course of a pursuit, or how he will find the break that cracks a case. His only lead on Anton Fehringer, a sadistic guard in the Plaszow, Poland, concentration camp, was that he reportedly came from northern Austria. While checking wartime newspapers for information in a library one day, Wiesenthal overheard two genealogical experts discussing family trees. A few days later the conversation popped into his consciousness, and he sought out a genealogist to ask, "Is there any particular place in upper Austria where there is a cluster of families by the name of Fehringer?"

Within 48 hours the expert reported, "Several Fehringer families live in the Krems Valley between Kirchdorf and Micheldorf."

When an aide found an Anton Fehringer living in Kirchdorf, Wiesenthal told a photographer: "Go to Kirchdorf. Pretend you're a tourist. Take lots of pictures, but get me a photograph of this Anton Fehringer." The man turned out to be *the* Fehringer. He was later convicted.

On several occasions, Wiesenthal has been spurred by a note, a phone call or a casual street meeting. This kind of happenstance produced the Hermine Braunsteiner case which was first heard before the Immigration and Naturalization Service in New York City on August 22, 1964. The previous April Wiesenthal was in a café in Tel Aviv in April 1964 when a woman recognized him. In considerable agitation, she blurted, "I was at the Majdanek concentration camp in Poland. There was a guard there named Hermine Braunsteiner who used a vicious dog and a leadweighted whip on women prisoners. She must answer for her crimes."

Braunsteiner was a name new to him, and he held little hope of finding out anything about her. But legal records showed that 15 years earlier Braunsteiner had been tried and sentenced to three years in prison for torturing female inmates at the Ravensbrück, Germany, concentration camp. She had been acquitted, however, of charges involving her service at Majdanek, a death camp where more than 100,000 perished.

Wiesenthal then called on his worldwide network of friends. He obtained incriminating statements about Braunsteiner's actions at Majdanek from survivors in Poland, Israel and Yugoslavia. He picked up her trail at the prison where she was released, "followed" her through Austria to Germany, where she had met and married an American construction worker. In 1963, she had obtained U.S. citizenship, and was now living in Maspeth, N.Y.

Knowing that she could never have acquired citizenship without denying that she had been "convicted of a crime," Wiesenthal informed the U.S. government. In August 1973, Hermine Braunsteiner was deported to West Germany as an undesirable alien. In June 1981, she was sentenced to life imprisonment for her criminal activities in the Majdanek camp.

For Wiesenthal, the dead can never rest until justice is done. And neither can he. That's why he keeps scratching for information about Martin Bormann, Hitler's chief adviser who was thought to have escaped to South America, until 1971 when Wiesenthal established with certainty that Borman had committed suicide in May 1945. That's why Franz Stangl was finally convicted after a 20-year chase.

Stangl had been arrested at the end of the war, but escaped and vanished with his wife and three daughters. No break came until February 22, 1964, when a shabby, shuffling, middle-aged man appeared at Wiesenthal's office. He said, "I was a rank-and-filer with the Gestapo during the war. I read an article in the paper about you the other day, and you said that Franz Stangl was wanted for war crimes. I know where he is. You'll have to pay for the information."

They finally agreed on $7000, if the information led to an arrest.

The tip—that Stangl worked at the Volkswagen plant in São Paulo, Brazil—proved correct. He was leading a pleasant, inconspicuous life in São Paulo and owned a house, two cars and several guns. A relative had informed him of the newspaper story mentioning his name—the same article that had brought in the Gestapo man. Stangl wasn't worried. What could a powerless private citizen, sitting in an office 6000 miles away, do to him? Besides, Brazil had never been coöperative in efforts to track down Nazis. He was safe.

Locating Stangl, verifying his identity and finally having him imprisoned in West Germany took Wiesenthal three years of patient, cautious, skillful undercover work. "Secrecy was all important," Wiesenthal explained. "Obtain the coöperation of Brazil, but limit knowledge of our plans to the smallest possible number of people. In the past, deliberate bureaucratic leaks had enabled wanted men to escape."

The plan worked. And when Wiesenthal was informed of the arrest by cable, he felt the excitement of triumph, not for any personal achievement but, "for the fact that the capture proved that justice knows no limits in time or distance." Subsequently, the justice departments of West Germany and Austria prevailed on Brazil to extradite Stangl.

Each arrest or trial greatly increases his usually heavy load of mail. Some of it is vaguely addressed: "Simon Wiesenthal, Office of Humanity, Vienna" or "The dirty Jew, Wiesenthal; Austria." There are checks, congratulations, new information, pleas to find certain war criminals and, always, threats.

The latter make him wary, but never frighten him. In fact, they bolster his dedication. "Threats indicate to me that criminals at large know they are being sought," he reflects. "I simply have a moral obligation to keep after these men. They must know that they are still held accountable, and none of them at this moment knows whether or not justice is just a step behind him." Wiesenthal also looks on his work as a warning to the 'murderers of tomorrow.' "My hope," he says, "is that my work will serve to remind those who commit acts of genocide that they will never be allowed to rest easy. At a time when human rights conventions seen barely worth the paper they are written on, perhaps my example is one way of ensuring that justice is seen to be done."

"I'm Still Alive!"

by Stanley L. Englebardt

THEY HAD COME up to the high mountains of Arizona's Co-
conino National Forest that June day in 1975, to trim and clear
small pines and oaks from a powerline right-of-way. Steve
Hackleman, 32, was deeply tanned, with arm muscles like
bullwhips from 13 years of wielding axes and heavy-duty power
saws. His 22-year-old partner, Jim McGregor, was new at the
trade but already a skilled tree trimmer.

Steve had just finished a half-hour stint with a high-speed,
compressed-air saw. This is a device resembling a land-mine
detector: a 6½-inch handle and, at the end of it, a fully exposed
ten-inch circular blade spinning at 4500 r.p.m. Now Steve was
stacking brush while McGregor used the saw.

Both men had handled an air saw many times before, though
usually to clear low-lying brush. They knew that if the blade
hit harder wood at a sharp angle it would kick back abruptly,
with the centrifugal force created by the whirling blade sending
it in a sweeping arc to the right.

213

At 2:12 p.m., working behind and to the supposedly safe left side of McGregor, Steve bent down to pick up some cut brush. He did not notice that Jim was having trouble cutting a stubborn branch, or that he had turned the saw completely over to gain a better angle of attack. As it touched the branch, the spinning blade glanced off and—because of its upside-down position—arced back *to the left*.

Steve saw, or sensed, it coming at him. Instinctively, he threw up his right arm to protect his head. The whirling blade entered his chest at mid-point, about six inches below his neck, slicing through his rib cage and lung like a scalpel through butter before coming out three inches under his right armpit.

He felt no impact or pain, only the sensation of a hot knife-edge against his skin. Almost immediately, though, he could feel the warm trickle of blood wetting his side. He didn't look down but he knew the blade had sliced in as far as it could go.

My God, he thought, *it's cut right through my heart!*

But he could still hear and see and think. If it had sliced through his heart, wouldn't he be dead? *I'm not dead, though,* he realized. *I'm still alive!*

Events now seemed to unfold in slow motion. McGregor, his face drained of color, dropped the saw and bolted for the shortwave radio in their truck. "Emergency 837," he shouted into the microphone, identifying his truck to another crew working down the line. "A man's been cut. We need an ambulance!" Steve came along behind him, ignoring his wound, which was now beginning to open. He knew that an ambulance might not get there in time. He leaned over McGregor and whispered, "Better get a helicopter."

McGregor relayed the message and, for the first time, took a close look at Steve. His eyes focused on the edges of raw bone, the exposed tissue and spreading stain of blood. "I've killed him," he said aloud. Overwhelmed, the young tree trimmer slumped against the truck.

For the moment, Steve was on his own. He glanced around at the peaceful forest; nearby, a bird sang. He still had no pain, but the feeling of wetness was spreading inside his pants and down his leg. *First aid,* he thought. *I've got to stop the bleeding.*

He tried to visualize the six main pressure points that had been demonstrated in a recent first-aid class. He could see them for wounds of the face, shoulder, arms and legs, but couldn't recall any places where pressure would stop bleeding from a chest wound. Yet, somehow, he'd have to press down on the cut vessels and stop the blood flow.

Holding his gloved left hand as rigid as possible, Steve rammed the meaty heel of it into the mouth of the wound. Then he clamped his right arm over the hand to apply still more pressure.

Foreman Jim Babcock was working about six miles down the line with another Arizona Public Service crew when McGregor's emergency call came in. A note in the voice told him the accident was bad. He vaulted into his four-wheel-drive vehicle and raced up the dirt access road.

"Nothing could have prepared me for that scene," he recalls. Steve was sitting on the ground, propped against a water can. His face was waxlike and he was covered with blood. McGregor, still visibly shaken, hovered over him.

"I'm cut bad," Steve whispered. "I'm going to die."

"Listen," Babcock snapped back, despite his own wave of nausea. "I've never had anybody die on one of my jobs, and you damn sure aren't going to be the first. Now, let's do something about this wound."

A glint of anger flashed in Steve's eyes. Here he was, nearly cut in half, and Babcock was chewing him out. "Then see if you can help me stop the rest of this bleeding," he said.

The pressure being exerted on Steve's hand had acted like a seal on the wound. Except for some oozing around his outspread fingers, the bleeding had stopped. Babcock got some ice from the truck and packed it around the still-wet spots. Almost immediately, they began to clot. Satisfied that at least the external blood flow was halted, Babcock reached for the radio microphone and began giving directions to the accident site. At this point an Arizona Department of Public Safety helicopter, piloted by Duke Moore and carrying paramedic Mike McArthur, was already on its way from Phoenix.

Steve's mind drifted, then focused on his four young children. A few weeks before, he'd got custody of them after a lengthy divorce action. Now they were at home with a housekeeper. "What's going to happen to the kids if I die?" he asked no one in particular.

Here was another wedge to keep Steve fighting. "It's up to

you *not* to die," Babcock said. "You can't desert those kids."

Benumbed, nauseated, Steve resolved to get back to his children. But his determination couldn't prevent the symptoms of shock from creeping up like a silent enemy. Cold drops of perspiration beaded his face and ran down his body. His teeth began to chatter, and a glaze crept over his eyes.

"Don't quit on me now," Babcock pleaded.

"Don't worry," Steve whispered *"I'm not going to die."*

The helicopter was now over the accident site, but getting down to it would be another matter. With mountain winds gusting up to 35 m.p.h., Moore wanted to stay well clear of the 230,000-volt, high-tension power lines. But a quick sweep of the terrain revealed a solid carpet of tall timber and dense brush. The only clearing was the right-of-way itself, directly under the lines.

Moore descended slowly, on an approach parallel to the power lines. At a point between widely spaced pine trees he dropped to just below the level of the lines and held the craft in a hover while McArthur leaned far out to check the clearance of their tail rotor. He gave a thumbs-up gesture. Moore then side-slipped the bird to the right, under the cables, and brought it to rest dead center from Steve Hackleman.

As the craft touched down, McArthur jumped out and raced to Steve's side. After a quick look at the wound, the men loaded Steve into the helicopter. Moore then lifted a few feet off the ground and flew forward—directly under the wires— to a point where the height of the trees bordering the right-of-way on one side tapered off. He swung the craft right, rose to treetop height, and eased out over the young pines. Then, with plenty of blue sky above, he rapidly headed up and out.

At Flagstaff Community Hospital an emergency medical team stood by while the hospital's security staff blocked a nearby road for the helicopter to land on. When Steve was lifted out, Dr. John Hildebrand, the surgeon-on-call, took one look at his wound and groaned. "Civilian doctors seldom see such wounds," he explains. "Injuries like that usually happen only in combat."

As they rushed into surgery, the doctor tried to remove Steve's hand from the wound. "Two of us pulled on his arm," he remembers. "But even though the patient was only semi-conscious, we couldn't get it to budge. It wasn't until we gave him a sedative, in fact, that he relaxed enough for us to get the hand out."

Examination revealed that the saw had cut through three ribs and the lower half of his right lung—starting just an inch from the heart. The wound was full of sawdust and pine needles from Steve's glove, and the doctors used almost a gallon of saline solution to flush it clean. "I didn't think he'd make it," says Dr. Hildebrand. "Be we operated, closed the wound, gave him antibiotics, then sent him off to the intensive-care unit. And crossed our fingers.

That evening, Jim Babcock, Jim McGregor and other friends kept a tense vigil outside the ICU. Inside, the unexpected was taking place. Slowly, inexorably, Steve's vital signs stabilized. When the doctor came out to tell them that he'd make it, McGregor buried his face in his hands. "Oh, thank God," he whispered. "Thank God!"

Incredibly, Steve was out of the ICU in seven days, and discharged from the hospital ten days after that. He was back on the job in less than four months—with nothing more to show for his near-fatal accident than a long red scar and some occasional shoulder pain. Looking back, Dr. Hildebrand credited this "miraculous" recovery to Steve's superb physical condition and to the fact that he'd so effectively sealed off the wound with his hand. "No medic could have done a better job. The hand pressure helped shut off all those severed vessels and, even more important, it maintained a lifesaving pocket of air in the upper part of his lung. In a very real sense, Steve saved his own life."

Jim Babcock agreed, but insisted there was another factor involved. "Any time you pull through an accident like that," he said, "the good Lord must be on your side."

New Profiles in Courage

by Kenneth Y. Tomlinson

ED MILLER gets up early. By 6:30 a.m., he leaves a small frame house near Palisade, Colo., and heads for the barn to gas his tractor. Miller, 35, is a farmer, a good one. Neighbors say his crops are among the best; his cattle bring top prices. Miller also is paralyzed from the waist down—crippled in Vietnam by an enemy sniper's bullet.

With the aid of a motor-powered pulley, he hoists himself from his wheelchair to the seat of a tractor equipped with special controls and drives off to work. At day's end, he will have harvested nearly 35 tons of oats and hay.

It seems a long way back to August 8, 1968, a hot, rainy day in South Vietnam's central highlands. Ed Miller was sitting in an armored personnel carrier when the bullet entered his back, punctured a lung, creased his spinal column and shattered his left arm above the elbow. Airlifted out by helicopter, he lay unconscious for six days. Doctors performed several operations, but the spinal injury had left his legs paralyzed—for life.

Miller refused to believe he would never walk again. "I kept hoping for a miracle," he recalls. He was discharged and assigned to the Long Beach VA hospital before he realized that the miracle had already happened: he was alive.

At first, progress was slow. Lying helplessly in bed, he watched football on TV. But the sight of an end catching a pass, as he himself had once done, was too much to bear. "To hell with it," he thought. "You're a helpless cripple, and that's all you'll ever be. You'll rot in this bed until you die."

Eventually, such periods of depression faded. Working with weights, he spent hundreds of hours building strength in his injured arm. Realizing that other patients were far worse off, he tried cheering them up, all the while thinking: "There are others who need this bed more than I do." Finally, when he could watch an entire football game without a thought about his own condition, he knew he was mentally prepared for his release.

Since childhood, Ed Miller had wanted to farm. But as a paraplegic, how could he? One evening sitting at home, he asked his father the question that had been gnawing at him for weeks: "Dad, do you think there is any way I can get back on the tractor and be useful—I mean, *really* useful?"

His father smiled. "I've been waiting for that question. We've been working on it since long before you came home." Indeed, his father rigged up the motor-operated pulley device that enabled his son to hoist himself from his wheelchair.

That first day on the tractor, Miller was the happiest of men. Soon he knew the joy of strangers stopping by his fields and saying, "That sure is a pretty crop. Whose is it!" He could tell them it was his—"and did that ever make me feel proud!"

GARY LEE FORMET learned the meaning of hard work early. He was 12 when his father died, and from then on he held part-time jobs to add to his mother's meager income. In college he worked a 40-hour week and more—scrubbing floors, waiting tables, washing dishes. He was R.O.T.C. brigade commander at Stetson University (Fla.) and, on graduation, was awarded a regular Army commission. On January 4, 1967, after paratroop and jungle-warfare training, Formet kissed his wife Jane and three-month-old son goodby and left for Vietnam.

Six months later, the young first lieutenant was leading his platoon on an assault mission when he tripped the wire of a camouflaged booby trap. Gary suffered such severe wounds that both legs had to be amputated, the left one above the knee, the right below. Flown to an intensive-care unit at an Army hospital in Japan, he worried constantly about his family. Would he be considered less than a man because he had no legs? What would his young son think, growing up with a father who could not run and play with him?

Three weeks later he was transferred to Augusta Military Hospital in Georgia, and Jane and the baby moved into an apartment nearby. Months passed with Formet spending countless hours in therapy, strengthening what was left of his legs. Then one day, without telling Jane, doctors fitted Gary with artificial limbs. The first day he wondered, "How in the world will I ever make these things work?" But they did work. Determined, Gary Formet *made* them work. One evening as Jane entered the hospital, she noticed patients looking at her with excited smiles. Wondering why, she looked toward Gary's room and there was her husband walking out to meet her.

Six months later, Formet entered Stetson's law school, where he was elected president of his class, president of his legal fraternity, president of the student bar association. And Jane had their second child.

Graduating in January 1971, Formet accepted a position in one of Orlando's leading law firms and also became active in civic work. When I met Gary Formet in his plush office I was surprised at his mobility. Because one knee was saved, he walks freely with the aid of a cane. He drives a car without special equipment. Gary has since learned to play golf although he gave up a regular game when he opened his own law practice. "For lack of time," he explained, "not interest." Today, an Orange County judge and recipient of community service awards from President Carter and the Military Order of the Purple Heart, Formet says one of his greatest pleasures was being assistant coach for his son's Pop Warner football team.

BILL MANNING checked his horse's saddle for a third time. In ten minutes they would enter the show ring. He was clearly nervous. It was, after all, his first competition in a horse show since he had lost his left shoulder and arm, and the fingers of his right hand.

Rebel Lady had great potential. But what about himself? He had trained her, but could he handle her before hundreds of people? "Will I make a fool of myself?" he thought repeatedly.

Then, it was time. A friend helped Manning mount and wrap the reins around his good arm. The ring announcer called for a walking gait; the horse and its rider performed smoothly. Then a faster saddle gait. Then the greatest test—the still faster racking gait. Manning nudged the horse with his knees. His nervousness gone now, he was concentrating on building up speed without losing rhythm. At 26 miles an hour, they circled the ring, seemingly flawlessly.

Waiting afterward for the judge's decision, Manning thought he and the horse had done well. They had—third place in the 45-horse event—and it was no fluke. In the next few months Manning won 32 ribbons in shows through central Tennessee and Kentucky. By 1978, when Manning gave up horse shows for race-car driving, he had collected 350 trophies, half for first place.

Willie D. Manning, Jr., a career military man, had dropped out of high school and enlisted soon after his 17th birthday. In his first Vietnam tour he had won two Bronze Stars and a Purple Heart as a recon platoon sergeant. In late 1969 he was 33 and back for a second tour which was to earn him another Bronze Star and Purple Heart.

One day, while he was patrolling with his men through dense jungle, North Vietnamese troops opened fire. For Manning, all went blank. When he regained consciousness, he was racked with pain and gasping for each breath. Gunfire echoed all around him, and for nearly 45 minutes he lay there helplessly. The faces of his wife and two sons flashed vividly in his mind. He was certain he was going to die.

Then the fighting ended, and the sergeant was evacuated. In Japan he underwent surgery nine times in 29 days. Four fingers of his right hand had been blown off, and doctors now had to remove the thumb. His left arm and shoulder were also amputated, and he contracted pneumonia. Manning's wife, flown to his bedside, was told there was little hope for her weakened husband. Nevertheless, Bill Manning survived. He soon realized, however, that he was totally helpless, dependent on others for even the simplest functions of living. He lay in despair. The sergeant was no churchgoer, but for the first time in his life he was praying.

Transferred to Nashville's VA hospital, he was fitted with

an artificial left arm and on his right hand a hook device, which opened and closed with the movement of his shoulder. Each day he adopted a project for self-improvement. He learned to pick up a paper cup by the rim without crushing it and to shave himself with a straight-edge razor.

After settling in Bradford, Tenn., he wanted very much to drive. But how does a man without hands turn a steering wheel? Manning finally devised a steering knob that he could grasp with his hook. He put a similar device on a tractor's steering wheel and plowed and planted a one-acre vegetable garden. Turned down for a job as a car salesman, he scraped together $700 and opened a tack shop to sell saddles and bridles.

Soon his sons, ages 11 and 13 at the time, became involved in his work. "When I had hands, I didn't have the patience to teach my boys how to hammer a nail or saw a board," he recalls. "Instead, I have learned to depend on them." When the tractor's carburetor needed overhauling, for example, Manning stood beside his older son, Mike, advising him step by step.

Indeed, as never before, the activities of his sons became entwined in his own life. Only months out of the hospital, he coached their Little League baseball team. "I couldn't throw a ball or swing a bat, but I could teach them how." He bought horses for the boys.

One day, watching his son ride a horse, Manning decided he, too, should be able to ride again. His son pulled a large wooden box over next to the horse and helped his father mount. Manning began riding almost daily, expanding his interest to training and trading horses. He learned to do all grooming himself, even handling the delicate chore of shearing his horses with electric clippers. He now hunts with a pistol and uses power tools with the more refined hook he and a business partner invented and patented. They built the factory in 1976, the same year the Army presented Manning with the Silver Star and the governor proclaimed December 30 Bill Manning Day in Tennessee.

M&W Handicapped Enterprises won the American Legion's national award in 1979 for employing the largest percentage of handicapped. Manning has since sold his interest in the business but continues as County Register and supervises a used-car lot he owns. And he's still winning prizes. With younger son Mark he competes in International Hot Road Association drag races, using a special gear shift he devised. Last year, his 1965 racing Corvette came within 1/300th second of the world record.

"The old Bill Manning was a selfish man," he says today. "He didn't have time to spend with his family. He had no interest in helping other people. I wouldn't trade places with him for the world."

MICHAEL NARANJO was on a journey of nostalgia. As a youth he had spent countless days in northern New Mexico's Pecos Wilderness, climbing peaks thousands of feet high, tracking and killing bear, elk and deer; living, as had his Indian forebears, off the land for weeks at a time. Now, once again, he stood amid the splendor of the jagged Rocky Mountains after a rugged five-day climb with a friend to the top of a 13,000-foot peak.

Only this time he was blind.

Michael Naranjo received his draft notice in June 1967, a year after he had dropped out of New Mexico Highlands University. Friends urged him to join the National Guard to avoid Vietnam. He answered the draft notice instead. He had mixed feelings about the worth of the war. Even after he got to Vietnam, he felt little sympathy for the South Vietnamese cause. But with so many others going, "I could not have lived with myself as a man if I had stayed behind."

The war lasted less than two months for Naranjo. During fierce fighting in the Mekong Delta, a Vietcong grenade exploded near him, knocking him unconscious. When he awoke, he couldn't see, and his right arm and shoulder were shattered. Doctors were able to restore limited movement to his badly mangled hand. But Michael Naranjo, the Indian outdoorsman, was now sightless and left with only one good arm.

Naranjo did not allow himself the luxury of despondency, however. "Why make the suffering worse?" he thought. "There is both happiness and pain in life. One makes you appreciate the other."

While his body was mending, first in Japan, then at Fitzsimons Army Hospital in Denver, Naranjo asked for some modeling clay. It would help pass the time, he thought, as it had when he was a child playing with clay at his mother's feet while she molded colorful pots. The animals and images he made as a child had been considered quite good, and he soon realized that the grenade blast had not destroyed his touch. Most important, he could still hold images in his mind's eye. He started sculpting horses and Indians. They were incredibly good, and as time went on they became even better. Cautiously, Naranjo began nurturing a dream that he would someday become a sculptor of wide acclaim.

One day after his release, a VA counselor, stopping by to check on him, became immensely interested in Náranjo's sculptures and volunteered to arrange a showing at the Albuquerque VA hospital. This led to an exhibit at VA headquarters in Washington and at the Library of Congress. During his visit to Washington, Naranjo and his family were escorted into the Oval Room of the White House for a meeting which ended with the sculptor and President Nixon on their hands and knees on the carpet feeling the contours of its woven Presidential Seal.

In a 1972 showing at the prestigious Heard Museum in Phoenix, Michael Naranjo's work was enthusiastically received. Subsequent exhibitions at museums across the country have established his reputation. He has been featured on the "Today" show and "PM Magazine" segments. Naranjo, his wife Laurie and two children live in a passive solar adobe home he designed to include a gallery and studio where he produces limited-edition bronze sculptures. But he is not content to rest on his success. "There is so much I want to learn." Then he pauses and adds softly, "I wouldn't trade sculpting for anything—not even my sight."

Shot Down Over Russia!

The Mysterious Saga of Flight 902

---

by Anthony Paul

KOREAN AIR LINES Flight 902 took off from Paris's Orly Airport at 12:39 p.m. on April 21, 1977 bound north for Seoul via the polar route. On board were 97 Japanese, Korean, French, British, West German and Chinese passengers, and 13 crew members. Although once considered perilous, polar flights in recent years have become routine. Flight 902's captain, Kim Chang-kyu, 46, had flown the polar route more than 30 times without incident; navigator Lee Kun-shik, 46, had covered the same ground some 70 times.

But no matter how experienced the air crew, the curious nature of the top-of-the-world makes navigation a tricky business. Maps are next to useless: from 35,000 feet, the Arctic Ocean is a vast stretch of ice as featureless as a freshly laundered sheet. Moreover, any point on the surface below moves about 15 degrees an hour, with the rapidly rotating earth. Thus reliance must be on instruments, closely watched.

Most airliners flying the polar route today are equipped with

227

Inertial Navigational Systems—on-board computers allied with highly advanced gyroscopes and fed with constantly updated information from radar stations and from observations of sun, moon and star positions. But Flight 902 did not have such computers. Instead, the 11-year-old Boeing 707 was equipped with the older Doppler Navigational System. This requires the navigator to check star or sun positions as frequently as every 10 or 15 minutes, and then adjust the directional gyroscope.

For the first two or three hours out of Paris, everything was normal aboard Flight 902. Then, somewhere near Iceland, the airliner encountered its first problem. Because of "atmospheric conditions," Captain Kim was unable to reach air-traffic control at Reykjavik, Iceland, to report his position. At about 5 p.m., therefore, he notified the next ground station—on Spitsbergen, 400 frozen miles off Norway's North Cape—that he was passing beyond Greenland's west coast, and asked them to notify Reykjavik. They did not acknowledge.

At that moment, according to Captain Kim's report, Flight 902 should have been heading into Canadian airspace. Instead of flying westward, however, the jetliner—in what must surely be the worst navigational error in modern aviation history—had somehow made a turn of 112 degrees. The plane's actual course was southeastward, straight toward the Soviet Union!

According to unofficial Moscow sources, the first Soviet radar sighting of the Korean jet was made by stations in the vicinity of Franz Josef Land, a group of Soviet islands above the 80th parallel, 700 miles north of Murmansk. Increasingly puzzled, the Russians reportedly queried the plane "on every available commercial radio frequency." No response, insist the Russians. High officials in Moscow were alerted.

In the airliner's passenger cabin, a group of Korean construction workers returning home from a project in Gabon, West Africa, called for more beer and whiskey. Two British clothing manufacturers—Benson Cohen and William Howard—dozed, chatted, read. Howard glanced at his watch. A scheduled stop in Anchorage, Alaska, would permit them to stretch their cramped legs. "We should be going down soon," he said.

Seiko Shiozaki, a Japanese English-language student, nudged her dozing fiancé, artist Moto-o Uota, and suggested that he look at the sun, now offering a striking display of gold, red and gray as it shimmered just above the icy horizon to the right of the aircraft. The sun also caught the eye of Kineo Ohtani, owner of a Tokyo camera store. "Something's wrong," he said to his wife. "The sun's on the wrong side."

At about the same time, Captain Kim also sensed something wrong with the sun's position. Then the plane's radar began indicating islands far beneath. "Check our position!" he ordered navigator Lee. By then, however, it was too late.

Han Young-choon, a Korean air-conditioning technician, may have been the first passenger to spot the fighter plane. Sipping a whiskey, he watched quietly as a needle-nosed V-winged aircraft rose toward the airliner, then drew level about 100 yards from the 707's right wingtip. Though most passengers saw only one fighter, the pilots later reported that at least two jets intercepted Flight 902.

Inside the airliner's cockpit, the arrival of the mystery jets was at first something of a relief. "I think they're Canadian," said co-pilot Cha Soon-do.

"Then ask them where we are!" ordered Captain Kim.

Using the international emergency radio frequency, the Koreans tried repeatedly to talk with the fighter pilots. But no answer came.

For at least ten minutes, the fighter off the right wing kept its position. Then it veered away into the twilight and the clouds. Suddenly, an odd thud came from the airliner's left side, along with a flash of light and a deafening explosion. Red-hot metal fragments slammed into the airliner, tearing holes—from nail-size up to the size of a melon. Shrapnel sprayed through the rear of the cabin.

Choi Bong-ki, section chief for a large Korean trading company, had leaned forward to write a translation of some camera instructions for a fellow passenger. That saved his life. A small piece of metal punched through the window beside him and, instead of slicing into Choi's left temple, grazed the back of his head. In the seat ahead, a Japanese tourist was saved by his cowboy belt, which stopped a bullet-sized fragment.

Two other passengers, however, were not so lucky. Technician Bang Tai-hwan had left his seat to talk with a friend; now he tumbled, dying, into the aisle. The top of his skull had been shaved off by shrapnel. Yoshitaka Sugano, a Yokohama coffee-shop proprietor—who moments before had switched seats with his older brother—slumped over, fatally wounded by shrapnel that pierced his elbow, chest and knee. Shrapnel wounded 13 other persons, some of them seriously.

Unofficial Soviet sources say Moscow feared the airliner was carrying electronic equipment for spying, and would soon turn westward and escape across the Finnish border. According to these sources, the fighters, supersonic Sukhoi Su-15s, tried unsuccessfully to communicate with the Koreans. The order was then given to "force the plane down by firing on it, but to bring it down in a condition that would permit a thorough examination."

These claims are highly doubtful. Between 6:35 p.m. and 6:41 p.m., air-traffic control at Rovaniemi, Finland, taped three Korean efforts to contact the Soviet fighters. From the Russians, the tape shows, there was no reply.

The blast, apparently from an exploding missile, battered Flight 902's wing and fuselage. The Boeing rocked violently; then, from 35,000 feet, it plunged into an uncontrolled dive. Electric wires crackled and the lights went out. Acrid smoke filled the aisle. The wounded screamed; blood trickled down the steeply sloping floor. The falling air pressure in the cabin threatened to burst eardrums, and several passengers fainted.

Captain Kim fought to regain control, managing to pull the airliner's nose up slightly. But then, because of continuing rapid decompression at a dangerously high altitude, he put the 707 once again into a steep dive. Meanwhile, chief steward Chu Myong-yong grabbed the public-address microphone and, with more coolness than accuracy, reassured passengers in Korean, Japanese and English: "There is nothing wrong with the plane. Passengers should be calm and cooperate with the crew." But then, in Korean, he ordered the cabin staff: "Prepare for an emergency landing!"

At 3000 feet, Captain Kim brought the airliner out of the dive and took stock. In addition to ripping holes in the fuselage, the missile blast had torn off the left wingtip and ten feet of the wing's leading edge. One passenger was dead. By the light of a pocket flashlight, two young Japanese doctors, one wounded himself, were trying to save Sugano with tourniquets fashioned from a necktie and a belt.

Just where Flight 902 was remained unclear. But somewhere in the rapidly gathering darkness, Captain Kim realized, jet fighters were still stalking his stricken Boeing. There was only one thing to do: try a crash landing. To find a suitable site, he began making wide, meandering circles above the eerily moon-lit snowscape.

Thrust hurriedly into life jackets, passengers were told to take off their shoes, sit in a fetal position and fasten their seat belts. At her fiancé's urging, Seiko Shiozaki kept her mind off the future by starting a diary: "Left wingtip gone. Plane continues flying. Moto-o kisses me."

A young Japanese, determined to protect his face, wrapped his head in every piece of spare clothing he was carrying or could borrow from others. The two British businessmen shook hands solemnly, wished each other luck, and shared the consolation that at least their wives would collect ample insurance.

Lin Shing-yueh, a Taiwan artist, recalls: "To the chilling question 'What can I do with the short time left to me?' there was just one answer: reminisce. Events that had caused me pain, I quickly cast away as I greedily tried to remember only the best and the beautiful. Why was I never so aware before?"

Three times, Captain Kim started to put the airliner down in grainfields or on roads, but each time hills or high-tension wires obstructed his approach. Finally he spotted a frozen, tree-lined lake. Would the ice hold the 100-ton Boeing? He would have to try.

The touchdown, raising an enormous cloud of snow, was smooth though the damaged wing was finally demolished in a collision with a grove of lakeside cedars. Seiko Shiozaki continued scribbling: "Landing. Flames [or sparks?] briefly seen outside window. Atmosphere of relief fills cabin. The captain appears—to passengers' standing ovation!"

After peering into the gloom, a German passenger announced with some authority, "We're in Alaska." A stewardess opened an emergency door and several passengers went down the chute onto the snow-covered lake, only to be driven back into the plane by the extreme cold. Inside it was dark and growing more chilly. The doctors continued to labor over Sugano.

Nearly two hours passed. At first, jets had been heard circling nearby. "Where, then, are the Americans and their rescue teams?" stewardess Yu Hae-ja wondered.

But now something was moving out from the trees, slowly, cautiously, toward the airliner. There were men out there, about 20 or 30. Several passengers cheered.

The forward door opened. Into the cabin stepped a tall, burly man in fur cap, jackboots, an imposing, ankle-length military greatcoat. Totally expressionless, he took in the scene, then walked slowly down the aisle. In the silent cabin, passengers caught a glimpse of a red star on the cap, red flashes on the collar. Through Miss Yu's mind flashed a scene from the movie *Doctor Zhivago*. This wasn't Alaska, she realized. He's a Russian officer!

Many of the South Koreans aboard were convinced the Russians would turn them over to North Korea. Surreptitiously, over the course of the next few hours, they tore up their passports and letters from home, hoping they could pass themselves off as Japanese or Chinese. Section chief Choi was carrying company documents listing construction projects—possible military targets—in South Korea. With Miss Yu's help he burned them, flushing the ashes down the toilet.

At last, large troop-carrying helicopters landed, while smaller helicopters hovered nearby. Sugano was the first passenger moved. Too late: he died a short time later in a Soviet hospital.

For two days, the Russians kept their uninvited guests in makeshift quarters in Kem, a fishing port 230 miles south of Murmansk. Finally, following overtures from the U.S. and Japanese embassies in Moscow, a chartered American airliner was permitted to pick up the 95 surviving passengers, 11 crew members and the bodies of the two who had died, and fly them to Helsinki. From there, another KAL airliner completed the journey to Seoul. After eight days' interrogation in the Soviet Union, the pilot and navigator were also released.

Some gravely important questions about Flight 902 remain unanswered. First of all, how could such an experienced crew take their airliner so far off course? And why, if Soviet ground stations really did try to contact the Korean jet, are there no known radio transcripts? Also, why did the Soviet fighter pilot make so little apparent effort to communicate with the airliner before firing?

The Russians have retained the single most important item of evidence: The Boeing's flight recorder, the "black box" which preserves a tape of everything said in an airliner's cockpit during a flight. So long as they refuse to release the tape, the full story of Flight 902 will not be known in the West. But if even deadlier incidents are to be avoided, the Russians owe it to the world to make the recorder available, and to publish a full, factual account of what they believe happened.

As the London *Guardian* put it: "Arctic navigation is a

difficult area, and humans make mistakes. But there ought to be a foolproof system, short of gunfire, whereby a military aircraft can warn a civilian one that it is committing an offense. What went wrong with the navigation? Was 121.5 megahertz [the emergency radio frequency] dependable or not? The sooner the Russians answer these questions the better, for international action may have to hinge on them."

Ron Woodcock's Long Walk Home

by Joseph P. Blank

RONALD WOODCOCK SAT on the trunk of a fallen tree, stared at the ground and tried to think. He was lost in the trackless, unspoiled wilderness of northwestern British Columbia. He marked the date on the calendar that he kept in his backpack: "June 5, 1971."

Woodcock wasn't worried about himself. He felt comfortable in the wilderness, and figured he had plenty of time to find the cabin that he had been using. But he was concerned about his family; he had been out of touch with them now for 40 days. His wife and six children were living in a rented house in Endako, more than 200 air miles to the south. The February before, his own home and his possessions—all uninsured—had been destroyed by fire. Financially, he had been wiped out.

That really, was why he had made this trip to the wilderness. He needed more money than he was earning at his railroad job, so he had taken a leave of absence to trap beaver. A good pelt brought $20. In late April he flew to Damdochax Lake, after arranging for a bush pilot, Bill Jenkins, to pick him up eight weeks later.

Woodcock, 48, was brown-haired, blue-eyed and stocky at 170 pounds. This venture was his third trip to the bush in ten years, and he loved it. He often thought, "If there was a way to have my family with me, I'd spend my life here. You're at peace. You're your own boss. Fish and game are plentiful. You're in a world you're making for yourself, and no other world exists."

The trapping went smoothly, and Woodcock garnered more than 50 pelts in his first three weeks. On May 31 he left his cabin to retrieve skins that he had cached 20 miles north. He wore rubber boots, a wool shirt and a light jacket. His 30-pound backpack included a sleeping bag, an ax, food, a rifle and 15 rounds of ammunition.

He worked his way up Slowmaldo Creek and into Ground-hog Pass, where he located his skins and spent several days cleaning them. Then he packed half the skins, a 60-pound load, and his remaining three-day supply of food. Because of the weight he was carrying, he decided to seek a shorter route back to Slowmaldo Creek.

After trudging south for six hours through high underbrush, he broke out onto a creek that was backed up by several un-familiar beaver dams—and from which he had a stunning view of strange mountains. For a long minute he was hypnotized by the beauty of the panorama. Then, sitting down, he faced the fact that what had so quickly happened to other woodsmen had now happened to him. He was lost. He had no means of know-ing whether Slowmaldo Creek was east or west. In this land of untapped mineral deposits, he thought his compass might not register true. He couldn't backtrack because there was noth-ing to follow. His best course, he reasoned, was to stick with this unfamiliar creek downstream to the south. It might bring him to recognizable land or a river. And south was the general direction of the closest town, Hazelton, 125 air miles away.

Woodcock pushed along the creek, still carrying the heavy beaver pelts. Every step was work. The creek was so overgrown along its banks that there was no simple path to follow. He was continually climbing and descending hills and fighting through underbrush; worse, he met an endless obstacle course of windfalls—dead trees that had accumulated over the years and sometimes built themselves into impasses 25 feet high.

On the evening of the second day, Woodcock reluctantly abandoned his furs. He cooked a handful of rice and zipped himself into his sleeping bag. As he lay awake, he realized that he was in trouble; other men in his predicament, he knew, had panicked, exhausted themselves and not survived. This would not happen to him. He resolved to pace himself and be finicky-careful. He *would* make it out, however long it took.

Although he plodded on for about 13 hours a day, he always stopped when he was tired, rather than spent. He doled out his food sparingly, always on the lookout for game. He shot a woodchuck and a grouse, and on the tenth day he shot a moose. He spent the following day dressing a hindquarter and cooking it down to some 20 pounds of meat to pack with him.

About six o'clock that evening, as he prepared his campsite, he looked up to see a giant grizzly approaching the moose carcass. Although he was 100 feet downwind from the carcass, he knew he had to kill the bear. "The grizzly must have stood nine feet tall and weighed more than a thousand pounds," he remembers. "Those bears are touchy in the spring, and inclined to attack. I couldn't have him around my camp while I was sleeping."

Woodcock's first shot slammed through the bear's neck and into his spinal column, paralyzing him. Reluctant to use another bullet, he waited for the wounded animal to die. Finally, as light grew dim, he had to finish off the bear with a second shot.

On the 14th day Woodcock's path toward home was blocked by an icy river too broad and deep to ford. He shoved his way westward for a day until he encountered a wildly running creek. He felled two 40-foot trees across the water, but the current swept each away. Now he was blocked to the south and the west, so he moved north along the creek, hoping that it would narrow enough to enable him to cross.

On the evening of the 15th day a storm struck. The wind howled, trees crashed and rain slashed down. He fixed a shelter and a high "mattress" out of spruce limbs. For two days, while the storm raged, he lay in his sleeping bag, hardly moving. He thought about his family and about what the bush pilot, Bill Jenkins, would think and do when he returned for their rendezvous at the Damdochax Lake cabin and found no one.

(In fact, the pilot did return. Alarmed at Woodcock's absence, he searched the area for two days, went home and then came back again with Woodcock's brother and brother-in-law. In four days they found only an overturned raft, where the lake emptied into a creek. They concluded that Woodcock must have been on the raft when it capsized and that he had drowned.)

After the storm subsided, Woodcock, still totally lost, continued northward, looking for a place to cross the creek. "Take it easy," he told himself aloud. "You'll get out." He found a narrowing of the stream, managed to cross and turned back southward.

On about the 25th day he ate the last of his food. Exertion already had chipped about 20 pounds off him. "Have to eat what grows," he ruminated. "But be careful. Don't get sick." He tried the young tender shoots of the Solomon's Seal plant; he had watched dairy cows munch on them. Squawberries, savored by moose, made his mouth pucker, but he assumed they contained some nourishment.

One morning, as he worked through the underbrush, he suddenly caught a glimpse of a rotting pole—a telegraph pole! He had, he knew, chanced on the old telegraph trail, put through the wilderness by government packhorse expeditions in the late 1800s, now abandoned for many decades. If he could follow signs of the trail—a pole here and there, a piece of telegraph wire still nailed to a tree—the clues would lead him to Hazelton.

Although the trail was overgrown now, it had been trampled for many years by men and animals. Woodcock cut himself a walking stick. By poking it gently into the ground, he could differentiate between the packed earth of the old trail and the soft virgin soil on either side of it.

Now, his odyssey became a step-by-step ordeal as he kept prodding the earth and looking for old poles and pieces of wire. Frequently, he lost the trail in foot-high moss, dense brush and trees. He had to detour for swamps and stands of impenetrable willows. When he lost the trail, he patiently zigged to the east, zagged to the west, sometimes repeating the pattern for days until he picked up the trail again. All movement was a struggle. During one two-week period he estimated that he had progressed no more than 20 miles.

By about the 43rd day his stamina was ebbing, and he couldn't remain on his feet more than six or seven hours a day. Since the 25th day he had eaten only wild berries and leaves.

His belt could no longer hold up his tattered trousers, so he removed the sling from his rifle and fashioned a single suspender out of it. In climbing, he had to pause after three or four steps, and he relied increasingly on his rifle and a walking stick for support. The sole flapped off one boot, and he tied it to the upper with a piece of string from his pack. His clothing was progressively shredded by the sharp brush. Mosquitoes were turning his forehead into raw, bleeding meat. He found nothing to eat except heavily seeded high-bush cranberries. The seeds lodged immovably in his intestines, doubled him up with cramps that shot through his middle like electric shocks.

On what he figured was about the 50th day, he lay on the ground, writhing and panting in pain. "Maybe it's time to give up," he thought. But that's not what he wanted to do; he wanted to see his family. "Rest awhile," he told himself. "You don't have much farther to go." Somewhere ahead, he knew, was the dirt road to Hazelton.

So he got up and stumbled on. His rubbery legs felt boneless. He had to squint to focus his eyes. Saliva thickened in his mouth and throat, and he choked when he tried to scrape it out with his fingers. He knew he couldn't climb each new incline, but somehow he did. He had to make it in two more days. He could not last a third day. Yet, even in his condition, he did not let himself indulge in hopeless thoughts.

Suddenly, around noon of the 57th day, he found himself in the open, on a road—the dirt road to Hazelton! The scene around kept wavering and swimming. He tried to lock his knees so they wouldn't buckle.

A car approached him. The two men in it, intent on an afternoon of fishing, stared at the mangy scarecrow of a human being and continued past him. One hundred and fifty feet down the road the car stopped, then backed. Woodcock staggered toward it. He opened his mouth to talk, but he couldn't utter a sound. He weakly motioned for a pencil and paper.

"I need water," he laboriously scrawled. One man opened a bottle of beer and handed it to him. He slowly got it through the saliva that clotted his mouth. Then he wrote, "If it's not too much trouble, please take me to my mother in Hazelton." Her house was closest.

The two men helped him into the rear seat. His head swam. He felt a mild sense of satisfaction and relief. He had made it. The fishermen helped him to the door of his mother's house.

She couldn't believe the apparition before her. Woodcock's face was gaunt behind a three-inch beard. His eyes were glazed. He had lost 70 of his 170 pounds. The rips in his trousers revealed thighs that looked like white sticks.

He was hospitalized two weeks for treatment of malnutrition, exposure and intestinal disorders, and it took an additional two months for him to recover his health and strength. In the hospital, it was three days before he could talk even in a whisper. His wife sat by his bed and asked no questions. After four days, Woodcock's feelings surfaced. When friends asked him about his experience, he began whispering the details, then broke into tears, not even aware that he was going to cry. The visitors misunderstood his tears. He couldn't explain that he had passed through a great adventure. It had given him a conviction that all human beings seek: that he had the courage to face and deal with whatever test life brought.

My Second Chance to Live

by Robert Strohm

I WAS at the Mayo Clinic in Rochester, Minn., for a life-or-death decision in April 1972. Ever since a streptococcus infection riddled my kidneys when I was eight, slowly spreading scar tissue had gradually choked off the kidneys' ability to filter wastes from my body. At 25, my kidney function was down to four percent, and the accumulating wastes in my blood were making me itch all over—one of the first signs of uremic poisoning. This meant, I learned, that I had only weeks to live.

"Your only hope for a normal life," a Mayo specialist said, "is a kidney transplant. Treatment three times a week on an artificial kidney machine could keep you alive, but I doubt that you'd enjoy that sort of life."

When I first got nephritis in 1954, my doctor's basic aim had been to stretch the life of my kidneys. He told my parents: "No one really knows how long Bob's kidneys can last. But as long as he's alive, there's always hope. Maybe we'll find a cure."

241

There were glimmers of hope. The first kidney transplant was performed in 1954. And the artificial kidney machine came into limited use in the early 1960s. But I knew that neither method was a sure thing. I lived for the present and tried not to think about the future.

My doctors had given me a somewhat normal life for 17 years of progressive kidney failure by fine-tuning my diet to put the least possible strain on my kidneys and by the masterful use of a variety of drugs. Nevertheless, my diet grew increasingly restricted. I suffered from blinding headaches. My blood-pressure pills made me light-headed, and I passed out several times, once falling into the street while getting off a bus. I was in and out of hospitals because my weakened system had a hard time resisting infections.

Still, I managed to get through school, receiving a degree in journalism from the University of Illinois in 1968. I had been working as an associate editor of *National Wildlife* magazine until shortly before I went to Mayo's.

It was hard to face the realization that my kidneys were now almost useless, and that I needed a kidney from someone else. (Fortunately, one can do the work of two.) Still seeking an escape, I asked the Mayo specialist, "Could the transplant be put off for a while?"

Leaning back from a desk cluttered with my medical history and the results of the morning's tests, he spoke firmly: "There's nothing to gain by waiting." My next big question was: "Where will I get a kidney?"

The majority of transplant patients now receive their kidney from a cadaver—the body of a person whose brain has died, as a result of a fatal accident or illness, but whose heart and lungs have been kept operating to ensure an oxygen supply to the kidney until it is removed. Such a kidney would give me only a 60-percent chance for a successful transplant, the Mayo doctor said. But a transplant from a living relative would increase my chances for a normal life to 90 percent.

On my return to my family's home in Woodstock, Ill., each of my two brothers and three sisters offered me a kidney. Blood tests narrowed the field of potential donors to David, 19, a junior at the University of Illinois, and Karen, 26, married, with two small children. Dave insisted that he was the logical one. "Then I can claim everything Bob does as partly mine," he said.

The next week, Karen, Dave and I flew to Mayo's, where I was immediately put on the artificial kidney machine, so that it could begin cleansing my blood in preparation for the operation. Meanwhile, Dave and Karen underwent a rigorous battery of tests and examinations, including an interview with a psychiatrist to be certain that they weren't being pressured by the family into volunteering a kidney.

Physically, this was the most uncomfortable period in my life. I had the typical symptoms of end-stage kidney failure. My overall poor health, the buildup of wastes in my system and very high blood pressure combined to give me almost constant headaches and nausea. I lost 30 of the 150 pounds on my six-foot-two-inch frame and was extremely weak. But I was so excited about my second chance at life that these physical discomforts did not depress my spirits. In fact, an emotional "high" started building in anticipation of what I told myself would be at least 50 years of a healthy, rewarding existence.

The first tests brought the good news that Karen and Dave were both good tissue matches—and the better the tissue match between donor and recipient, the less chance there is that the transplant will be rejected. We were still all on edge about the last big hurdle: a renal arteriogram to see if they both had two kidneys and only one artery supplying blood to each. Some people have only one kidney; and it is fairly common for a kidney to have two or more arteries, which greatly complicates transplant surgery.

A profound sense of gratitude swept over me when a doctor told me, "Your sister Karen has been approved as a donor." But I was still counting on Dave: he was a better tissue match, almost as good as an identical twin. When I got the word from him the next evening, I wrote in my journal:

"At 7:10 Dave called, and he has two kidneys! Same size! Each has one artery! Called Mom and Dad. Celebration! Happiness! Elation! Thank the Lord! Better than a nine-out-of-ten chance for a normal life after a little plumbing!"

Surgery to take out my kidneys was scheduled for the next Friday, April 23. The transplant operation was set for June 9, six weeks later. Transplants at the Mayo Clinic are performed in two stages, because the surgeons have learned that the chance of success is better if the major shock of removing the old kidneys and planting a new one all in one operation is avoided. Between the two operations, the artificial kidney would keep me alive. For the first time in 17 years, I felt that a normal life was within my reach.

Dad was sitting by my hospital bed when I woke up nine hours after both my kidneys had been removed.

"How did it go?" I mumbled, feeling the bandage covering the long incision running down the middle of my front.

"Doctors say you're doing great," he answered. "Next, the transplant—and then a new life."

For the six weeks I was without kidneys, I was hooked up to that magnificent artificial kidney machine for dialysis eight hours a day, four days a week. Dialysis is a relatively simple process. A small plastic tube, called a cannula, was implanted in my left wrist. One end was connected to an artery, the other to a vein. Blood flows out of the artery into the machine, where it passes into a cellophane filter containing microscopic holes. Because the waste particles collected by the blood are smaller than blood cells, they pass through the filter and are washed away by the dialyzing fluid. The purified blood is then routed back to the patient's body through the vein. In each eight-hour session, the kidney machine removed from my blood one to three pounds of excess fluids and wastes that would have otherwise accumulated and killed me.

The last weekend before the transplant, Dad came up. We went out to a little state park and walked along a stream, photographed wild flowers, and sat on logs in the sun and talked. During these weeks, I felt very close to every member of my family. The sacrifices they had made over the years to accommodate me, and their wholehearted support of me now gave me tremendous confidence that everything would work out.

At last, the big day arrived. The operation would involve six surgeons, four nurses, plus anesthesiologists and technicians. Dave and I were lying on hospital carts next to each other. For about 40 minutes before we were taken into separate operating rooms, we talked about the family, about the future, about frivolous things.

Not surprisingly, I felt closer to Dave than I had ever felt to anyone. We had had the usual brotherly fights when we were younger, but in those days I couldn't have imagined that one day he would be giving me a part of his body that I might live. Then the blue-clad orderlies came for him, and I was alone with my thoughts.

The painstaking operation to remove Dave's kidney lasted 2 ½ hours, the surgical team working through a 14-inch incision made diagonally around his left side, just above the waist.

A few feet away in an adjacent operating room, an hour after the incision was made in Dave, another surgical team started the three-hour operation on me. Transplant teams develop intricate teamwork and timing, and are in constant communication, as I was to observe months later when I witnessed a transplant.

When the transplant surgeon finished preparing the site in my body where the new kidney would be placed—nowhere near the natural kidney location, but low on the right side of the abdomen so that if removal should become necessary later, the surgery would be simplified—he sent word to Dave's surgical team. And, at the last possible moment—making certain that the kidney was actually functioning—Dave's surgeon severed the artery and vein that still connected the exposed kidney to my brother's body. Another surgeon swiftly carried the fist-sized organ to my operating room. He handed it to the head of the transplant team, who placed it in an iced saline solution, then flushed it out with a special solution to both cool it and remove the remaining blood. Then, within half an hour, Dave's kidney became mine.

Surgery was finished by noon. I woke up about 8:30 that evening in the isolation unit. Dad was there, all wrapped up in a green plastic gown with a mask over his nose and mouth.

"How's the kidney working?" I asked.

"Great! The doctors told me it put out almost two liters of urine in the first hour and a half." He said as proudly as if he were telling how a son of his had scored 30 points in a basketball game.

"How's Dave?"

"He's fine. You're both doing great."

The third day after transplant, I was eating foods I hadn't eaten for years because of dietary restrictions on sodium and protein. I never knew bologna and crackers could taste so good. I had almost no pain, and began walking around the hospital, feeling better and getting stronger every day. Dave had a much rougher time of it, because the surgeons had to cut through three layers of muscle to get at his kidney. But he bounced back quickly, and within ten days was back in school.

A few days later, I walked out of the hospital, with a funny little bulge on the right side of my abdomen—my brother's kidney. My remaining concern was the one that every kidney transplant patient faces: Will the new kidney be rejected? Will it die and have to be removed?

If that happens, the patient must go back on the artificial kidney. If he is lucky, he may get another transplant—but kidneys are scarce. Today there are, according to the National Kidney Foundation, 60,000 persons on dialysis, most of whom are waiting for a transplant.

If my body were to try to reject Dave's kidney, the most likely time would have been in the first two weeks after surgery, when the anti-rejection drug doses, which I had started taking two days before the operation, were lowered. Anxiously I waited. The tell-tale signs of rejection—fever and a rise in serum creatinine (a measure of kidney function)—did not show up. I felt I had it made.

In three months, I was running two miles before work every morning, then plunging into nine-hour workdays. I seemed to have an entirely different body—one that never got tired or felt bad. My doctor was pleased, but not surprised. Almost 100 percent of his successful transplant patients were able to resume full normal activity, he said.

Dave was also doing well. After six weeks, he was playing tennis and doing all the other things he'd done before, with one exception: no contact sports. Doctors say his remaining kidney has greatly increased its capacity, and chances are he'll never miss the one he gave me.

The only price I pay for my new life is sticking to what my doctor called a "long, boring, post-operative regimen." I must continue to take anti-rejection drugs daily for the rest of my life. And because these drugs induced diabetes about a month after the operation—my only real setback—I now need insulin shots. But doctors say this need may disappear in the future as the anti-rejection drug dosage is reduced.

The first critical period is now past. And if my new kidney

is still functioning well after two years, Mayo specialists say, I can be 90-percent sure of a normal life-span. Most Americans with end-stage kidney disease are not so lucky. Of the 60,000 Americans on dialysis this year, only about 4500 will receive a kidney transplant for lack of suitable donors. Treatment on a home machine costs between $14,000 and $20,000 per year. And according to the National Kidney Foundation, the average cost of a transplant is about $25,000.

So I realize I have been given something very special.

To repay society for my new life in a small way, I carry in my billfold a Uniform Donor Card. It says that in the hope of helping others I give, upon my death, any of my organs or parts for the purposes of transplantation, therapy, medical research or education; or my body for anatomical study.

This is the least I can do. The possibility that I can help others, as I have been helped, is really what the Golden Rule is all about, isn't it?

Betty Ford's Triumph

by Betty Ford with Chris Chase

In the spring of 1978, former First Lady Betty Ford was putting the finishing touches on her autobiography, The Times of My Life, *when she discovered that the real ending had yet to be written. On April 10, 1978, she entered the Long Beach, Calif., Naval Hospital's Alcohol and Drug Rehabilitation Service for intensive treatment to rid herself of a debilitating addiction. Here, condensed from the final chapter of her book, is the story of her ordeal, and the courageous battle she waged against an insidious disease shared by millions of Americans.*

IT WASN'T UNTIL after we had left the White House and retired to private life in Palm Springs that my family realized I was in trouble. For 14 years I'd been on medications—for a pinched nerve, arthritis, muscle spasms in my neck and, in 1974, for relief during my recovery from a radical mastectomy. I'd built up a tolerance to the drugs prescribed for me. And just one drink, taken on top of so much medication, would make me groggy.

In the fall of 1977, I went to Moscow to narrate *The Nut-cracker* ballet for television. Later, there were comments about my "sloe-eyed, sleepy-tongued" performance. Jerry and the children were worried, but I had no idea what was happening to me or how much I had changed. Only now do I realize that after the trip to Russia I began to suffer lapses of memory.

Finally my daughter Susan discussed my condition with our doctor. He recommended direct intervention. The thinking used to be that a person chemically addicted to either alcohol or pills had to hit bottom, then decide he or she *wanted* to get well, before recovery could begin. But it has now been demonstrated that a sick person's family, along with others important to the patient, can intervene to help. With this new intervention method, the recovery rate has increased significantly.

In March 1978, while Jerry was in the East on a speaking tour, the doctor, along with Susan and my secretary, Caroline Coventry, marched into my sitting room and confronted me. They started talking about my giving up all medication and liquor. I got very angry, and was so upset that after they left I called a friend and complained about the terrible invasion of my privacy. (I don't remember that call; the friend has since told me about it.)

Why was I so disturbed? Perhaps because drinking is so much a part of our society. We get to know one another over drinks, and associate feasts and celebrations with liquor. We think we have to drink, that it's a social necessity, that it's romantic. Well, that's fine as long as you can handle it. For years I could and did.

I don't think everybody has to stop drinking; I just think I had to stop drinking. When I add up the number of pills I was taking, and put a drink or two on top, I can see how I got to the breaking point. I realize now that members of my family used to run to fix me my nightly libation because they could keep it light, whereas when I poured it, I'd make it stiff. Jerry would hand me a mild vodka and tonic, and I'd sigh, "Why don't you give me a *normal* drink?"

On the morning of April 1—it was a Saturday—I was thinking about phoning my son Mike and his wife, Gayle, in Pittsburgh, when the front door opened and in they came, along with the entire family. I was thrilled, thinking they'd gathered because I wasn't feeling well. We hugged and kissed and went into the living room—where they all proceeded to confront me a second time. And they meant business. They had brought along Capt. Joe Pursch, the Navy doctor who is head of the Alcohol and Drug Rehabilitation Service at Long Beach.

I can tell you where every single person in that room was sitting. The floor plan is burned into my brain. But I can't remember their exact words; I was in shock. Mike and Gayle spoke of wanting children, and wanting those children's grandmother to be healthy and in charge of her own life. Jerry mentioned times when I'd fallen asleep in the chair, and times when my speech had slurred, and Steve brought up a recent weekend when he and a girlfriend had cooked dinner for me and I wouldn't come to the table on time. "You just sat in front of the TV," Steve said, "and had one drink, two drinks, three drinks. You hurt me."

Well, he hurt me back. They all hurt me. I collapsed in tears. But I still had enough sense to realize that they hadn't come around just to make me cry; they were there because they loved me and wanted to help me.

Yet I resisted any suggestion that liquor had contributed to my illness; all I would confess to was overmedication. Captain Pursch told me it didn't matter. He gave me the book, *Alcoholics Anonymous,* and told me to read it, substituting the words "chemically dependent" for "alcoholic." Since a tranquilizer or a dry martini each brings the same relief, you can use the same book for drugs and alcohol. And when I say drugs, I'm talking about legal medications, prescribed by doctors.

At first I was bitter toward the medical profession for all those years of being advised to take pills rather than wait for the pain to hit. I took pills for pain, and pills to sleep, and I took tranquilizers. Today, many doctors are beginning to recognize the risks in these medications, but some of them used to be all too eager to write prescriptions. (The odd thing is that I had already tapered myself off one medication, and was beginning to work on letting go of another when the intervention started.)

Two days after my 60th birthday, I entered the hospital at Long Beach. I could have gone to a private facility, but I decided that it was better to seek treatment publicly rather than to hide behind a silk sheet. A statement which said I'd been overmedicating myself was to be released to the press once I was safely ensconced.

Captain Pursch met me on the fourth floor and escorted me to a room with four beds. I balked. I'd expected privacy. I was not going to sign in; I was not going to release my statement. Captain Pursch handled the situation perfectly. "If you insist on a private room," he said, "I will have all these women moved out. . . ." He put the ball right in my court.

"No, no, I won't have that," I said quickly and self-consciously. An hour later, I was settled in with three roommates and my statement was being read to reporters.

On April 15, at the end of my first week in Long Beach, my son Steve—caught by a reporter outside the hospital—said I was fighting the effects not only of pills, but of alcohol as well. I wasn't enchanted; I wasn't yet prepared to admit that. All week I had been talking about medications, and everyone had nodded respectfully.

Five days later there was a meeting in Captain Pursch's office. Jerry and I were there, along with several doctors. Now they told me that I should make a public statement admitting that I was also an alcoholic. I refused. "I don't want to embarrass my husband," I said.

"You're trying to hide behind your husband," Captain Pursch said. "Why don't you ask him if it would embarrass him if you say you're an alcoholic?"

I started to cry, and Jerry took my hand. "There will be no embarrassment to me," he insisted. "You go ahead and say what should be said."

With that, my crying got worse. When Jerry took me back to my room, I was still sobbing so hard I couldn't get my breath. I hope I never have to cry like that again. It was terrifying. But once it was over, I felt a great relief.

That night, propped up in bed, I scrawled yet another public statement: "I have found that I am not only addicted to the medications I have been taking for my arthritis, but also to alcohol. I expect this treatment and fellowship to be a solution for my problems, and I embrace it not only for me, but for all the others who are here to participate." It was a big step for me to write that, but it was only the first of many steps that I would have to take.

The reason I had rejected the idea that I was alcoholic was

that my addiction wasn't dramatic. So my speech had become deliberate and I forgot a few telephone calls. So I fell in the bathroom and cracked three ribs. But I never drank to ease a hangover, and I hadn't been a solitary drinker, either. I'd never hidden bottles in chandeliers or toilet tanks. There had been no broken promises (Jerry never came to me and said, "Please quit") and no drunken driving. And I never wound up in a strange part of town with a bunch of sailors.

Until Long Beach.

I loved the sailors at Long Beach. We were all on a first-name basis—everywhere I went, people called, "Hi, Betty"—and as we struggled with our dependencies and our terrors, each of us held out his hands to the others.

The drug and alcohol rehabilitation program was started at Long Beach in 1965, mostly to help active-duty Navy personnel and their dependents. While I was there, Jerry went through a two-week participatory course; so did Susan. They had therapy, though not in my group, and Steve spent a few days in the program, too.

Each day the alarm clock went off at 6 a.m. I got up, made my bed, fixed myself a cup of tea and then answered the shout, "Muster!" which meant roll call. (I was in the Navy, after all.) Cleaning detail came next, each of us being given a housekeeping task. Frequently there was an 8 a.m. "Doctors' Meeting." This was a period in which patients interacted with visiting doctors, most of them Naval officers. These doctors were being trained to recognize addiction, and not to push medication to solve people's problems.

Some doctors responded well to the training, some badly. There was one who was very unsympathetic. "I resent being waked up at three o'clock in the morning to have to go and de-tox an alcoholic," he said. We didn't let him get away with that! "What if the patient had cancer or diabetes?" someone asked. "Well, that would be different," he said. We told him it wasn't different. Addiction is a sickness, a terminal sickness; it can be arrested by abstinence, but there is no cure for the disease.

On mornings when I didn't have a Doctors' Meeting, I had group therapy at 8:45, and there was always a second group-therapy session right before lunch. After lunch there would be a lecture or a film, then another class. Each group is composed of six or seven patients and one counselor. In these groups you begin to feel the support, the warmth and comradeship that will be your lifeline back to sobriety. In my group were a 20-year-old sailor (a jet mechanic who'd been drinking since he was eight years old), a young officer (twice married, twice divorced) and a clergyman (addicted to drugs and drink, living on the thin edge of his nerves).

At first, I loathed these sessions. I was uncomfortable, unwilling to speak up. Then one day another woman said she didn't think that her drinking was a problem. I became very emotional and got to my feet. "I'm Betty," I said. "I'm an alcoholic, and I know my drinking has hurt my family." I heard myself, and couldn't believe it. I was trembling; another defense had cracked.

Nothing you hear is to be repeated outside the group. You can freely admit to having wrecked your car and your liver, broken your teeth and your marriage and your dreams. Your group-mates will nod and say yes, but you're not alone, and after all it could be worse. You could still be conning yourself or cursing your genes or your doctors.

In the end, what it comes down to is that you have to take the responsibility for yourself. Never mind that your wife kept a dirty house, or your mother didn't like you, or your husband can't remember your wedding anniversary. Everybody's had disappointments, and anyone can rationalize his actions. But none of that matters. Blaming other people for your condition is a total waste of time.

After I entered the hospital, flowers and bags of mail from well-wishers followed. So many kind people were pulling for me. The Washington *Post* ran an editorial recalling that my candor in discussing my mastectomy had given heart "to countless other victims and prospective victims of breast cancer." And the paper praised me for revealing my addiction to pills and alcohol: "Whatever combination of emotional and psychological stress and physical pain brought her to this pass, she is, characteristically, determined to overcome it. And she is unafraid and unembarrassed to say so."

I thank the *Post,* but I don't deserve the accolade. I've been both afraid *and* embarrassed. I've gone through loneliness, depression, anger, discouragement. Here, for example, is the April 21 notation from a diary I kept at Long Beach:

Now to bed. These damn scratchy wool blankets. Little did I know when I signed in that it was going to be so rough, and

*I don't mean just the blankets, either. It's a good program,
but mighty hard for someone who turned 60 a couple of weeks
ago. What in hell am I doing here? I've even started talking
like the sailors. I could sign out, but I won't let myself do that.
I want it too badly. Guess I'll just cry.*

You get better when you least expect to, when you're not
even trying, when you're down by the coffee machine kibitzing
with two card-playing seamen. In my everyday life, I would
never have met these men, but they and I helped to heal one
another.

Toward the end of my month at Long Beach, I tried to tell
my group—we were Group Six and called ourselves The Six
Pack—what they had meant to me, but I couldn't express it
in words. I started to cry, and one of the fellows handed me
some tissues and said, "Now we know you're going to get
better."

Serenity is hard-won, but I'm making progress. I don't want
to drink anymore, and it's been a great relief to stop. The Betty
Ford Center on the Eisenhower Medical Center Campus houses
a program for the treatment of chemically addicted patients,
and I am participating to help others, which is the best possible
therapy.

There are plenty of chemically dependent people like me,
women who aren't recognized as problem drinkers until con-
frontation is forced on them or they crack. I've heard stories
about women who are business successes and leaders of their
communities—but the iced tea in their hands or the coffee at
their desks is laced with vodka just to keep them going. It's
crucially important to realize how easy it is to slip into such
dependency on pills or alcohol. And how hard it is to admit
that dependency.

I'm grateful to Captain Pursch and the rest of the believers
at Long Beach for their skills and their caring. I'm grateful to
thousands of strangers for their kindness and encouragement.

Through all this, I've learned a lot about myself. When I
add up the pluses and subtract the minuses, I think I come out
pretty well. As I continue to study and learn and work toward
an aware future, I'm sure more will be revealed to me, and
I'm looking forward to that. I intend to make it!

MAYDAY at 19,000 Feet

by James H. Winchester

ON MARCH 28, 1978, Maj. Dale Fowler, a 34-year-old combat pilot in the U.S. Air Force, was in a full power dive over the Gulf of Mexico 55 miles east of Pensacola, Fla. With his one-man, F-5E supersonic jet fighter pointed downward at a 30-degree angle, he was plummeting from 35,000 feet to begin a mock attack in a simulated air battle.

At 22,000 feet, traveling faster than a bullet fired from a .45 revolver, Dale was suddenly slammed against the padded back of his seat by an invisible force. A deafening, shockingly cold 800-mile-an-hour wind filled the tiny cockpit. The temperature dropped almost instantaneously from 60 degrees F. to well below zero. The plane plunged to 10,000 feet before Dale reacted. Pressing the radio-transmitter button, he shouted, "Mayday! Mayday!" It was 11:06 a.m.

The ¾-inch-thick plexiglass cockpit canopy had unexplainably disintegrated. One fragment, about the size of a clenched fist, smashed into the right side of Dale's helmet visor, shattering it like a jagged, broken windshield. (With a special Air Force waiver, he was wearing prescription glasses with metal frames.) The projectile pulverized the right lens, driving glass particles and the twisted frame into his right eye socket.

Though his right eye was gone, he thought he just had a bad cut. Blood coated the still-intact left lens of his glasses, and streaked down the instrument panel. His remaining vision was further blurred by tears caused by the blasting wind.

Ducking behind the instrument panel for protection, Dale instinctively pulled back the throttles to slow his speed, and with his thumb pulled the switch to extend the speed brakes, two 1-½-foot-square panels that drop out of the bottom of the fuselage. Then he called again: "Mayday! Mayday! Dale* has lost his canopy at 19,000. Some damage to right eye!"

Capt. David McCloud, a 33-year-old instructor-pilot from Nellis Air Force Base in Nevada, Dale's home unit, was pulling out of his own dive at 16,000 feet when he heard the Mayday. About eight miles away, the pilots of two F-15s also heard the distress signal. The four fighters were undergoing war-game training at nearby Eglin Air Force Base.

With directions from ground radar, the three fighters rushed to the damaged plane. One F-15 took the left, the other trailed behind and Captain McCloud eased into position on Dale's right. Only a few feet separated their wing tips. Dale could not see McCloud's plane, and the jet on his left was only a dim shape. Deafened by the shrieking wind, he could barely hear McCloud on the radio: "Dale, can you see?"

"I can see some out of one eye," Dale responded. Attempting to make out the altitude and direction indicators, he rubbed his hand across his blood-streaked left lens but the gore had already frozen solid. He found his radio dial by touch, turning it to the Eglin control-tower frequency. Tersely, he detailed the emergency.

Senior Airman Frederick Gardell, the tower controller, told Dale to use runway 30, extending 12,000 feet in a northwest-southeast direction. He next initiated emergency crash procedures by alerting the base fire department, hospital, operations office, and scattering the other airborne jets near the Eglin

---

*In actual or simulated combat, some U.S. Air Force units use first names as call signs, because they are easier to recall than numbers in stress situations.

runways. Less than two minutes had elapsed since the canopy exploded.

Following faint radio instructions from McCloud, Dale made a sweeping turn to head north toward Eglin. At 15,000 feet, he was getting only a trickle of oxygen from his leaking breathing tube. Blood was filling his face mask. With near hypoxia (an inadequate oxygen supply in the organs and tissues) and increasing weakness from loss of blood, Dale realized he had to descend to a lower altitude where he could breathe on his own. It was 11:08 a.m.

McCloud, the war-game flight leader, took charge. He told the F-15 on the left to drop back and act as a relay on a separate frequency with the ground, then pass the information along to him on another channel. To avoid confusion, the flight leader would be the only one talking directly to Dale.

Desperately seeking more oxygen, Dale dropped lower, McCloud close at his side. His dizziness receded. McCloud didn't know how badly Dale's eyes were injured, but from 40 feet away, he could clearly see that the canopy was missing and the pilot was hunched behind the instrument panel.

To get the injured man down as quickly as possible, McCloud decided that Dale should land on runway 01. It was 2000 feet shorter than runway 30 but extended north-south, the course Dale was already on. McCloud kept reassuring him: "Cut back your power a little! . . . Ten miles out. Let's go down gradually!"

Dale, a veteran of 428 combat missions over Southeast Asia, fought to remain patient. The pain in his eye was a dull throb, and blood continued to stream from the wound. But flying was his life, and a drilled-in professional pride kept him sounding normal on the radio.

The approach and landing, critical parts of any flight, were still ahead. McCloud repeated his reassurances and directions every few seconds. As both jets neared the coastline, with the end of the runway just beyond, they were flying below 4000 feet at about 250 m.p.h. McCloud said, "Drop your landing gear!"

Even a trivial mistake now was an invitation to death. Over and over Dale repeated in his mind, "I must remember what to do!" His left hand instinctively found the lever to lower and lock the wheels.

Seeing the wheels down, McCloud gave Dale confirmation

by radio. Perhaps, at the lower speed, it would be safe for him to parachute. McCloud told him: "If it's too bad on approach, I'm going to have you jump!"

"Aw, I'm going to make it!" Dale replied. But he added, "Depth perception is going to be a problem. Can you give me my altitude from the last 200 feet on down?"

This was terribly dangerous. It meant that McCloud had to stay at the side of the other plane until they were both only a few feet off the runway. Could McCloud help Dale complete a safe landing and, at the same time, control his own plane and ground approach? There was no hesitation: "Will do, Dale!"

On the ground, the Eglin emergency equipment rolled into position. More than two dozen firemen and medics waited. In the control tower, Gardell still warned other traffic away from the area. In the radar station, another controller kept his eyes on the moving blips on his screen. It was 11:15 a.m.

Dale was having problems. At the lower altitude, the warmer air was turbulent, causing his jet to bounce. With his one partially working eye on the instruments, he couldn't see beyond the cockpit. Every slight head movement sent searing pains through the right side of his face.

With the wing tips of their jets no more than ten feet apart, McCloud and Dale passed over the end of the runway at 200 feet. McCloud talked constantly: "Fifty feet and 170 speed!... Twenty-five feet! Still 170... Fifteen feet! Ten feet and 170!... Five feet!"

This was McCloud's last message. With his jet just five feet off the ground, McCloud pushed his throttles forward, climbing as he passed Dale's plane. Dale pulled the nose of his own jet up slightly, and the plane settled. The back wheels touched down; then the plane bounced several feet into the air. The pilot maneuvered his controls slightly. Feel and instinct were everything. The wheels touched again, bounced, hit the runway for a third time and gripped the concrete. Dale dropped the nose, and the front wheel hit hard. It was 11:19.

Landing much faster and at least 1500 feet farther down the runway than normal, Dale had to slow his speed to keep from careering off the end of the strip. As the nose wheel was making contact with the ground, he pulled the handle to release a nylon parachute to act as a brake. Nothing happened. From the control tower came frantic warnings; "No chute! No chute!"

The jet still raced at more than 140 miles an hour; the end

of the runway was only split-seconds ahead, with dense woods beyond. Dale wondered if he should apply the regular brakes. At this speed, the wheels could lock, causing the tires to explode. Yet he didn't have a choice.

He pressed down on the brake pedals and held his breath. Miraculously there was no explosion and the speed began to slow. The end of the runway was only yards away when the plane finally stopped. It was 11:21 a.m. Radioing the tower, Dale said, "I'm clear and I need some assistance! Where is that flight surgeon?"

As rescuers reached the cockpit, civilian Kenneth Spicknall unbuckled the injured man's parachute harness. The oxygen connections were unsnapped and, as the mask was pulled away, blood poured down the front of Dale's flight suit. Next his helmet was removed, fully revealing the horror of his torn-up face.

With help, Dale descended a boarding ladder. A flight surgeon placed a bandage over the bleeding hole that was once the pilot's right eye, and helped him to an ambulance. Says medic Lt. Col. Donald Wright, "The pain had to be intense, but he never complained. It was unbelievable how he coped."

In the ambulance, Dale began to cry, overcome by his anger at the accident. A corpsman told him gently, "Go ahead and let it all out!"

He was in the operating room over four hours, but his eye could not be saved. He recalls hearing opthalmologist and surgeon Col. Barry Shaklan say that his eye looked like a glass marble smashed by a hammer.

In a week he was out of the hospital. Fitted with an artificial eye, he has few obvious scars but no longer has full peripheral vision. Although he will never fly again as a fighter pilot, he has stayed in the Air Force.

Dale gives much of the credit for his being alive to Captain McCloud. Others, including the Air Force, see Dale's own strength and skill as the essential elements responsible for his one-in-a-million survival. When the Air Force awarded him the Distinguished Flying Cross on April 11, 1978, the accompanying citation read: "His high degree of performance under extreme physical stress demonstrates exceptional professionalism, aerial skill and devotion to duty."

The Remarkable Saga
of Ray Charles

by James Lincoln Collier

HIS HAS BEEN one of the most astonishing careers in the history of American show business. For over two decades he has been a dominating figure on the popular-music scene, creating a legacy of memorable records that range from his first hit, "I Got a Woman," to his startlingly original rendition of "America the Beautiful." Perhaps more than anybody—Bing Crosby, Frank Sinatra, the Beatles—he has written his mark on the popular culture of his time. Indeed, Sinatra himself has said, "He is the only genius in our business." Yet even more amazing than the extent of his success is the saga of how Ray Charles got there.

He was born Ray Charles Robinson (he later dropped his last name to avoid confusion with boxer Sugar Ray Robinson) on September 23, 1930, in the abject poverty of the Depression South. A few months after his birth, his parents moved from Georgia to the small sawmill town of Greenville, Fla. Because his father was frequently away from home working for the railroad, Ray's principal support and direction came from his mother. "She didn't have much education," he says. "But she had great common sense. She had parables for everything, and I live by a lot of them today."

Charles' mother worked as a domestic and occasionally at the sawmill. At best, there was $40 a week to support the family, which included a second son born a year after Ray. But, as Charles says, "One thing about country people is that when they're poor it brings togetherness. When everybody is in the same boat, you do things for each other."

As hard-working and honest as the family was, it might have deserved a little good luck. What it got was nearly all bad. In 1935, when Ray was five, his younger brother toppled into a washtub and drowned, despite Ray's frantic efforts to pull him out. Then something began to go wrong with Ray's eyes. In the mornings, they would be stuck closed with mucus, so that he would have to pry them open. At times they ached excruciatingly. His area of vision began to narrow. His parents took him to the local doctor, but a specialist was needed, and there was no money for that.

By the age of seven, Charles was blind—probably from glaucoma, doctors have since told him. Charles could easily have sunk into apathy and lived out his life as a beggar. What saved him was the intelligence and courage of his mother. "You're blind, not stupid," she would tell him. "You've lost your eyes, not your mind." And, painstakingly, she began the arduous task of making him into a self-sufficient human being. She had him scrub floors, sweep, even chop wood. "She made me understand that if I thought about something enough, I could figure out a way to do it myself. She used to tell me, 'Someday I'm not going to be around to help you. You'll have to help yourself.'"

Charles also had something else going for him: music. A neighbor had a piano and started showing Ray how to make little melodies and put together notes to make chords. A second source of music for Charles was the church. "The kind of singing we did wasn't so much this finger-popping music that they call gospel music today," Charles says. "It was slow hymns. I loved that type of service."

By the time Charles was seven, and old enough to go to a school for the blind in St. Augustine, he had developed a passion and considerable facility for music. The school encouraged him to study a variety of instruments and he learned some classical piano fare. Then one more blow fell—his beloved mother, only in her early 30s, suddenly died. Charles could not weep, he could not eat. He sat at home for two weeks and had to be force-fed. Finally, a neighbor woman told him that his mother would have demanded that he go on. She spoke to him about his mother's goodness and her courage. Ray wept at last. When his father died a year later, he was able to absorb this new blow. "My mother had given me a toughness," he says. "I knew I was going to take care of myself. I was never going to beg."

By 16, Ray was beginning to work with bands around Jacksonville, then Orlando and Tampa. He sang, played the piano and arranged music, earning three or four dollars a night. Brewing in him was a determination to make a career of his music. He was afraid to tackle New York or Chicago, so he asked a friend to pick out on a map a medium-sized city as far from Jacksonville as he could get. The choice was Seattle.

Thus, in 1948, when Charles was not yet 18, he climbed on a bus with $600 saved over the years and five days later arrived in Seattle, exhausted and hungry. He went to a small hotel and slept for 21 hours. When he awoke, he asked the desk clerk where he could find a restaurant. The woman said, "It's two o'clock in the morning. Nothing open." Then she remembered that a small after-hours club nearby might serve food. Charles found the place and knocked on the door.

"What do you want, kid?" a man asked.

"Some food."

"We don't serve food. We've got a talent night on here."

Charles saw his chance; he announced that he could play the piano and sing. The man tried to shoo him away, but Charles was stubborn and he was finally admitted. When all the other aspirants had left, Ray was guided to the piano and sang a song called "Driftin' Blues." As he came off the stand, a man stopped him and said. "I'm from the Elks Club. Get yourself a trio and you've got a weekend job."

That was Tuesday. By Friday, Charles was working regularly. After that he never looked back. In the first years, jobs were low-paying, the musicians he worked with were sometimes inadequate and the traveling life was arduous. But he was young, excited by his small success, and he loved music. "Money didn't mean much to me," he says. "What I wanted was to be accepted in the profession as one of the best."

For the next several years Charles worked with various groups, mostly in the West, recording for a small local label. Then, in 1954, Atlantic Records bought his contract and the same year issued "I Got a Woman." It was an important moment in the history of American popular music, because for the first time an uncompromisingly black sound found wide acceptance. And from that beginning there flowed a great deal of what happens in popular music today, with its emphasis on "soul" or "rhythm and blues."

Life after "I Got a Woman" was hardly all peaches and cream. For one thing, there was Charles' much-publicized bout with drug addiction. When the law finally caught up with him, he was put on probation with the proviso that he get medical help. Today, Charles says: "I wanted to get rid of that part of my life, and I did." It was not easy; he had to take a year off from his career, but in the end, he succeeded.

Thereafter, one hit followed another—from his classic version of "Georgia On My Mind," which he still sings at virtually every performance, to "I Can't Stop Loving You." Then followed the awards: ten Grammies, given by the National Academy of Recording Arts and Sciences, five consecutive awards as top male vocalist in the prestigious *Down Beat* International Jazz Critics' Poll, a bronze medallion from the government of France on behalf of its people.

What is the magic that draws so many people? Most obviously, there is his great musical sense, flawless timing and thoroughgoing professionalism. But there is more. Whitney Balliett, one of our foremost jazz critics, has written. "He is, in his naked, powerful manner, in a class with Billie Holiday, Bessie Smith and Louis Armstrong. He is revered by every class, color and creed, perhaps because he *touches* his listeners' emotions with his voice." Charles himself says, "I try to bring out my soul so people can understand what I am. I try to make it so true that people believe that what I'm singing about really happened to me."

Ray Charles today heads two music publishing firms, a record-production company and an organization which manages the affairs of some two dozen musicians, singers and aides. Though he is on the road nine months of the year, he constantly returns to Los Angeles, his home base, to be with his family and to deal with business matters. Whenever he can, he goes to a little church where the slow hymns he so loved as a boy are still sung. He and his wife, Della, have three sons (Charles has a grown daughter by an earlier marriage).

He runs his business with a firm hand, demanding that his employees come up to a high standard of professionalism. And he still operates under one of his mother's rules: "When you meet a new person, give him a clean sheet and let him mark it up himself."

Asked why he recorded his own special version of "America the Beautiful," Charles says: "America is the greatest country in the world. We have a lot of things that need to be changed and a lot of things we have to accomplish. But when you travel to other places you realize how great this country is. And that's what I'm saying in this song."

Face to Face
With Hurricane Camille

---

by Joseph P. Blank

JOHN KOSHAK, JR., knew that Hurricane Camille would be bad. Radio and television warnings had sounded throughout that Sunday, August 17, 1969 as Camille lashed northwestward across the Gulf of Mexico. It was certain to pummel Gulfport, Miss., where the Koshaks lived. Along the coasts of Louisiana, Mississippi and Alabama, nearly 150,000 people fled inland to safer ground. But, like thousands of others in the coastal communities, John was reluctant to abandon his home unless the family—his wife, Janis, and their seven children, aged 3 to 11—was clearly endangered.

Trying to reason out the best course of action, he talked with his father and mother, who had moved into the ten-room house with the Koshaks a month earlier from California. He also consulted Charles Hill, a longtime friend, who had driven from Las Vegas for a visit.

John, 37—whose business was right there in his home (he designed and developed educational toys and supplies, and all of Magna Products' correspondence, engineering drawings and art work were there on the first floor)—was familiar with the power of a hurricane. Four years earlier, Hurricane Betsy had demolished his former home a few miles west of Gulfport (Koshak had moved his family to a motel for the night). But that house had stood only a few feet above sea level. "We're elevated 23 feet," he told his father, "and we're a good 250 yards from the sea. The place has been here since 1915, and no hurricane has ever bothered it. We'll probably be as safe here as anyplace else."

The elder Koshak, a gruff, warm-hearted expert machinist of 67, agreed. "We can batten down and ride it out," he said. "If we see signs of danger, we can get out before dark."

The men methodically prepared for the hurricane. Since water mains might be damaged, they filled bathtubs and pails. A power failure was likely, so they checked out batteries for the portable radio and flashlights, and fuel for the lantern. John's father moved a small generator into the downstairs hallway, wired several light bulbs to it and prepared a connection to the refrigerator.

Rain fell steadily that afternoon; gray clouds scudded in from the Gulf on the rising wind. The family had an early supper. A neighbor, whose husband was in Vietnam, asked if she and her two children could sit out the storm with the Koshaks. Another neighbor came by on his way inland—would the Koshaks mind taking care of his dog?

It grew dark before seven o'clock. Wind and rain now whipped the house. John sent his oldest son and daughter upstairs to bring down mattresses and pillows for the younger children. He wanted to keep the group together on one floor. "Stay away from the windows," he warned, concerned about glass flying from storm-shattered panes. As the wind mounted to a roar, the house began leaking—the rain seemingly driven right through the walls. With mops, towels, pots and buckets the Koshaks began a struggle against the rapidly spreading water. At 8:30 power failed, and Pop Koshak turned on the generator.

The roar of the hurricane now was overwhelming. The house shook, and the ceiling in the living room was falling piece by piece. The French doors in an upstairs room blew in with an explosive sound, and the group heard gun-like reports as other upstairs windows disintegrated. Water rose above their ankles.

Then the front door started to break away from its frame. John and Charlie put their shoulders against it, but a blast of water hit the house, flinging open the door and shoving them down the hall. The generator was doused, and the lights went out. Charlie licked his lips and shouted to John, "I think we're in real trouble. That water tasted salty." The sea had reached the house, and the water was rising by the minute!

"Everybody out the back door to the cars!" John yelled. "We'll pass the children along between us. Count them! Nine!"

The children went from adult to adult like buckets in a fire brigade. But the cars wouldn't start; the electrical systems had been killed by water. The wind was too strong and the water too deep to flee on foot. "Back to the house!" John yelled. "Count the children! Count nine!"

As they scrambled back, John ordered, "Everybody on the stairs!" Frightened, breathless and wet, the group settled on the stairs, which were protected by two interior walls. The children put the cat, Spooky, and a box with her four kittens on the landing. She peered nervously at her litter. The neighbor's dog curled up and went to sleep.

The wind sounded like the roar of a train passing a few yards away. The house shuddered and shifted on its foundations. Water inched its way up the steps as first-floor outside walls collapsed. No one spoke. Everyone knew there was no escape; they would live or die in the house.

Charlie Hill had more or less taken responsibility for the neighbor and her two children. The mother was on the verge of panic. She clutched his arm and kept repeating, "I can't swim, I can't swim."

"You won't have to," he told her, with outward calm. "It's bound to end soon."

Grandmother Koshak reached an arm around her husband's shoulder and put her mouth close to his ear. "Pop," she said, "I love you." He turned his head and answered, "I love you"— and his voice lacked its usual gruffness.

John watched the water lap at the steps, and felt a crushing guilt. He had underestimated the ferocity of Camille. He had his head between his hands and silently prayed: "Get us through this mess, will You?"

A moment later, the hurricane, in one mighty swipe, lifted

the entire roof off the house and skimmed it 40 feet through the air. The bottom steps of the staircase broke apart. One wall began crumbling on the marooned group.

Dr. Robert H. Simpson, director of the National Hurricane Center in Miami, Fla., graded Hurricane Camille as "the greatest recorded storm ever to hit a populated area in the Western Hemisphere." In its concentrated breadth of some 70 miles it shot out winds of nearly 200 m.p.h. and raised tides as much as 30 feet. Along the Gulf Coast it devastated everything in its swath: 19,467 homes and 709 small businesses were demolished or severely damaged. It seized a 600,000-gallon Gulfport oil tank and dumped it 3½ miles away. It tore three large cargo ships from their moorings and beached them. Telephone poles and 20-inch-thick pines cracked like guns as the winds snapped them.

To the west of Gulfport, the town of Pass Christian was virtually wiped out. Several vacationers at the luxurious Richelieu Apartments there held a hurricane party to watch the storm from their spectacular vantage point. Richelieu Apartments were smashed apart as if by a gigantic fist, and 26 people perished.

Seconds after the roof blew off the Koshak house, John yelled, "Up the stairs—into our bedroom! Count the kids." The children huddled in the slashing rain within the circle of adults. Grandmother Koshak implored, "Children, let's sing!" The children were too frightened to respond. She carried on alone for a few bars; then her voice trailed away.

Debris flew as the living-room fireplace and its chimney collapsed. With two walls in their bedroom sanctuary beginning to disintegrate, John ordered, "Into the television room!" This was the room farthest from the direction of the storm.

For an instant, John put his arm around his wife. Janis understood. Shivering from the wind and rain and fear, clutching two children to her, she thought. *Dear Lord, give me the strength to endure what I have to.* She felt anger against the hurricane. *We won't let it win.*

Pop Koshak raged silently, frustrated at not being able to *do* anything to fight Camille. Without reason, he dragged a cedar chest and a double mattress from a bedroom into the TV room. At that moment, the wind tore out one wall and extinguished the lantern. A second wall moved, wavered. Charlie Hill tried to support it, but it toppled on him, injuring his back. The house, shuddering and rocking, had moved 25 feet from its foundations. The world seemed to be breaking apart.

"Let's get that mattress up!" John shouted to his father. "Make it a lean-to against the wind. Get the kids under it. We can prop it up with our heads and shoulders!"

The larger children sprawled on the floor, with the smaller ones in a layer on top of them, and the adults bent over all nine. The floor tilted. The box containing the litter of kittens slid off a shelf and vanished in the wind. Spooky flew off the top of a sliding bookcase and also disappeared. The dog cowered with eyes closed. A third wall gave way. Water lapped across the slanting floor. John grabbed a door which was still hinged to one closet wall. "If the floor goes," he yelled at his father, "let's get the kids on this."

In that moment, the wind slightly diminished, and the water stopped rising. Then the water began receding. The main thrust of Camille had passed. The Koshaks and their friends had survived.

With the dawn, Gulfport people started coming back to their homes. They saw human bodies—more than 130 men, women and children died along the Mississippi coast—and parts of the beach and highway were strewn with dead dogs, cats, cattle. Strips of clothing festooned the standing trees, and blown-down power lines coiled like black spaghetti over the roads.

None of the returnees moved quickly or spoke loudly; they stood shocked, trying to absorb the shattering scenes before their eyes. "What do we do?" they asked. "Where do we go?"

By this time, organizations within the area and, in effect, the entire population of the United States had come to the aid of the devastated coast. Before dawn, the Mississippi National Guard and civil-defense units were moving in to handle traffic, guard property, set up communications centers, help clear the debris and take the homeless by truck and bus to refugee centers. By 10 a.m., the Salvation Army's canteen trucks and Red Cross volunteers and staffers were going wherever possible to distribute hot drinks, food, clothing and bedding.

From hundreds of towns and cities across the country came several million dollars in donations; household and medical supplies streamed in by plane, train, truck and car. The federal

*government shipped 4,400,000 pounds of food, moved in mo-
bile homes, set up portable classrooms, opened offices to provide low-interest, long-term business loans.*

*Camille, meanwhile, had raked its way northward across
Mississippi, dropping more than 28 inches of rain into West
Virginia and southern Virginia, causing rampaging floods, huge
mountain slides and 111 additional deaths before breaking up
over the Atlantic Ocean.*

Like many other Gulfport families, the Koshaks quickly
began reorganizing their lives. John divided his family in the
homes of two friends. The neighbor with her two children went
to a refugee center. Charlie Hill found a room for rent. By
Tuesday, Charlie's back had improved, and he pitched in with
Seabees in the worst volunteer work of all—searching for
bodies. Three days after the storm, he decided not to return to
Las Vegas, but to "remain in Gulfport and help rebuild the
community."

Near the end of the first week, a friend offered the Koshaks
his apartment, and the family was reunited. The children appeared to suffer no psychological damage from their experience; they were still awed by the incomprehensible power of
the hurricane, but enjoyed describing what they had seen and
heard on that frightful night. Janis had just one delayed reaction.
A few nights after the hurricane, she awoke suddenly at 2 a.m.
She quietly got up and went outside. Looking up at the sky
and, without knowing she was going to do it, she began to cry
softly.

Meanwhile, John, Pop and Charlie were picking through
the wreckage of the home. It could have been depressing, but
it wasn't: each salvaged item represented a little victory over
the wrath of the storm. The dog and cat suddenly appeared at
the scene, alive and hungry.

But the blues did occasionally afflict all the adults. Once,
in a low mood, John said to his parents, "I wanted you here
so that we would all be together, so you could enjoy the children, and look what happened."

His father, who had made up his mind to start a welding
shop when living was normal again, said, "Let's not cry about
what's gone. We'll just start all over."

"You're great," John said. "And this town has a lot of great people in it. It's going to be better here than it ever was before."

Later, Grandmother Koshak reflected: "We lost practically all our possessions, but the family came through it. When I think of that, I realize we lost nothing important."